American
Religious
Heretics

American
Religious
Heretics
FORMAL AND INFORMAL TRIALS

EDITED BY GEORGE H. SHRIVER

ABINGDON PRESS

NASHVILLE •• NEW YORK

American Religious Heretics

Copyright © 1966 by Abingdon Press

Library of Congress Catalog Card Number: 66-21972

Set up, printed, and bound by the
Parthenon Press, at Nashville, Tennessee,
United States of America

To the obedient heretics
and their bewildering offspring

Foreword

Between 1880 and 1905 American Protestantism experienced a flurry of heresy hunting. This may seem rather surprising in view of America's long tradition of religious freedom. But in the late nineteenth century a new situation had arisen. During most of our earlier history the main concern was to achieve equal freedom of the denominations to propagate their distinctive forms of faith within the same political jurisdiction. This goal was attained when the nation adopted the principle of the separation of church and state. The struggle in the 1880's, on the other hand, involved a doctrinal contest between conservatives and liberals within the same denomination.

Two major factors lay at the root of the rift of this period: (1) the Darwinian theory of evolution, and (2) the historical criticism of the Scriptures. Both factors created unrest, but biblical criticism caused greater alarm than did Darwinism, since it sharply challenged the orthodox idea of biblical authority. Under the impact of these two forces many Protestant theological seminaries became centers of conservative-liberal conflict, and dismissals or forced resignations were not uncommon. Professors who lost their positions included James Woodrow (Columbia Presbyterian Seminary), Alexander Winchell (Vanderbilt University), Crawford H. Toy (Southern Baptist Seminary), Henry Preserved Smith (Lane Seminary), Nathaniel Schmidt (Colgate University), and Hinkley G. Mitchell (Boston University School of Theology). Meanwhile, several well-known ministers, such as Algernon S. Crapsey became denominational casualties.

Yet, despite these suppressive measures, Christian liberalism continued to spread, and by the opening of the twentieth century many of the foremost theological schools were firmly in the liberal camp. The fundamentalist counterattack of the 1920's was a rear-guard attack, and it failed to restore its scheme of orthodoxy in a single leading seminary.

The present splendid book tells a story that should be better known among churchmen of today. Although the essayists confine their attention to five men in five denominations, the cases they have examined give a representative picture of the methods generally employed to prevent the growth of academic freedom. The authors have carefully explored the original documents and their conclusions seem solidly grounded. Hopefully, their pioneer labors will inspire others to undertake further investigations in this significant aspect of American church history.

H. SHELTON SMITH
James B. Duke Professor Emeritus of American Religious Thought, Duke University

Preface

This book is the result of Louis Nizer's *My Life in Court* and a coffee break. During the course of a conversation concerning the former at the latter, I suddenly came to the realization that such days in "church court" had never been described in a separate volume. Why not a volume of "church court" trials? Furthermore, with so much recent interest on the part of American Protestants in dissent, heresy, and infidelity, such a book might best be limited to American Protestantism and its major communions. Since enough interpretive works have been written concerning the impact of the new science upon religion, it was decided that these chapters should concentrate primarily upon the individuals and their trials. After a bibliographical search it was apparent that no such project had ever been attempted. Discussions of the major heresy trials in American Protestant Christianity are limited to a few lines in the general works and to a few pages in the denominational histories. No full accounts are to be found, and certainly no collection from several communions. And yet these heresy trials, in addition to making a scholarly contribution to denominational and ecumenical self-understanding, have an inbuilt interest. Fiction's Perry Mason was never more intriguing nor thrilling.

But which trials and what authors? Granted, other selections might have been made. And perhaps another editor someday will do just that. But I considered that these trials were major ones and offered the best cross section of subjects and communions. The contributors themselves should also be a cross section of communions and scholars, yet well versed in the primary sources of the communion and the trial itself. And so they are. Three of these chapters are in part the result of many years of dissertation research at several major universities and seminaries. The other two are written by leading scholars in the particular denominational context of the trial they describe. The order in which the chapters appear is strictly chronological—from Schaff's trial in 1845 to Crapsey's in 1906.

The volume would not have appeared without the fine participation of these four other contributors. Each worked as an independent scholar and did so in real diligence. Special appreciation must be given to Max Gray Rogers for his willingness to write a chapter without a publisher's commitment.

I owe a personal word to Dr. Ray C. Petry, who introduced me so well to the heretics of the church and gave me a valid ecumenical outlook. Dr. H. Shelton Smith, dean of American church historians, has been most helpful throughout the production in mature suggestions and encouragement. Mrs. Kathleen McCormick Daughtry, Mrs. Norma Owens Hash, Mrs. Hanne Rogers, and Mrs. Donna Shriver performed expertly as typists. Dr. John E. Steely gave valuable technical assistance and the kind of encouragement only engendered by deep friendship. To such friends no word of appreciation is expected, but it is sincerely given. The Alumni Association of Southeastern Baptist Theological Seminary was thoughtful to lend partial material assistance for the typing of the manuscript. My wife, Donna Newcomer Shriver, knows the pain and joy of even an edited volume, and has patiently shared both with me.

GEORGE H. SHRIVER

Wake Forest, North Carolina

Contents

11

Introduction
The Image

The image of the heretic has been one of the most useless and abused images in the history of the Christian church. The course of American Protestant Christianity has not appreciably altered this tragedy.

Originally the words "heretic" and "heresy" referred simply to "choice." One man chooses a particular opinion while another prefers the contrary, or at least a variant. There is nothing particularly tragic or negative about this. But in the course of Christian history, as soon as truth became identified with orthodoxy or one particular canonized viewpoint, such choice was deadly. And it was deadly not only for the ideas but also for the persons. The pages of church history are marred in every chapter by the story of the persecution of the heretic—from Simon Magus to twentieth-century American Christian forms. The Christian heretic, then, is one who has deviated within the fold of Christian faith from some established or accepted doctrine or set of doctrines. Or, as Belloc has put it, "heresy is the dislocation of some complete and self-supporting scheme by the introduction of a novel denial of some essential part therein." [1] In brief, the heretic is one who challenges a closed system of orthodoxy.

As a result of his challenge he has always paid some kind of penalty. The way of the heretic has been courageous but costly. Generally the penalty occurred after the procedure of a formal or informal trial. Even the medieval inquisitors held trials—farcical as they sometimes were. Too often the Thomistic rationale was followed. For if society puts the murderer of the physical body to death, how much more responsible is it to rid itself of one who damns the soul.

Protestantism did no better. It merely raised other issues as the ostensible reasons for trial and penalty. Sedition was a favorite charge among the magisterial reformers. In so doing, the reformers rejected in part the very principle of Protestantism which they had themselves originally conceived. Openness to the fresh and renewing hand of God, which had been the genius of their attack upon Roman Catholic forms, was partially rejected in their own persecution of certain "seditionists."

Even the complexity of American Protestantism did not bring to an end the trials of heretics. One might expect to find victims in the colonial period and a cessation during the national period with its greater religious liberty. But this was definitely not the case. Instead of one orthodox opinion there were many orthodoxies with attendant trials. Our ultra-modern twentieth century has made few improvements; it has fallen heir to some of the most insidious trials in the history of Christendom! These trials have not always been exactly formal ones.

Carl F. H. Henry is not completely correct in his judgment as he states, "Heresy trials became an oddity in contemporary church history, not because of an absence of heresy, but because of the lack of zeal to prosecute heretics." [2] In the contemporary period one witnesses more than enough misplaced zeal in regard to the so-called heretic. He is not always put to the test of a formal trial, but he undergoes multiplied pain in informal trials which also result in devilish penalties. So, heretics and heresy trials are not things of the past. Some of the most intriguing cases have appeared on the American scene during the nineteenth and twentieth centuries.

But what of the image of the heretic in the American

religious tradition? No precise definition or description can really be given. And the denominational complexity in America further confuses the issue. An accused heretic in one denomination might be considered a conservative and orthodox churchman in another. One must not oversimplify when dealing with and trying to define the heretic. Whenever the heretic has been reduced to a stereotype or common denominator, a distorted picture has resulted. This must not be done. He does not hate Jesus, despise the church, or corrupt youth. He does not conceive of his task as that of troublemaker, nor is he obsessed with arrogance and an infallibility complex. He is not a wicked man, nor un-American. These are some of the false images, however, which have discredited him even before he has spoken.

This is part of the caricature drawn by those who have always retreated from the ultimate questions which the heretic has raised. They are in retreat because their legitimacy has been threatened. Their use of the word "heretic" is as a battle cry to rally around the flag. And the tenor of voice in which they cry is more conducive to negative action than to clear thinking. Sadly enough, their battle cry has intentionally obscured the real issues and led to false simplifications. In fact, those who have hunted down the heretics have generally displayed an absolute perversion of Christian ethics. The denominations have too often been arrogant with those they should have tried most to understand. As a result, the heretic has paid a price of tremendous suffering and the denominations have paid the price of forestalled self-criticism and examination.

Actually, the only useful image of the heretic in the American religious tradition would be synonymous with that pictured by the word "saint." Without a manual of church history as a program guide, it would be very difficult to tell the saints from the heretics in the course of Christian history. Both have been the most religious of men in their own generation! Is not Christianity itself a heresy? And may not those who experience Christianity at its deepest levels be called "heretics"? [8]

This new image of the heretic pictures him as a creative precursor of new ideas in a particular context—whether within a single denomination or in a complete generation. Implicit in this observation is the fact that, perforce, he must "live dangerously." What he is about does not lead to peace in Zion, but it is rather generative of a healthy restlessness. These avant-gardists attempt to lead the denominations to fresh assessments and interpretations within the context of self-criticism. In this respect the heretic becomes a healthy cathartic agent, but often the churches are unaware of the medicinal properties of his activities. So they fight. And they fight these individuals. The sincere attempts of the heretic are branded as the fruits of bitter malice. Ironically enough, the prosecutors become illustrations *par excellence* of this kind of malice. Tragedy of one kind or another results—whether internal, external, or both. There is a haunting loneliness about the role of the heretic as he passes through valleys of shadow, often with unspeakable burdens. Can it not be said that he, more than any other, enters into the mysticism of Gethsemane suffering? It is not then strange to observe that the interrogation of Jesus on that last morning was the "prototype of all heresy trials!" [4]

Up to this time there has been no attempt to gather under one cover the stories of the major heresy trials in the history of American Christianity. The selection made here is not all inclusive, but it is believed that these are the major heresy trials among the various denominations.[5] It is evident that no one religious group in America has dominated these trials. Further examinations of heresy trials in America would only substantiate the cross section in this book. Further, the word "informal" seems valid as a description of heresy trials. The informal trial sometimes even leads to more devastating results than the formal ones. In fact, within the context of formal trial procedures there is less likely to be a gross miscarriage of justice.

P. T. Forsyth once said that a "live heresy is better than a dead orthodoxy." [6] It will be noted in these chapters that both the heretics and the orthodox churchman are "lively ones." So there is no option between living forms and dead expressions. But perhaps the question ought to be raised as to whether the heretic or the orthodox is the more valid heir of the faith.

NOTES

1. H. Belloc, *The Great Heresies* (London: Sheed and Ward 1938), p. 4.
2. "Dare We Renew the Controversy? The Evangelical Responsibility," *Christianity Today*, July 22, 1957, p. 38.
3. Cf. Walter Nigg, *The Heretics* (New York: Alfred A. Knopf, 1962), p. 11.
4. *Ibid.*, p. 411.
5. The original plan of this volume included a chapter concerning the heresy trial of James Woodrow of Presbyterian, U.S., fame. Unfortunately, the contracted writer was unable to complete his essay for this volume.
6. Cited by Robert McAfee Brown, *The Spirit of Protestantism* (New York: Oxford University Press, 1961), p. 128.

1. Philip Schaff
Heresy at Mercersburg

GEORGE H. SHRIVER

Nestled in the foothills of the Appalachian mountain range lies the friendly Pennsylvania village of Mercersburg. Though today the major academic institution in the town is the Mercersburg Academy, in the mid-nineteenth century this village was the home of the college and seminary of the German Reformed Church in the United States. Contemporary allusions to the "Mercersburg theology" or the "Mercersburg movement" arouse little recognition generally.[1] The name Philip Schaff would be more widely known, but he would probably not be identified as having had anything to do with Mercersburg. And even those persons involved in the specific field of church history are surprised to learn that this dean of nineteenth-century American church historians underwent two heresy trials!

Philip Schaff [2] was a Swiss-born German who received his theological training in three distinguished European schools—Tübingen, Halle, and Berlin. Because of his early background, he was attracted to those professors who could be considered as representatives of the conciliatory or mediational theology. This young theological student with his pietistic orientation was drawn by the evangelical [3] emphases and approaches of C. F. Schmid and J. A. Dorner at Tübingen, of F. A. Tholuck and Julius Müller at Halle, and of the matchless Augustus

Neander at Berlin. At the same time, he was cognizant of and influenced by the leading scholars of neo-Lutheranism and radicalism who taught at these three institutions. Schaff was especially indebted to E. W. Hengstenberg of Berlin and F. C. Baur of Tübingen who were of these two respective viewpoints.[4]

In 1841 the itinerant student completed his studies at Berlin and was awarded the licentiate in theology. Encouraged by all his former teachers, Schaff entered the educational field and commenced the ordeal of the German *privat-docent*. For his right to lecture he published a trial essay on James, the Lord's brother, and a monograph entitled *Die Sünde wider den Heiligen Geist*.[5] The views expressed in this early work on a purgatorial "middle state" were to cause grave trouble for him several years later. As he set himself to the classroom task, he did so not only with the tools of the scholar but also with a sense of pietistic and evangelical dedication. He expressed in his own career the antithesis of his description of a faithless theologian: "A theologian without faith is like a sky without a star, a heart without a pulse, light without warmth, a sword without edge, a body without soul."[6]

The occasion of the coming of Philip Schaff to America was a unanimous invitation from the Eastern Synod of the German Reformed Church in the United States to a professorship in its theological seminary at Mercersburg. Originally, Frederick W. Krummacher, one of the foremost pulpit orators in Germany, had been extended the call to teach. The Eastern Synod had sent T. L. Hoffeditz and B. S. Schneck in July, 1843, to Elberfeld, Germany, to convey its invitation personally to Krummacher. It appears that he was actually favorably inclined to accept, but, because of his popularity and influence as a preacher, the King of Prussia, Frederick William IV, refused him a passport.

At this point Krummacher recommended the young scholar, Philip Schaff, for the position.[7] In its investigations the com-

mittee was also impressed with the glowing reports concerning
Schaff given it by many of his former teachers, including
Tholuck, Müller, Neander, and Hengstenberg. After two inter-
views with Schaff, Hoffeditz and Schneck received his permission to present his name before the Synod.

Arriving back in the States, they found the Synod in session
at Winchester, Virginia, October, 1843. After reviewing the
professors' testimonials on Schaff's behalf and reading copies
of *Die Sünde,* the Synod by a unanimous vote extended a call
to Philip Schaff of Berlin, Germany, to the chair of Church
History and Biblical Literature in the Theological Seminary
at Mercersburg.[8] He would be paid a salary of one thousand
dollars *per annum* quarterly and would be furnished a house.
It is most ironical that the document was signed by Joseph F.
Berg, president of the Synod, for only a few months later
he became the chief prosecutor of Philip Schaff on the charge
of heresy.

The call was formally accepted by Schaff, and the official
governmental sanction was given shortly thereafter when
Frederick William IV granted him permission to accept the
position.[9] A young *privat-docent* could be spared more easily
than a seasoned and popular preacher!

On April 12, 1844, Schaff was ordained to the Christian
ministry in Elberfeld. The conditions of his ordination were
prophetic of the ecumenical interests of his later career, for he,
a Swiss, was ordained by the Prussian Evangelical Union
Church in the Reformed Church in Elberfeld according to the
Lutheran form in preparation for service with the German
Reformed Church in the United States! Krummacher himself
preached the ordination sermon and delivered the charge to
the young ordinand. At the close of his sermon and after a
congregational hymn Schaff stepped into the pulpit and delivered a sermon, as was the custom. His text was Acts
16:8-10 with its discussion of Paul's Macedonian vision.

This sermon is of considerable importance in two respects.
First, an insight is given concerning Schaff's early view of

the American scene and of the task to which he felt himself dedicated. Secondly, copies of the sermon preceded him to America, and, because of his negative picture of the religious conditions of the Germans in the United States, he was heavily censured even before his arrival at Mercersburg.

At the outset of his message he confessed that he felt over-powered with anxiety and fear upon contemplating the dimensions of the task to which he had been called. His emotion was that of the novice sculptor, standing before a colossal rock with only a slender chisel in his hand. He expressed depression upon a consideration of all that he was leaving in Germany, "to place me down in the midst of relations wholly new and strange, among a people and in a land, which seem to have become estranged from the deeper life of the soul in the pursuit of that which is material and outward." [10] Exhorting his listeners themselves to hear the call, "Come over and help us," he shared the fervent feeling that in such a situation as he faced, the sense of divine call was a necessity—even that of a missionary. Schaff pictured the man in America who called for help as standing on the brink of a threefold abyss—heathenism, Romanism, and sectarianism. These three foes of the German churches in America then became the subjects of the body of the sermon. Though he mentioned Romanism as one of the primary foes of the church, shortly he would be condemned himself as a papist!

Schaff's description of the religious condition of those Germans who had emigrated to America was less than complimentary. "If the German emigrants had only half the earnestness of those rigid Puritans and quiet Quakers, I would scarcely presume to bespeak your sympathy in their behalf." [11] Under his major division of heathenism, in a derogatory manner he named five groups of German emigrants: (1) those who go seeking only monetary values, leaving all Christian influence behind, not even bothering to take a minister with them; (2) vagabonds and adventurers; (3) "ranters" and "friends of lawless freedom"; (4) those who escape the proper penalty of their crimes or a secret sin which they fear might catch up with them; and (5) those who hate the gospel! One can easily see how such material in the hands of Germans in America would result in adverse criticism of this young minister/teacher.

The second major division of his sermon concerned itself with the threat of Romanism. Catholics in America were characterized as engaged in malicious laughter at the divisions among Protestants—while thousands of Protestants cried to Europe for help and assistance. At this juncture Schaff gave a penetrating critique of the indifference and false security of the Evangelical Church in Germany. Of course, Germans in America who read the sermon later overlooked this criticism of the homeland and saw it only as a bitter attack upon the German Church in America.

Of the sectarian fragmentation of Protestants in America Schaff was most pessimistic. He spoke of those fanatics who dream up a new religion overnight, build a chapel in their own name the next day, and bequeath it as a legacy to the future generations. At bottom he named conscious and unconscious pride and vanity as the leading impulses of all sectarianism and separatism.

He closed his sermon with a use of catholic and eschatological symbols designed to arouse the sentiment of hope within the Christian community, which is assured that history is moving forward to a conclusion which will enhance the meaning of all that has gone before. For the German and German-American Church—as well as the universal church—ardently and zealously await the time when all discords will be solved in the final concord of divine truth. Schaff's poetic prose certainly must have captivated the audience as he delivered his concluding statements:

It is our fond hope and earnest desire, that this occasion may form the commencement of a new era of intimate and friendly correspondence between ourselves and our brethren of the same faith in Germany, that may work with salutary influence on the churches of both countries in all time to come.

The interest to be labored for is the fraternal, spiritual and outward confederation of the professors of the same faith on both sides of the ocean; a firm union among all the true members of the evangelical, apostolical, and on this account only truly Catholic Church; that Europe, and especially Protestant Germany, the heart of Europe, with its hard won moral wealth of eighteen hundred years, may be brought to live, flourish and bloom in America; that the new world, big with the future, may be drawn closer to the old world; in its growing age; so that this last shall be secured from decay and reanimated with youthful vigor; and thus the time appear when both hemispheres shall see eye to eye entirely in their love to the same crucified Saviour, and join hands together across the waves of the great sea in everlasting charity and peace.

On the strong pinions of hope we pass far beyond sea and land, mountain and valley, yea beyond all space and time, and sin and death into the land of true liberty endlessly manifold and yet one, the realm of the blessed where there shall be no Europe, no America, no Catholicism and no Protestantism, but an undivided Kingdom of God: No old and no new world, but the one glorious church of the redeemed, resplendent in immortal youth.

Here we gaze by faith into the ever-during city of God and behold all the living members of the body of Christ, now separated, gathered into one triumphant throng around the throne of the Lamb that was slain.[12]

Though the central thrust of his sermon was thoroughly Christian and sane, those few items of a negative note were picked up by some Germans in America as soon as it was published by the religious and secular German press. Unwittingly, the twenty-five-year-old teacher had alienated some Germans in America, the community in which he would serve for several decades—even before he docked in New York harbor!

On his journey to America he spent six weeks of orientation in England. He met English Christians with whom he would have important relationships for the rest of his life. Schaff recorded in his journal an important conversation with Pusey during this visit. It is crucial because it vividly illustrates Schaff's principle of organic development in his historiographical approach which would never allow him to become a Puseyite as he was charged with being early in his American career.[13]

The young Swiss-German scholar was coming to a very restless United States of America. Not only was the German Reformed Church in the United States in a state of flux, but also the general scene was one of political, social, economic, and religious unrest. The third and fourth decades of the nineteenth century are examples *par excellence* of this restlessness. In such turmoil, stress, and strain the professor would soon take his place. It is only miraculous that he remained in America instead of leaving immediately for the security of a state church and complete academic freedom.

It was an age of sectionalism, nativism, revolution, immigration, democracy, and sectarianism. The young slumbering giant was rising from his couch, but as he did there were the usual juvenile diseases which threatened the health of youth. The air was charged with emotionalism and individualism as these factors crisscrossed on the American scene. Rapid changes were occurring economically, for the industrial revolution was under way. Streams of immigrants, especially from Ireland and Germany, were flooding the eastern seaboard and contributing to the phenomenal rise of cities with their legion of problems. Native American Protestant laborers despised this flooding of the cheap labor market by the foreign born and reacted to the influx by seeing it as an economic, political, and religious threat to security, democracy, and Protestantism. The results of this fierce opposition to immigration were the nativist movement, generally, and the Know-Nothing party, specifically. Politically, this movement was anxious to restrict immigration and naturalization. In the Jacksonian age of the elevation of the common man there was a rising suspicion of the Catholic immigrant who seemed to pose a threat to the democratic principle. This nativist movement later became a frank anti-Catholic movement and gravely affected both the popular

Protestant opinion of the Roman Catholic Church and the history of the Christian church itself.[14] Philip Schaff was to encounter false judgments of the latter variety.

The social, economic, and political bias against Catholicism simply added fuel to the fire of deep-dyed Protestant suspicion. When Catholic leaders began to ask for a share in public school funds for the support of parochial schools, Protestants raised the banner of separation of church and state. Press crusades, lecture tirades, and even the use of violence against Catholic churches followed. Catholicism was branded as undemocratic and un-American. Out of such a milieu it is not strange, then, to see the development of such a radical Protestant reaction. Catholicism became completely identified with "popery," and if the principle of "popery" is undemocratic and completely opposed to the Protestant principle, it is only a quick step to conclude that the Roman Catholic Church and its history are not even Christian! In one instance this was done by formal action from the floor of a Presbyterian Old School General Assembly,[15] and in many instances it was the end result of opinionated Protestant historiography. Protestant groups were prone to trace their "trail of blood" through Waldensian and other medieval sect forefathers directly to Christ and his apostles, completely ignoring the fact that the Catholic Church of the middle ages was part of their lineage. Within such a context many would consider it crass heresy for any historian, of famed or infamous reputation, to suggest that an appreciative study of the medieval Catholic Church had any Christian value whatsoever for Protestants. In these circles it would be hazardous for any historian to dare suggest that the medieval Catholic Church played the major role in the organic development of Christianity from the days of Christ to the Protestant Reformation. In fact, for a century scholars of certain denominational types who expressed such ideas continued to face the danger of being branded as heretical.

However, Protestant opposition to Catholicism was by no means the only problem to confront Schaff as he entered the

American church situation. Denominational loyalty was expressing itself in a spirit of sectarianism. The divisive principle was at work within denominations as well as without. Divisions and subdivisions occurred in several large communions as the result of theological disagreement and dispute concerning the slavery question.

After the General Assembly of 1837 the Presbyterians had split over theological and disciplinary matters into New School and Old School. Within Lutheranism there were strong rumblings between the liberal and conservative elements. The liberal party was interested in Americanizing the Lutheran Church and in making liberal interpretations of the Augsburg Confession. The conservative element demanded the use of the German language in its worship as well as a strict adherence to the Augsburg Confession. The years 1844-45 witnessed the division of two of the greatest American denominations of the soil—the Baptists and the Methodists. The irrepressible conflict over slavery saw the funeral of the Baptist Triennial Convention and the birth of the Southern Baptist Convention in the South and the American Baptist Missionary Union in the North. From the Methodist Episcopal Church came the Methodist Episcopal Church, South. The name of the new group itself was indicative of the primary cause of bisection.

In addition to the turmoil among Protestant denominations, strange movements began to spring up on the American religious scene. The "burned-over district" of central western New York acted as a type of watershed for the variety of sects which sprang from the general background of revivalism and disturbed economic conditions.[16]

During the course of tracing the operations of religious liberty and political equality in America, Alexis De Tocqueville gave a continental nonclerical description of the religious situation. He adumbrated Schaff's critique of the rise of sects which the Swiss-German had presented at his own ordination. De Tocqueville's vivid description follows:

Here and there, in the midst of American society, you meet with
men, full of a fanatical and almost wild enthusiasm, which hardly
exists in Europe. From time to time strange sects arise, which endeavor to strike out extraordinary paths to eternal happiness. Religious insanity is very common in the United States.[17]

The religious scene became crowded with Joseph Smith,
William Miller, and Charles G. Finney. The latter was followed
by a host of post-Finney revivalists who did a less worthy work
than he. With no formal education and little common ground
with the settled ministry, these free-lancers "swarmed over
Yankeedom, old and new, preaching every shade of gospel,
heresy and reform to a people who for a generation had been
saturated with spiritual and moral intensity." [18]

Mercersburg itself had been plagued by this type of roving
evangelist before the arrival of Schaff, and he was to be in
complete accord with the reaction toward it of John W. Nevin,
his only colleague at the Seminary. When the "anxious bench"
measure of the enthusiastic evangelists was employed in the
Reformed Church at Mercersburg, Nevin strenuously objected
and defended his viewpoint in 1843 in his publication of *The
Anxious Bench*. In this work he did not attack a proper revival
of religion; he rather exposed that variety of revival which is
mechanically imposed upon the church from without. A true
revival, he insisted, must grow out of the very life of the church.
He urged the German churches to remain loyal to their cate-
chetical system and to their history.

Such were the major aspects of the American religious
setting when Philip Schaff came to the Mercersburg Seminary.
That aspect of his historiographical approach which emphasized
the growth of the Protestant movement in its organic and
intrinsic relationship to the medieval Catholic Church was
certain to be attacked severely. The sectarian spirit of American
Christianity completely bypassed the Catholic Church of the
middle ages in tracing its lineage through the Waldensians
and other medieval sect groups directly to the Apostolic Church.

To favor any aspect of the Catholic Church or to appreciate its history as organically related to the Protestant Reformation was to subject oneself and one's ideas to widespread contumely.

Sectarianism and the principle of congregational independency were also inclined to deny any historiography which stressed the church universal, creedal symbols, or liturgical forms. The political, economic, and religious *Zeitgeist* was totally unfavorable to the projection of such emphases. Not only was the young historian ill received in America because of his ordination sermon's critical statements concerning the German immigrant in America, but he was also misunderstood and resisted by a conservative and sectarian element in the German Reformed Church when he delivered his inaugural address.

Upon his arrival in the States his first responsibility was the pastor's pulpit rather than the professor's lectern. Before arriving at Mercersburg he preached in New York and Chambersburg. The weekly news organ of the German Reformed Church reported its first impressions of the new teacher as preacher.

His manner was simple, dignified, earnest, and affectionate, and it could not escape any observor, that the large audience which hung upon his lips, was frequently thrilled with the bursts of eloquence which occasionally broke forth, and which were at once natural and graceful—the eloquence of truth, rather than the flourishes of rhetorick.[19]

On August 12, 1844, he arrived at Mercersburg and was surprised by a tremendous reception. He was overwhelmed by the greeting, and in his first speech to his future students expressed the ecumenicity which marked the pedagogical method he employed throughout his career as an educator.

I came in your midst, to labor for the Church, which is far removed beyond the boundaries of Language and Nationality— for the Church, the spiritual mother—hearth of all Christians, which binds together those that are far distant in one fold, feeds them upon the same green pastures of the Word of God, and refreshes them with the same sweet water of eternal life.[20]

He closed the address by stating his judgment concerning the proper function of German learning in America. It was his opinion that the thorough European mental culture, when mixed with American freshness and practicality, would yield tasty fruit. German learning in this way would be adapted and appropriated rather than merely transferred and adopted *in toto*.

At the conclusion of the evening meal in the home of Professor Nevin the students gathered outside and sang a final welcome in German which was then followed by the thrice-repeated shout: *"Vivat hoch unser Professor!"* Schaff answered with a *"Vivant studiosi."* This momentous day was closed with the students' singing of the Latin air "Gaudeamus Igitur." *The Weekly Messenger* noted concerning his reception that the students were "fully alive to the acquisition which their *Alma Mater* has received in the person of a distinguished scholar from the capital of Prussia." [21] In a few months and in another setting there would be a completely different reaction to the "distinguished scholar." In some instances, such as this one, ministerial students have shown keener insight and deeper awareness than have seasoned pastors.

Schaff's only colleague on the Seminary staff was John W. Nevin, a young graduate of Princeton Seminary who was already influenced in his thought patterns by German theology. Soon after arriving, Schaff mentioned Nevin in his journal: "I think I could not have a better colleague than Dr. Nevin. I feared I might not find any sympathy in him for my views of the church; but I discover that he occupies essentially the same ground that I do and confirms me in my position. He is filled with the ideas of German theology." [22]

Nevin was more the speculative theologian, while Schaff was the constructive church historian. It is very apparent, however, that the greatest difference between these two men was their

psychological composition and temperament. While Nevin
was polemic and bombastic, Schaff was conciliatory and sooth-
ing. Nevin was intolerant and divisive; Schaff was tolerant
and irenic. Though Nevin was judged as the prime leader of
the "Mercersburg theology," it must not be concluded that he
and Schaff were opposed to one another in basic thought patterns. They were not; they stood together. The difference
between the men was one of method and approach. Schaff's
biographer, his son David, concluded with others that the
negative attitude toward Nevin was often also transferred to
Schaff because of their personal relations.[23] This was probably
true. Schaff's ideas, expounded apart from his relationships
with the polemical-spirited Nevin, would have had a quicker
and more positive hearing. As to essential theological position,
however, the two professors agreed.

On October 17, 1844, the Eastern Synod of the German
Reformed Church convened in Allentown, Pennsylvania, and
a committee composed of John W. Nevin, T. L. Hoffeditz,
E. Heiner, and Henry Shade was appointed to hold the traditional *Tentamen* with Schaff with a view to his reception as a
member of the Synod. The committee submitted a positive
report.

That they have had satisfactory evidence of his being in regular
ecclesiastical connection as a minister with the Evangelical Church
of Prussia, having been ordained in the Reformed Church of
Elberfeld last April. They have satisfied themselves also that as
he was born in the bosom of the Reformed Church, so he continues to be still true to its faith as exhibited in the Heidelberg
Catechism, and that he is prepared moreover to conform to the
constitution and order of the same Church as established in this
country. They recommend therefore that he be received as a member of this Synod.[24]

Insofar as the Synod was concerned, Schaff had now received
his official theological "clean bill of health."

This same day Joseph F. Berg, pastor of the First German

Reformed Church in Philadelphia, delivered a sermon at the opening of the Synod in which he espoused the Waldensian theory of the church. The would-be-historian pastor chimed:

If we had time, we might present no mean array of historical facts, establishing a claim to apostolical order and *succession* if you will, which is based upon a foundation of acknowledged truth; but I must content myself with remarking that from the latter half of the second century to the present day, Christian churches have been in existence in the South of France and adjacent countries, and from the Waldensian records which have been preserved, it is evident that the doctrines of the Reformation in their purity and strength were maintained from the days of the Apostles until the age of Luther.[25]

Berg then proceeded to place the Reformed Church in this apostolical tradition by claiming, "The fathers of the Church of the Palatinate were Waldensian Brethren, and the Church of the Palatinate is the mother of the Reformed interest in America." [26] He concluded his sermon by calling for a particular *esprit de corps* or proper denominational spirit while condemning "innovators" and "new-measure men" who forsook what he defined as denominational landmarks. Just one week later Berg was himself to hear one of these "new-measure men."

On October 25, 1844, the Synod reconvened in Reading, Pennsylvania, to hear the traditional inaugural address of the new professor. Here, as a young professor of only twenty-five years, Philip Schaff delivered his masterful "The Principle of Protestantism." Though he was certainly unaware of it at that time, he was flinging a firebrand marked with the words "Romanizer" and "Tractarian!" Schaff's theory of the organic development of the church with its attendant appreciation of medieval Catholicism simply could not be accepted by the Berg element in the German Reformed Church. To speak of the Reformation as developing quite naturally out of the medieval Catholic period and as a normal growth of the church was utter nonsense and heresy to those who held the Waldensian view of the church. To them Schaff was merely playing into the hands of the papists and Puseyites and thus leading the Reformed Church astray.

An immediate notice of the address in *The Weekly Messenger* was quietly complimentary, though no involved or absolutely committed statement was made.

Dr. Schaf's inaugural . . . was a masterly performance. It abounded in deep and solid thought, and was delivered in a peculiarly happy manner. Though it was somewhat lengthy, and many portions of it were evidently elevated above the usual sphere of thought of most of the audience, it still was listened to throughout with marked attention and interest. The prevailing topic of his address was the true life and spirit of the Reformation. As it will doubtless be given to the public in a permanent form, we forbear any further comment upon its merits.[27]

The "permanent" and expanded form did appear early in 1845. Originally published in German, the address appeared soon afterward in English translation by Nevin, prefaced by Nevin's introduction and carrying an appended sermon by him on "Catholic Unity," along with 112 theses for the times penned by Schaff.[28] The entire introduction and conclusion of *The Principle of Protestantism* were also carried in two issues of *The Weekly Messenger*.[29]

Because of an anti-Catholic mental conditioning, the conservative element within the German Reformed Church was not disposed to accept the major thrust of *The Principle of Protestantism*.

The 'Principle of Protestantism,' by Dr. Schaff, the first successful defense of this principle against Romanism, was strangely enough charged with teaching doctrines of a Romanizing tendency. The public mind had become so much accustomed to mere negative protests, that it was not prepared for the truth unfolded in a positive form. This is a two-edged sword and because it was wielded with great power and skill against the errors of Pseudo-Protestants

Catholic Church; (3) the Reformation must be viewed as the product of the previous life of the church under its Roman Catholic form; (4) Protestantism is more than a mere retrogression to the position it occupied in the beginning; (5) Christianity is a continued inward movement; and (6) the principle of Protestantism makes room for something more glorious in the future.[34] Against the unhistorical mood of the American Church, Nevin lucidly stated:

How cheap and easy is that championship of Protestantism, which just plants its heel on the article of a universal Christian Church, at the very outset of its polemic crusade, and then carries the whole question, caricatured to its own content, to the bar of common sense, there to be settled in pure lynch law style, without the least regard to the mystery of Christianity, as a past fact in the history of the world.[35]

Philip Schaff was already breaking ecumenical ground—and Nevin recognized the tremendous value of his efforts for the American Church! Nevin concluded his lengthy review by judging *The Principle* to be the most able argument ever presented against the pretensions of the Roman Church; yet, ironically enough, it was "looked upon widely as a sort of semi-jesuitic stab to the whole cause it pretends to support." [36]

Before such favorable reviews appeared, however, heresy-hunters had already sighted their quarry. At the time of his inaugural Schaff was not under the impression that his ideas would arouse a flight of hornets, but soon after the publication of his premises it was evident that he would be opposed openly by a conservative element within the German Reformed Church.

Schaff wrote to Elias Heiner, one of the pastors of this element, inquiring about the impact which the publication of *The Principle* would make on the general public. Heiner answered with a clipped frankness and insisted that it would raise a "host of antagonisms" in sister churches as well as opening the door for divisions in the German Reformed Church. Heiner seemed to have more concern for the institutional church

as well as against the errors of the Romish Church, it could nc
the nature of the case, be popular.[30]

Evidently those who opposed the work were so blinded in th
predispositions that they could not even see that *The Princi*
was the finest argument against Romanism they would ev
read! And, it is difficult to understand how anyone could accu
Schaff of being a Puseyite after having read his excelle
critique of this movement in *The Principle*.[31]

There *were* some positive value-judgments, however. Charle
Hodge of Princeton had thoroughly read the book and, thougl
disagreeing with certain views expressed by Schaff, had close
his formal review of the work by generally praising the autho
and by noting that neither Schaff nor Nevin was leaning toward
Puseyism or Rome. He correctly observed that such a "leaning"
would completely contradict the expressed position of the principle of progress.[32] Hodge displayed in this observation an
important insight which was absolutely missed, or ignored, by
Schaff's critics. Tayler Lewis, a layman in the Dutch Reformed
Church, also gave a favorable review of *The Principle*. He
praised Schaff's presentation of the article of justification by
faith as the most truly evangelical statement he had read. Expressing agreement with Schaff's contention for the continuity
of the church, Lewis concluded that he was most certainly not a
Romanist nor a Puseyite.[33]

In a positive and perceptive review four years later Nevin
complained that the book had not yet received the measure of
attention to which it was entitled. He felt that the work continued to be overlooked by the American Church. The "anti-
popery panic" of the times had called forth criticism of *The
Principle* but, Nevin asserted, no scientific criticism had as yet
been given. Then, in a fine summary, Nevin pointed out those
elements in *The Principle* by which the American Church
would profit through a proper investigation: (1) Christianity
is historical; (2) the stream of life belonging to Christianity
before the Reformation lay mainly in the bosom of the Roman

than for the intellectual honesty of its professors as he chided: "As you and Dr. Nevin entertain so high a regard for Church Authority, decisions, traditions, it is marvelously strange that in this respect also, you do not bow to the opinion and decisions of the Church." [37] In a typically dogmatic fashion Heiner also presumed to be speaking for the entire church when he exhorted the professor.

Illustrative of the sarcastic bitterness which confronted Schaff was an article by the Baltimore Correspondent ("S. R.")[38] of *The Weekly Messenger:*

Well, really Doctor, you have done remarkably well, considering your brief sojourn at Jericho, and the distance you have lived from "Oxford and Rome." You seem to have made rapid advances indeed, considering the time you have been journeying towards the celestial cities, and the difficulties you had to encounter on your way! And may we not hope that you will at length safely arrive at the seven hilled city, having passed a night at Oxford on your route, and then and there have the unspeakable joy of throwing yourself into the loving arms of Holy Mother!—enjoying to your heart's content her fond and affectionate caresses! She will no doubt be overjoyed to see an erring son restored to her embrace.[39]

As charge after charge was directed toward Schaff and Nevin, Nevin reacted in August, 1845, with a series of five articles in *The Weekly Messenger* entitled "Pseudo-Protestantism." [40] In this series he defended his refusal "to unchurch" the entire Roman communion as well as his doctrine of the spiritually real presence of Christ in the eucharist. Nevin characterized his attackers as being "loveless, intolerant, harsh—a new incarnation in fact of the papacy itself." [41] Continuing, he identified what he considered the greatest threat to the church: "The Protestant Church at this time has no greater enemy to her prosperity than this bastard zeal, which affects to usurp her name and pass itself off before the world as the true expression of her life." [42] Concluding his fifth article, he charged that the cry of heresy against the doctrines and teachings of the

Mercersburg teachers was a "loud ecclesiastical libel." [43] One is not surprised to see Nevin bear the brunt of the attack in later years after reading from his vitriolic pen. Though he was correct in his judgments, he antagonized people by the way he formulated them.

At the instigation of Berg the matter of *The Principle of Protestantism* was taken up by the Philadelphia Classis which met September 16, 1845. Schaff's book was examined by a committee with Berg acting as chairman. With Berg presiding the outcome of their study was a foregone conclusion. The committee brought the following resolutions to the Classis for adoption :

1. Resolved, That we regard the doctrine, that the Scriptures are the only rule of faith and practice as fundamental and essential to the existence of Christianity, and that we utterly deny the propriety of asserting that Scripture may under any circumstances be undervalued in favor of human addition or tradition. (Rev. 22:18, 19)

2. Resolved, That we regard faith in Christ as the life-giving principle of Christianity, (Gal. 2:20) and that under no circumstances may the efficacy of the sacraments be represented as superior to that of faith.

3. Resolved, That we deem the sentiment, that the sacraments depend not for their efficacy upon the spiritual state of the receiver, as contravening the great truth that the sacraments without faith are unavailing. (Remember Judas)

4. Resolved, That we hold as a fundamental doctrine that we derive our religious life from Christ by the truth, through the quickening influence of the Spirit, and that whilst the ordinances of the Church are channels through which spiritual blessings are conveyed, they cannot confer religious life.

5. Resolved, That we hold that Christ is not bodily present with his people in the celebration of the Lord's Supper, in any other way than symbolically, but is spiritually present with them to the end of time, and that this institution is intended to remind us of his death, till he come the second time in his glorified body; that we cannot admit that the presence of Christ

in the Lord's Supper is corporeal as it was in the days of his flesh, because his presence with his Church on earth is no longer human, but divine and spiritual, and that in all cases in which the flesh and blood of Christ are said to be received in the Sacrament of the Supper, the language is to be understood symbolically and not literally.

6. Inasmuch, as it is believed by many that sentiments contrary to the above essential doctrines of God's word are inculcated in a work entitled the 'Principle of Protestantism,' (p. 122-124) therefore Resolved that the attention of Synod be called to the work in question.[44]

It is observed that the technical intent of the resolutions is to place on trial a book instead of a man. The practical result, however, is much more personal than inanimate objects! Interestingly enough, Schaff could have subscribed to the first five resolutions himself. Nothing expressed in *The Principle*, if read in its entirety and within context, was inconsistent with these resolutions. But, as is often true of heresy hunters, here was an attempt to obtain a quick discreditation of a man and his work by the use of generalities and "holy-mouth" defenses of the faith which has ostensibly been attacked! The person or group who shouts "heresy" enjoys the psychological advantage of the vicious rumor. By thus shouting they place the burden of proof upon the object, whether or not such proof is needed. This is exactly what happened in the case of Philip Schaff.

The resolutions presented to the Philadelphia Classis by the Berg committee were adopted by a vote of eleven to one. The Reverend J. F. Foulk protested the adoption of the articles, not because he disbelieved them, but because of their express and implied object of fastening upon Schaff's work the charge of inculcating dangerous and Romanistic errors. He concluded his objection by confessing:

While I do not feel prepared to endorse all the sentiments in *The Principle of Protestantism*, by our theological professors at Mercersburg as really true, *especially* when wrested from their

connection, and made to assume a mere isolated form, I feel as
little prepared to pronounce them false, either expressly or im-
pliedly.[45]

According to the Minutes of the Classis, C. R. Kessler, J. R.
Rooken, and A. L. Young entered a similar statement. A final
resolution was adopted which seemed to be an outright blow to
Schaff's interpretation of church history. Though it carried a
rider stating that no implication was intended concerning
Schaff's work (probably insisted upon by the less radical element), the resolution bitterly attacked the Catholic Church.

Resolved, That in accordance with the general sentiment of the
Protestant Church we regard the *Papal System* as the great
Apostasy under the Christian dispensation—'the man of sin'—'the
mystery of iniquity,'—'the mother of abominations of the earth'
(I Tim. iv. 1-3; II Thess. i. 7-12; II Thess. ii. 3, 4) ; and as such,
is destined to utter and fearful destruction (II Thess. i. 8; Rev.
xviii and xix).[46]

The Berg faction, by its action, had put the icing on the cake.
Little did they realize, though, that the recipe was faulty and
the icing too bitter for the Synod's taste.

It must be said that another classis reacted against this
criticism. Before the opening of the Synod, the Classis of
East Pennsylvania met and, on October 1, 1845, passed a resolution endorsing the orthodoxy of the professors with regard
to the attack made upon them by the Philadelphia Classis.[47]

When the Synod met at York, October 16, 1845, it received
the complaint of the Philadelphia Classis. The Synod actually
bypassed constitutional technicality in even considering the
charges made by the classis because such complaints were supposed to come before the Board of Visitors of the Seminary
before the Synod received them. At the request of the professors themselves, however, the case was opened.

A special committee consisting of one member from each
classis was appointed to consider the charges. Upon the com-

pletion of its work the committee brought back to the Synod for adoption the following resolutions:

That after a most earnest and thorough examination of the Book referred to them, together with its Introduction and Appendix, the committee is entirely persuaded that it does not contain anything by which the charges preferred by the Philadelphia Classis can be sustained, or that should lead to the suspicion or fear that our professors are disposed to depart from the true protestant standpoint;—on the contrary that they are disposed firmly to maintain it; and that the Book if fairly understood is well calculated to promote the true interests of religion, and entitles its author to the respect and affectionate regard of the protestant community.

That the Professors in our Theological Seminary are deserving and should receive the affectionate sympathy and cordial support of every friend of the Church in their earnest and untiring efforts to build up our Institutions and to advance the honor and welfare of the Church.

That without desiring for a moment to limit the right, or to restrain the disposition of any individual, or religious body in the Church, freely to inquire into the doctrines or conduct of those having charge of our institutions, or to question, or reflect upon the motives which led to the recent movement on the part of a majority of the Philadelphia Classis, Synod is decidedly of the opinion, that the course indicated by the Constitution and sanctioned by the custom of the Church, is the only safe, true and proper course to be pursued in bringing to the notice of Synod complaints against our Theological Professors.[48]

The Berg group had been annihilated by these resolutions in more ways than they realized. The first paragraph practically accuses the professors' opposition of sheer ignorance! The professors are then complimented, and the wrists of the Berg faction are further slapped for not using the proper constitutional procedure.

The full report of the committee answered the accusations item by item and then summarized them in the above resolutions. There resulted quite naturally an "acrimonious discussion." The discussions and speeches lasted for several days, but, unfortunately, no records were kept. If a court recorder had been present the most interesting aspect of the trial would have been preserved for posterity. But one can only imagine the course taken by the speeches. Joseph Berg spoke for two hours in opposition to the report. Nevin's defense lasted two hours and Schaff's four and one-half hours in all. J. H. A. Bomberger spoke lengthily in favor of the report, and Jacob Helfenstein attacked it. When the vote was finally taken, it was strongly in favor of the report. There were forty "yeas" and three "nays" recorded. The Synod, in voting so positively, had also placed its sanction on the longer section of the report which, among other things, had criticized the action of the Phila-delphia Classis as being "characterized by an entire absence of consideration and forethought."

Philip Schaff, then, was completely exonerated of all charges by the action of the Synod of York in 1845. But the opposition was far from being silenced. Heresy hunters never die; they just change their basis of attack. Since *The Principle* had been declared orthodox, Berg and his friends were forced to find other writings which might serve their purpose just as well. So they did.

When the members of the Philadelphia Classis met in the fall of 1846 they expressed anger at the Synod of York's censure of their Classis in the Mercersburg matter. The Classis renewed its statements of faith, and Helfenstein offered a resolution that the Classis approve the protest of the delegate, the Reverend Dr. Berg, and his "firmness under the trying circum-stances." [49] New resolutions were passed in opposition to *The Principle of Protestantism* and to Schaff's more recent produc-tion, *What Is Church History?* The Classis also condemned anew the idea that the Roman Catholic Church be regarded as belonging in the main stream of Christian history. The last resolution of the Classis finally revealed the Berg group's fresh attack upon Schaff. It was as follows: "Resolved, That Synod be requested to inquire into Dr. Schaff's views concerning the intermediate state; to ascertain whether he believes that death terminates the probation of all men, and closes to them the gospel offer of pardon." [50] The heresy hunters had finally landed upon a highly speculative aspect of eschatology—a favorite area of investigation for such hunters.

In 1898 *The Reformed Church Messenger* received a letter requesting information about a so-called second trial of Philip Schaff.[51] The letter asking the question was sent because Schaff was in the habit of saying he had been twice tried for heresy. But his son's recent and supposedly definitive biography did not mention any second trial. Though not brought before the Synod for a formal trial, Schaff did undergo in 1846 a second heresy trial which was not merely a continuation of the 1845 affair. The accusations assumed a different form and, from all appearances, a man stood trial instead of a book this time. Although this second trial was conducted privately by the Board of Visitors, if the report presented to the Synod concerning Schaff's views had been negative, it would very likely have resulted in his resignation.

The events leading up to this second trial are most interesting and especially revelatory of the moral character of the opposition. On July 9, 1846, *The Christian Intelligencer,* a Dutch Reformed news agency, published the Reverend Guldin's translation of extracts from Schaff's work *Die Sünde wider den Heiligen Geist.*[52] The translation ended with Schaff's conclusion that for all men "there is a middle state, which begins with death, and continues to the final judgment." [53] Schaff designated three categories which participate in this middle state: (1) Those despising salvation in Christ are put in a Hades prison to await the final judgment. (2) For the undecided, who had no opportunity in the temporal life to respond to Christ's way of life, and for all the heathen, there is a time of grace after death and the possibility of the remission of sins and repentance—but only by faith. Schaff retained a high Christology even in the midst of this eschatological speculation. His soteriology remained dependent even here upon his Christology with its emphasis upon a positive response to the Christ act in time. Also included in this second category are those in whom, before death, faith had begun but had not matured to full communion with the Lord. Each one in this category, he asserted, must pass through a period of trial and purification, but not in the Catholic sense of self-works. (3) For Christians there awaits a childhood of communion which will be matured fully only at the Resurrection and final day of triumph.[54] It was quite normal for a young theological student, and perhaps for an older one as well, to be concerned about the question of ultimate destiny and to speculate along such lines. But to the unquestioning orthodox, the issue was closed and there was no room for speculation.

In the next issue of *The Christian Intelligencer,* an unsigned article thanked the translator of Schaff's *Die Sünde* on behalf of the Dutch Reformed Church, whose suspicions concerning the orthodoxy of professors within the German Reformed Church had now been verified! The article expressed the opinion that if there were to come about any organic relationship between these two communions (which had actually been anticipated and planned), a more complete answer to the German Reformed professorial doctrinal standpoint would have to be given. The writer correctly claimed that a quick excuse of Schaff's "German-mind and terminology" would not be an adequate answer to the Dutch Reformed.[55]

The following week *The Christian Intelligencer* was fair enough to print Schaff's answering letter. In it he criticized the motives of the translator, accusing him of only wishing to bring Schaff's orthodoxy into discredit by publishing the selections from *Die Sünde.* Schaff pointed out that Guldin's method of selection of the passages printed was to choose those which would most likely conflict with the general thinking among Protestants. He also implied that Guldin's motivation was to cultivate negative feelings between the German Reformed and the Dutch Reformed communions. The young professor felt, and rightly, it was strange indeed that his opponents were not satisfied with attacking what he had published in the United States, "but must carry their inquisition also to an Essay which appeared several years ago in the old world, before I dreamed of ever seeing the shores of the United States." [56] The author of *Die Sünde* pointed out that the writing was a juvenile performance prepared with the freedom of thought and inquiry common to the German educational scene. To go back to this product of his student days as a basis for his present relation to the German Reformed Church was deemed unfair treatment. Schaff was also eager for the readers to know that the investigating committee which extended him the invitation to come to Mercersburg was acquainted with the essay and had also been told of his desire not to have it translated. The Schaff correspondence definitely proves that Guldin was aware of Schaff's feelings about this matter.[57] And yet, in spite of the ethics involved, Guldin catered to base motives and wrote his translation. Rather cuttingly, Schaff advised the news organ to use a more competent translator next time and then concluded by declaring his willingness to state openly his present position on the doctrine in question.

Whether, after all, my views of the Middle State, as held with more mature judgment at the present time, (and as I may yet lay them before the world, if God sees fit, in a new edition of the Essay in question,) would be found to accord with the theology of your correspondent, I, of course, am not able fully to say. My apprehension is, that they would not. But all this is of no particular account. I stand responsible for them, as already said, to my own Church; and this responsibility I am perfectly willing to meet at any moment.[58]

A correspondent signed "N" (probably Nevin) sent to *The Weekly Messenger* a copy of Schaff's letter to the Dutch Reformed paper. It was printed in the *Messenger* along with the correspondent's advice to transfer the letter to the *Messenger's* columns "in reply to the attempt made in a previous number of that paper [*The Christian Intelligencer*] to injure his reputation, by some excerpts bunglingly translated from his juvenile performance '*Die Sünde wider den heiligen Geist.*' The whole case is one that demands some attention." [59] The last suggestion was certainly followed!

It was inevitable that the matter would come before the Synod of 1846 which met in Carlisle, Cumberland County, Pennsylvania. The Philadelphia Classis objected to the views of Schaff as expressed in his recent book *What Is Church History?* and to his doctrine of the intermediate state as set forth in *Die Sünde*. The former charge was not even considered by the Synod, and the latter was disposed of in a private interview between Schaff and the Board of Visitors.

The Board reported to the Synod that it had secured from Schaff the following modification of his views concerning the intermediate or middle state:

I object to my former view of the Middle State as contained in my essay on the sin against the Holy Ghost, written six years ago at Berlin,
1. That the scriptural and philosophical argumentation is by no means in all respects satisfactory to me at present.
2. That the statement is too general, and
3. That it is too positive and categorical.
I now hold hypothetically in regard to the subject in dispute,
1. That in the case of those heathen who have died without the knowledge of the gospel either before the coming of Christ or since, and who have been at the same time properly predisposed to embrace the Christian salvation, the opportunity of doing so (and thus completing the work already commenced) will not be withheld from them by an infinitely merciful God in the world to come.
2. That if persons thus described are saved at all, they cannot be saved on the ground of any personal merit, but only through Jesus Christ, as there is absolutely no salvation without him.
3. This involves the idea that Christ previously unknown must be exhibited to them in some way as the object of their knowledge of faith.

4. All this, however, and the whole subject of the Middle State
of the heathen, and of infants universally is involved in great
obscurity, nor can it ever be made properly the subject of doctrinal and symbolical teaching.[60]

Schaff recognized the speculative nature of such thought, but in
the midst of it he retained a very high Christology which could
be only satisfactory to the orthodox churchman.

In relation to the whole matter, the Board unanimously
adopted the following resolution:

Resolved, That whilst the Board cannot endorse the view of Dr.
Schaf as set forth in the above statement, they nevertheless do
not deem it of sufficient importance to call for any special action
of Synod. The Board deem it necessary to add, that the view has
not been taught nor is it contemplated ever to be taught in the
Theological Seminary.[61]

Though the Synod was in a "very nervous condition," the
report of the Board was adopted with the addition of a single
resolution:

Resolved, That whilst in consideration of the statement of the doctrine of the intermediate state contained in the report of the
Board of Visitors, the case is not thought to demand special action
on the part of Synod, we nevertheless cannot endorse the reported modification of the view in question.[62]

The Synod expressed its nervous condition by the added
resolution, but it refused to censure one of its professors simply
because his view on a single doctrine did not correspond with
that of the majority. Although not refusing to express disagreement, it did refuse to express its belief in its own infallibility,
a claim which would have necessarily stifled Schaff or any
other theological professor who might teach at Mercersburg.
The Synod preserved in a precedenting way the full freedom
of the teacher to search for truth and then to express it as he
believes he has found it.

For all formal purposes this closed the case for the Synod. Once again, however, at the Synod of 1847 which met in Lancaster, Pennsylvania, Berg and Helfenstein complained to the Board of Visitors that the professors of the Seminary varied in their doctrines from the standards of the church and the Word of God. The Board responded with the following resolution: "Resolved, That the Board cannot grant the request of the Reverend Doctor Berg, inasmuch as his specifications are not sufficiently distinct, and the request has been presented to the Board, at too late a period to receive regular attention." [63] The final *formal* "silence" had been placed upon Schaff's antagonists. Actually, more theological noise would be made by the opposition, but, formally, the Synod would take no action.

Though Schaff's views on the intermediate state were not approved by the Synod, action was not taken against him personally. Actually, the final attitude of the Synod was another step forward in the long struggle for academic and religious freedom. The descriptive adjective "religious" must not be underemphasized in this "Schaffian" context. Schaff, himself, was convinced that man, of necessity, must be completely free in his quest for religious truth. This intense conviction resulted from his principle of the unitary nature of truth. Over and beyond academic freedom, man's religious search for truth must never be hampered by denominational biases and creedal statements. This was no side issue; it was a vital concern of this dedicated Swiss scholar. He would later choose as a motto for his multivolume *History of the Christian Church* the following declaration: *Christianus sum: Christiani nihil a me alienum puto.*

Even though the Board stated that these views were not being taught at the Seminary (a good move in public relations, perhaps), there is definite proof that Schaff, in his classroom lectures, was speculating about an intermediate state as late as the academic year of 1859-60.[64] It naturally follows, then, that he, as well as others, was enjoying a large measure of academic and religious freedom by this time. After 1847 heresy trials are events of the past in the German Reformed Church.

Encouragement and congratulations were received by Schaff from varied sources during and after the trials. J. H. Good wrote to Schaff congratulating him on the triumph and expressed hope that the Mercersburg theology might live forever.[65] A letter was penned by George L. Prentiss wishing Schaff and Nevin success in their endeavor to inspire the American Church with deeper Catholic instruction. He understandingly said: "You no doubt find the *Theological* soil of the New World somewhat rough and uncongenial: but for all that it is full of life and power, only wanting a wise and liberal science to make it become the most excellent finish." [66]

Schaff's most formidable opponent, Joseph F. Berg, left the German Reformed Church in March, 1852, in order to align himself with a more conservative communion, the Dutch Reformed Church. That same year he became a teacher at Rutgers College. *The Weekly Messenger* gave notice of his departure, heavily censuring him for not having left much earlier and in a quieter manner. It reminded Berg of the words in his own farewell speech to his church, as applied to his relation to the German Reformed Church: "That man incurs a terrible responsibility who recklessly undermines a pastor's influence; not for ten thousand worlds would I encounter it." [67] Nevin, in *The Mercersburg Review,* agreed that Berg's departure should have been made quietly but that, instead, he had played Hannibal or Napoleon. Nevin complained that Berg had intended drastic changes for the German Reformed Church, and had left its communion severely feeling his failure: "He does accordingly the best he can; makes a merit of valorously forsaking its communion, and endeavors to carry away with him the laurels of a great and glorious martyr. *Requiescat in pace!*" [68]

On the count of Romanizing, however, Schaff was still attacked. As soon as his *History of the Apostolic Church* appeared in 1854, the radical Dutch Reformed journal, *The New Brunswick Review,* made a scathing criticism of his so-called

Romanistic tendencies. *The Review* condemned Schaff's theory of historical Christianity as being thoroughly papal in all its essential features and tendencies. Professor J. W. Proudfit, of Rutgers College, the writer of the article, also spoke disparagingly of Schaff's use of "poetico-romantic sentimentality." Proudfit sarcastically concluded his article by saying that if Schaff's book were used as a text in seminaries, as some persons had suggested, the schools would do well to apply to the General of the Society of Jesus for professors to teach it! [69] Benjamin S. Schneck, one of the members of the committee which had extended Schaff's original call to America, noticed the article and wrote Schaff an encouraging letter. It was one which probably reveals the general attitude in the German Reformed Church toward such vitriolic outside efforts.

The 'New Brunswick Review' contained an *extinguisher* on your Church History from Dr. Pr. More than 60 pp. of the most overstrained and merely clap-trap sort of fault-finding (not reviewing), are devoted to it. The printing was so heavy, that the canvas could not bear it. *The New York Observor* a few weeks back gave a most able, gentlemanly, and yet withering expose. It is really a masterpiece, and is supposed to be from the pen of Prof. McClelland. The *Observor* even prefaced it with decided commendatory remarks and expresses himself satisfied that the reviewer has acted courageously.[70]

Such efforts as Proudfit's could no longer jeopardize Schaff's position, but they could rupture any possible ecumenical relations between these two Reformed traditions.

The most caustic diatribe against Schaff's *History*, however, came from the pen of J. J. Janeway, minister in the Dutch Reformed Church. True to his orientation, Janeway attacked Schaff for finding Christianity in the Catholic Church of the middle ages and then developed his own Waldensian theory.

How easily, could this historian, (had not his eyes been **beclouded** by his attachment to Popery,) have traced an unbroken **perpetuity**

of Christianity through these different Churches; and discovered
the fulfillment of 'the Lord's precious promise to be and rule in
his Church continually.' Among these churches he could have
seen a *true, visible, Catholic* Church.[71]

Janeway refuted Schaff's developmental theory of history, called
the papacy anti-Christ, and assured his readers of a further
exposé which would save them from the expense of purchasing
the German professor's book! His review was actually printed
as a separate small volume and carried the lengthy title, *Antidote to the Poison of Popery in the Publications of Professor
Schaff*. But the efforts of Janeway and his kind were rather
futile by now, and Schaff was actually academically safe.

Mercersburg and its professors were battle-tried, but the
withdrawal of Berg in 1852 and the resignation of Nevin in
1851 appeared to be healing ointment for the wounds of war.
Although rumblings such as those caused by Proudfit and
Janeway would continue, the tensions were certainly eased by
these events.

Parenthetically, it should be mentioned that Nevin had
actually become the main target in the later phase of the attack
upon Mercersburg theology. It was even Nevin's conviction
that the post-trial criticism of Schaff was due to their personal
relationship.[72] As has been stated earlier, however, the primary
difference between Schaff and Nevin was not so much a theological variance as it was a psychological and temperamental
dissimilarity.

After 1852 Schaff enjoyed comparative theological quiet at
Mercersburg as he busied himself with his lectures and writing
and the liturgical movement within the German Reformed
Church. In 1863 Schaff secured a two years' leave of absence
from Mercersburg and, at the conclusion of that period, he
formally resigned his professorship there. Two very trying, yet
fruitful, decades in the career of Philip Schaff thus came to a
close as he took up residence in New York City—a city which
would afford him the research opportunities for which he had
so earnestly longed.

The Union Theological Seminary in New York extended an invitation in 1870 to Schaff to become its professor of theological encyclopaedia and Christian symbolism. He accepted and was destined to spend the rest of his academic career at this institution. His inaugural address at Union was delivered on October 10, 1871, and his subject was "The Theology for Our Age and Country." In this lecture he adumbrated those principles of ecumenical Christianity with which he would be so vitally engaged for the rest of his life. On the occasion of this, his second inaugural in America, there was no danger of a heresy trial resulting from the irenical views of a seasoned, thoroughly Americanized, German professor. The notices of his inaugural were most laudatory and commendatory—even from so great a distance as the *German Reformed Messenger*.

The last years of Schaff's life were caught up, to some degree, in the agitation and dissension caused within the Presbyterian Church, U.S.A. and Union Theological Seminary by the famous heresy trial which charged Charles Augustus Briggs with denying the infallibility and sufficiency of the Scriptures. Schaff had faced the same problem of academic and religious freedom in 1845 within the German Reformed Church and had been exonerated. He labored tirelessly toward a similar vindication of C. A. Briggs. This trial was not destined to end with the same happy results as had his own, but this was not through Schaff's neglect. Though in ill health, Schaff wrote numerous defenses of Briggs [73] and was actually at Briggs' side during the formal trials. He was convinced that the charges of heresy which were being hurled at Briggs were absolutely invalid, and made brilliant defenses of Briggs' orthodoxy. In fact, Schaff believed that Briggs was actually more orthodox on matters of the faith than were those who attacked him!

One hesitates to think of the loss which would have occurred to the American religious tradition if either one of Philip Schaff's heresy trials had been negative in its result. If Schaff had returned to Europe, the loss would have included his eight-volume *History of the Christian Church* and his classical *Creeds of Christendom,* in addition to the hundreds of other books and articles which he wrote. Lost also would have been his untiring efforts in Bible revision, the 1873 meeting of the Evangelical Alliance in New York City, and the foundation of the American Society of Church History in 1888. If the heresy hunters of 1845-46 had been successful, the American Church would have forfeited its most formidable prophet of the ecumenical age. At the Parliament of Religions meeting in Chicago, September, 1893, the most irenical and ecumenical production of his career was presented, *The Reunion of Christendom.* Inspired by an idealistic vision, he foresaw a peaceful end to all sectarian wars "when all the Churches shall be thoroughly Christianized and all the creeds of Christendom unified in the creed of Christ." [74]

At his death on October 20, 1893, amid all the comments and resolutions of praise was one which seemed best to capture the true spirit of the career which had *not* been lost to the American religious tradition. It was made by the Society of Biblical Literature and Exegesis:

Seldom does a man of foreign birth who has won a name as a scholar before becoming an American citizen succeed so completely as did Dr. Schaff in catching the spirit of our political and religious life, and coming to so thorough and sanguine a faith in our country's privileges and opportunities. So catholic was his spirit, so broad were his interests, so multifarious, so enterprising and many-sided his literary undertakings and achievements, that he has often been pointed out as the typical American scholar. . . . He possessed rare skill, for a scholar, in the popular presentation of learning; and no one could well surpass him in imparting the contagion of his own enthusiasm to others. Many were the young men of promise who were stimulated by the opportunities he opened for them, or by the association of their labors with his own.[75]

NOTES

1. For the most recent interpretation of this theological school see James Hastings Nichols, *Romanticism in American Theology* (Chicago: The University of Chicago Press, 1961). Also see Theodore

L. Trost, "Philip Schaff's Concept of the Church With Special Reference to His Role in the Mercersburg Movement, 1844-1864," unpublished Ph.D. dissertation, New College, Edinburgh University, 1958. The *Lancaster Series on the Mercersburg Theology,* edited by Bard Thompson and George H. Bricker (Philadelphia: United Church Press), projects six volumes of source readings from the Mercersburg Theology. Schaff's *The Principle of Protestantism,* volume I in the series, appeared in 1964.

2. Schaff's correspondence and manuscripts indicate that he spelled his name as "Schaf" and "Schaff" until *circa* 1847 when he settled on the latter spelling.

3. The mediational school proclaimed the authority of the Bible in matters of religion, though it did not admit either the infallibility of the canon or the plenary inspiration of the text. Both canon and text could be submitted to the test of historical criticism. Likewise, this school retained in a polar relation the authority of the church with its tradition and the authority of the individual in the name of his Christian consciousness.

4. For an excellent discussion of the German theological influences upon Schaff, see Klaus Penzel, "Church History and the Ecumenical Quest: A Study of the German Background and Thought of Philip Schaff," unpublished Th.D. dissertation, Union Theological Seminary, 1962.

5. (Halle: Johann Friedrick Lippert, 1841).

6. Cited in David Schaff, *The Life of Philip Schaff* (New York: Charles Scribner's Sons, 1897), p. 69.

7. Letters in Archives Collection of the German Reformed Church, Fackenthal Library, Franklin and Marshall College, Lancaster, Pennsylvania. This collection will be cited hereafter as F Letters.

8. The manuscript of the invitation is found in F Letters.

9. The manuscript of the permission, signed by the Prussian Secretary of Education, Eichhorn, is found in F Letters.

10. *The Weekly Messenger,* IX (Sept. 4, 1844), 1869. (Hereafter cited as WM.)

11. *Ibid.*

12. *Ibid.,* p. 1870.

13. An undated letter from Pusey to Schaff in F Letters also supports this statement. Pusey concludes the letter by stating: "I do not wish to envolve [*sic*] you or myself in controversy. I only wish to be true and honest."

14. Nearly a half century later Protestant writers still claimed that Romanism was a major threat to the democratic principle. See Josiah Strong, *Our Country: Its Possible Future and Its Present Crisis* (New York: The Baker and Taylor Co., 1885), pp. 46-59.

15. Schaff made reference to this incident in his class lectures of 1855 at Mercersburg. See C. C. Russell, "Notes of Dr. Schaff's Lectures on Church History (311-590)" (handwritten manuscript in Fack-

enthal Collection), p. 100. In his discussion of the Donatist schism he alluded to the contemporary scene: "The Old School Presbyterians at Cincinnati declared the Roman baptism *null* and invalid. This is the greatest piece of foolishness ever heard of. The Catholics even acknowledge protestant baptism when performed in the name of the Trinity. The principle [*sic*] men in the Presbyterian do not obey the decision of the Assembly."

16. See W. R. Cross, *The Burned-Over District* (Ithaca, N. Y.: Cornell University Press, 1950), *passim*.
17. *Democracy in America,* Henry Reeve, tr., II (4th ed. rev.; New York: Henry G. Langley, 1845), 142.
18. Cross, *The Burned-Over District,* pp. 187-88.
19. "Dr. Schaf's Reception at Mercersburg," WM, IX (Aug. 21, 1844), 1863.
20. *Ibid.*
21. *Ibid.*
22. Cited in David Schaff, *The Life of Philip Schaff,* p. 103.
23. *Ibid.,* p. 104. David states here: "It will appear, however, that this very relation put Dr. Schaff more than once in a position where his real views were subjected to serious misconstruction."
24. *Acts and Proceedings of the Synod of the German Reformed Church in the United States (Eastern Synod),* Allentown, Pennsylvania, 1844, p. 26.
25. J. F. Berg, " 'A Sermon' Delivered at the Opening of the Synod of the German Reformed Church at Allentown, Pennsylvania, October 17, 1844," WM, X (Nov. 20, 1844), 1913.
26. *Ibid.*
27. "Inauguration of Dr. Schaff," WM, X (Nov. 6, 1844), 1907.
28. Philip Schaf, *The Principle of Protestantism as Related to the Present State of the Church,* John W. Nevin, tr. (Chambersburg, Pennsylvania: "Publication Office" of the German Reformed Church, 1845).
29. WM, X (April 9, 1845), 1990-91; X (Apr. 23, 1845), 1998.
30. Moses Kiefer, "Theological Seminary at Mercersburg, Earlier Reminiscences, 1838-1851," WM, XXXVI (July 6, 1870), 2.
31. Pp. 121-28.
32. "Review of *The Principle of Protestantism* by PS," *Biblical Repertory and Princeton Review,* XVII (Oct., 1845), pp. 626-36. This review was reprinted in WM, XI (Nov. 12, 1845), 2113. Hodge criticized Schaff for giving no clear definition of the church, for not presenting prominently enough the opposition of the principle of justification by faith to a mediating Church (Catholic), for giving too much weight to the opinions and traditions of the visible church, and for what Hodge considered to be a false conception of sectarism. Hodge complains that German writers "are seldom very intelligible," and then admits that "there is a great deal that is due to the peculiar philosophical and historical training of the

writer; much that we do not understand." Hodge was evidently aware of his own deficiencies in German thought!

33. Tayler Lewis, "The Church Question," WM, XI (Jan. 21, 28, Feb. 5, 1846), pp. 2153, 2157, 2161.
34. J. W. Nevin, "Review of *The Principle of Protestantism* by PS," *The Mercersburg Review*, I (Jan., 1849), 63-104.
35. *Ibid.*, p. 94.
36. *Ibid.*, p. 104.
37. Letter from Elias Heiner to Philip Schaff, July 19, 1845, F Letters.
38. Nichols, *Romanticism in American Theology*, p. 153, identifies the correspondent as Heiner himself!
39. "The Protestantism of Mercersburg, as Contrasted with the Protestantism of the Bible and the German Reformed Church," WM, XI (Oct. 15, 1845), 2096. It is interesting to note that in this same edition (p. 2094) there is an article signed "a member of the church" which completely vindicates Schaff and Nevin, saying that there has been gross misrepresentation and misunderstanding of the professors' views.
40. WM, X (Aug. 13, 1845), 2061; (Aug. 20), 2065; (Aug. 27), 2069; (Sept. 3), 2073; (Sept. 10), 2077.
41. *Ibid.*, p. 2061.
42. *Ibid.*
43. *Ibid.*, p. 2077.
44. "Minutes of the Classis of Philadelphia, 1836-1868" (handwritten manuscript in the Fackenthal Collection).
45. *Ibid.*
46. *Ibid.*
47. "Minutes of the East Pennsylvania Classis, 1845" (Fackenthal Collection).
48. *Acts and Proceedings*, York, Pennsylvania, 1845, p. 80.
49. "Minutes of the Classis of Philadelphia, 1836-1868."
50. *Ibid.*
51. "Dr. Schaff's Second Trial for Heresy," *The Reformed Church Messenger*, LXVI (Oct. 6, 1898), 2-3.
52. " 'The Intermediate State,' from Dr. Schaf's work *Sin Against the Holy Spirit*," *The Christian Intelligencer*, XVI (July 9, 1846), 206.
53. *Ibid.*
54. *Ibid.*
55. "Our Relations to the German Reformed Church," *The Christian Intelligencer*, XVII (July 16, 1846), 2.
56. Philip Schaff, "Letter for *The Christian Intelligencer*," *The Christian Intelligencer*, XVII (July 23, 1846), 6.
57. Letter from B. S. Schneck to Philip Schaff, Dec. 3, 1846, F Letters. Schneck states that he and others had told Guldin of Schaff's desire not to have *Die Sünde* translated.
58. Philip Schaff, *The Christian Intelligencer*, XVII, 6. A feeble reply

to Schaff from Guldin was carried in *The Christian Intelligencer,*
XVII (July 30, 1846), 10.

59. "The Christian Intelligencer," WM XI (Aug. 5, 1846), 2266.
60. *Acts and Proceedings,* Carlisle, Pennsylvania, 1846, pp. 41-42.
61. *Ibid.,* p. 42.
62. *Ibid.*
63. *Acts and Proceedings,* Lancaster, Pennsylvania, 1847, p. 36.
64. E. R. Eschbach, "Notes on Church History taken under Philip
Schaff, 1859-1860" (handwritten manuscript in Fackenthal Collection). Schaff is especially bothered in these lectures with the
heathen who have died with no knowledge of Christ. He questions
the class: "There here arises a serious question. May there not be
an intermediate state for those who have never had the advantage of
becoming Christian?" He continues by observing that if the heathen
are to be saved, there must be a probationary period during which
Christ is preached. It is evident from this discussion that Schaff
did not give an absolute soteriological value to "general revelation."
The positive response to general revelation only qualifies one for
this middle state at which time special revelation of the Christ is
given. Only this revelation has ultimate soteriological value.
65. Feb. 24, 1847, F Letters.
66. May 17, 1848, Union Theological Seminary Letters.
67. "Farewell Words to the First German Reformed Church," WM,
XVII (Apr. 28, 1852), 3662.
68. J. W. Nevin, "Dr. Berg's Last Words," *The Mercersburg Review,*
IV (May, 1852), 284.
69. J. W. Proudfit, "Dr. Schaff's Works on Church History," *The
New Brunswick Review,* I (May, 1854), 61.
70. July 10, 1854, F Letters.
71. *Antidote to the Poison of Popery in the Publications of Professor
Schaff* (New Brunswick: J. Terhune and Son, 1854), pp. 35-36.
Also see Jacob Helfenstein, *A Perverted Gospel of the Romanizing
Tendency of the Mercersburg Theology* (Philadelphia: Wm. S.
Young, 1853).
72. Letter from J. W. Nevin to Philip Schaff, Feb. 22, 1854, F Letters.
73. Philip Schaff, "Other Heresy Trials and the Briggs Case," *The
Forum,* XII (Jan., 1892), pp. 621-33.
74. Philip Schaff, *The Reunion of Christendom,* Evangelical Alliance
Document XXXIII (New York: Evangelical Alliance Office,
1893), p. 29.
75. F Letters.

2. Crawford Howell Toy Heresy at Louisville

POPE A. DUNCAN

"An American heretic." [1] "The first to suffer for the Higher Criticism in the United States." [2] These descriptive phrases were both applied in honor to the subject of this chapter, Crawford Howell Toy (1836-1919). Seldom has a "heretic" been more beloved by his opponents than this one. No one of those who voted against him denied his ability, piety, honor, integrity, and candor. Indeed, they professed their admiration and even confidence in him.

If this all sounds strange, so it is! The "Toy Case" is one of the oddest, most complex in the annals of American church history. Its victim sought to draw the line of battle on the issue of the nature of inspiration. The opposition refused to question his orthodoxy and, in effect, made the decision against him on the issue of the nature of theological education. In truth, they may not have known what they were really doing, and he forgave them!

I. Toy's Early Career

Toy did not by chance become a scholar. His father, while a druggist, was himself an avid student. Languages particularly fascinated him. He lived in the port city of Norfolk, Virginia, and had reason to hear and use many modern tongues.

At times he served as an interpreter for merchantmen who came into port. Yet not satisfied with the ordinary languages, Thomas D. Toy studied Hebrew. His devotion to the Bible and his church made this a particularly interesting and attractive study to him. Thomas was active in the Freemason Street Baptist Church which he had helped found and was much beloved as a deacon.[3]

The eldest in a large family of four sons and five daughters, Crawford Howell Toy nevertheless was permitted an excellent education. After receiving his elementary training in Norfolk Academy, a military school, he attended the University of Virginia. The University was justly famous for its outstanding faculty, including Professor McGuffey of the classic reader, and its elective curriculum. Also at the University when Toy arrived in 1852 was John A. Broadus. He was serving as tutor in Greek but left to become pastor of the Baptist Church in Charlottesville before Toy began his study of the ancient languages at the University.[4]

After taking the Master of Arts degree in 1856 Toy continued in Charlottesville as a teacher in the Albemarle Female Institute for three years. This school had been organized as a result in part of the efforts of Broadus, who was president of its trustees. The principal, John Hart, Alexander Pope Abell, Toy, and Broadus broke with the current practice and put instruction in English on a par with the ancient classics and modern foreign languages.[5]

It was while teaching here that Toy first met Charlotte ("Lottie") Moon, who came as a student in 1857. Apparently a considerable courtship ensued, for in June of 1861 he called at her home and asked her to marry him. While she refused his proposal at this time, a later chapter in the story was to occur.[6]

Toy entered the first session of the Southern Baptist Theological Seminary in the fall of 1859. Broadus was there as a professor and had organized the curriculum on the University of Virginia elective plan. Other professors were James P. Boyce (who also served as President), Basil Manly, Jr., and William

Williams. In one year Toy finished about three quarters of the course which was supposed to take three years. In June, 1860, Broadus, who had baptized him in 1854, ordained him.

Toy became committed to the idea of going as a missionary to Japan and spent part of the academic year, 1860-61, at home apparently studying relative to this plan and visiting churches which had undertaken to sponsor him in Japan.[7] The last part of the year he served as professor of Greek at Richmond College. The outbreak of war prevented his missionary service, and in October, 1861, he entered the Norfolk Light Artillery Blues. He seems to have been a devoted supporter of the Confederacy.[8]

After serving for a time as private, he became an infantry chaplain in General Lee's army. He was in Longstreet's Corps at Gettysburg. During the retreat he remained behind with the surgeons and was wounded and captured on July 4, 1863.[9] Until December, when he was exchanged, he was a prisoner at Fort McHenry where he busied himself directing a glee club and teaching Italian.

Many stories have been handed down about the intellectual curiosity of Toy, but none are more revealing than those coming out of his period of service during the War. One which came from a friend related that during an interval in the battle of Cold Harbor in 1864 he was seen lying on his oilcloth "amusing" himself by studying Arabic. Another friend who saw him wrote a mutual acquaintance that Toy's Syriac books were in Norfolk and he had "to fall back on German for amusement." [10] It was also reported that "he tramped all the way from the Seven Pines battlefield to Richmond to consult a Hebrew grammar." [11]

After his exchange he was soon appointed professor of natural philosophy at the University of Alabama which was serving as a military training school for the Confederacy at that time. When the War was over, Toy returned to the University of Virginia where during 1865-66 he was "licentiate" in Greek.

One of the great formative periods in his life came in 1866-

68, during which he was in Berlin. (C. A. Briggs spent 1866-69 there also.)[12] Here he studied theology with Dorner, Sanskrit with Weber, and Semitics with Roediger and Dieterici.

On his return to the States Toy was appointed professor of Greek language and literature in Furman University, Greenville, South Carolina. Furman was a Baptist institution and had been a kind of mother to the much younger Southern Baptist Theological Seminary located in the same city. Indeed, Furman's theological library and endowment along with its young Professor Boyce had passed to the Seminary when it was founded in 1859.

Toy began his duties with Furman in January, 1869, with the clear understanding that he might resign at any time. Even during this period he gave private tutoring to students from the Seminary. Dr. Broadus' health was wretched, and in order to relieve him of some of his load the trustees invited Toy in May, 1869, to join the Seminary ranks as professor of Old Testament interpretation.[13]

II. Toy's Religious and Intellectual Development

We have already noted that Toy had the good fortune to be reared in a family which was both devout and intellectually curious. It must have been obvious from Toy's early years that here was a very bright youngster. No doubt the fact that he was sent to the University of Virginia reflects this recognition. The letters he wrote to friends during his college days[14] indicate that he was a discerning student. Sometimes critical of the laborious lecture method employed by some of his teachers, he was also a very normal student in his interest in fun and the girls. His letters also give evidence of an interest in religion and often mention revivals and other events in the local churches.

He seems to have fallen under the spell of the outstanding preaching of John A. Broadus in the Baptist Church in Charlottesville, and it is not surprising to learn that it was Broadus who baptized him in 1854.

Even as a young man he took a keen interest in the affairs of his denomination and demonstrated his progressive outlook. In a letter dated February 28, 1859, he pointed out to his friend Morton his strong opposition to the views of J. R. Graves. Graves was just at this time leading a movement in the Southern Baptist Convention known as Landmarkism which sought to win favor for a doctrine of the church which would deny a valid ministry, valid sacraments, and a right to be designated "church" to any other communion but the Baptist. Graves believed that Baptists alone had a continuous history as valid churches from the days of the apostles. In addition his exaggerated view of the autonomy and importance of the local church would have completely undermined the cooperative ventures of Southern Baptists, particularly the Foreign Mission Board. Toy's strong statement about all this was that those who supported Graves "are such as have read nothing but the *Tennessee Baptist* and are not men of reliable judgment in such matters." [15] Perhaps there were other than intellectual and religious reasons for Toy's opposition to Graves. R. B. C. Howell, the greatest personal enemy of Graves, was married to an aunt of Toy, a sister of his father. Howell and Graves had been involved in a bitter conflict in Nashville, Tennessee. Howell was for a number of years president of the Southern Baptist Convention.

Toy remained under the spell of Broadus. Not only was Broadus president of the trustees of the Albemarle Female Institute when Toy was teaching there, but when Broadus joined the faculty of the newly founded Southern Baptist Theological Seminary in 1859, Toy journeyed to Greenville to study with him. As a matter of fact, for at least some, if not all, of the time he was in Greenville Toy was boarding with Broadus.[16] Broadus was as impressed with Toy as he with Broadus. Broadus wrote in March, 1860, "Toy is among the foremost scholars I have ever known of his years, and an uncommonly conscientious and devoted man." [17]

Toy was a deeply devout young man and with some of his friends had decided upon a missionary career. He was particularly anxious to go to Japan. After the Seminary session was over Broadus journeyed back to Charlottesville, Virginia, to ordain Toy; John L. Johnson, who married Toy's sister, Julia Anna; John William Jones, who with Toy had boarded with Broadus in Greenville; and James B. Taylor, Jr., the son of the secretary of the Baptist Foreign Mission Board.[18] Because of the coming of war, the Foreign Mission Board decided not to send out Toy to Japan. Jones, in a letter to Broadus in December, indicated that Toy was talking of going on to Japan and taking his chances in spite of the unwillingness of the Board to send him.[19] Obviously, Toy's religious motivation was very deep and very strong.

We have already noted the remarkable strength of Toy's intellectual curiosity, which refused to allow him to put away his studies even in the midst of war.

It is difficult to assess the full impact of the years in Berlin upon Toy's intellectual and religious development. It would appear that they did not greatly alter his religious orientation at the time, but they did serve to sharpen his intellectual tools, to put him in touch with the best theological scholarship, and to whet further his appetite for research.

While his sojourn at Furman was brief, he made many friends in the University and among those who were related to it. By the time he entered upon his duties for the Southern Baptist Theological Seminary in 1869, Toy was a scholar and teacher of first-rate quality.

Toy's inaugural address before the Seminary community was entitled "The Claims of Biblical Interpretation on Baptists." It was a brilliant statement, but it could only be called orthodox. He noted that Baptists rested their case completely on the Bible, and it was therefore urgent that they undertake its right interpretation. He sought to point out some principles by which the Bible may be interpreted and made one of the fundamental principles to be "that the Bible, its real assertations being known, is in every iota of its substance absolutely and infallibly true." [20]

It is somewhat strange to hear Toy making such a strong statement of biblical infallibility in his inaugural when, several years earlier, 1861, he had written to John A. Broadus the following:

In fact, do you think mathematical proof possible in many of these collateral questions concerning the great doctrines of the Gospel? Rather, the Divine Word furnishes in its general tenor sufficient evidence for the truth, and in the minor points there is good ground for satisfaction, but yet pegs to hang doubts on.[21]

In any case Toy was a highly respected member of the faculty, the denomination, and his own First Baptist Church in Greenville. Broadus spoke of him as "our shining pearl of learning—not an ordinary star, but a brilliant meteor, dropped down among us." [22] Boyce "declared that in scholarship he was *facile princeps* in the Seminary faculty." [23] J. S. Dill, a former student of Toy, wrote, "No man could give a clearer or more positive expression to our Baptist principles than Dr. Crawford Toy did in 1869." [24] Dill went on to say that he did not remember the teachings of Kuenen and Wellhausen cropping out during the last year of Toy's teaching in Greenville.[25] Indeed, Toy is still honored in Greenville with a street named after him.[26]

In spite of the generally orthodox approach of Toy during the Greenville days, his brilliance continued to shine through. A. H. Newman, later to become a principal jewel in the Baptist crown of scholarship,[27] had finished Rochester Seminary and was intending to go to Germany for advanced study, particularly in Semitics. However, while journeying in the autumn of 1875 from Alabama to New York to board ship, he stopped at the Seminary in Greenville. There he met Toy and Broadus. Toy offered to give him private instruction, and Newman was so impressed that he stayed.[28]

In addition, Toy's inquiring mind was leading him privately on a great search. While in Greenville he continued to seek the harmonization of the first chapters of Genesis and the science which he had been learning. A letter to *The Religious Herald* dated from New York, March, 1880, recounts his own struggle in this regard.[29] Toy recalls that at an early age he began to read geological books at home and at school. In the beginning he held the opinion which many then were expounding that the creative "days" in Genesis 1 were geological periods, and that the chapter is a geological history of the earth. He indicated that he held this view during his residence in Germany and for several years after his return to the United States. However, as he continued his study in Hebrew, he became convinced that the word "day" must mean a natural day of twenty-four hours and further that the days of Genesis 1 did not correspond to the geological periods. For a time he had recourse to the theory of John Pye Smith and Hitchcock that the Genesis account dealt with only the last geological stage of creation just before the creation of man. However, he soon realized the conflict here with the geological record was even greater and, further, that the text would not allow such a view. He next tried McCaul's theory of "maximum effect," that is, that the "day" was to represent only the culminating point in each geological period. This, too, soon proved to be untenable. Toy now adopted yet another theory which seemed for a time to remove his difficulties. This one maintained that the author of the Genesis account was not narrating what took place in historical fashion but that he was simply dividing all created things into categories and had assigned them to "days" for poetic and rhetorical vividness. The main point of the author, then, was that God made all things. This soon ceased to satisfy him when he began to ask the question: Does not this chapter really represent simply the "crude cosmogonic ideas of the Israelites and of the Babylonians, from whom the Israelites seem to have got them?"

Other factors also began to play a part in Toy's development.

About the same time that he was concerning himself with these problems in the Old Testament the important works of Darwin began to appear. Thus in addition to the theological problem there also appeared the anthropological problem. Much impressed with the work of Herbert Spencer and Darwin, Toy became a convinced evolutionist. He even delivered a popular lecture in Greenville interpreting and advocating Darwin's theory of the origin of man.[30]

It was about this time that he also became acquainted with the work of Kuenen and Wellhausen. The views expressed by these men appealed to him and helped him in his own reconstruction of the Old Testament material. He had contemplated the failure of his own attempts at explanation and harmonization with great dismay, and had questioned seriously whether or not this would destroy the Bible's truthfulness and helpfulness. This mood did not last long, however, and he began to see that God permitted his servants "to convey the truth in the form proper to his time." He was now convinced that the proper approach to the Bible was to "take the kernel of truth from its outer covering of myth." [31] He said that his fear now vanished, and he no longer worried himself with attempts to reconcile the findings of Scripture with modern scientific views. He found himself "at peace and in a position absolutely beyond the reach of science." [32] He reached this conclusion about 1874 or 1875.

This was from two to three years before the Seminary moved to Louisville (1877). Apparently, however, it was not until the move of the Seminary to Louisville that he incorporated enough of these views in his teaching to give any concern to his colleagues or students. He was generally recognized as the most learned member of the faculty, possessed of prodigious knowledge.[33] While he was reverent and considerate in his attitude toward Scripture, he insisted that the student should face realistically the problems there. He would give the pros and cons relative to these problems and state his own view, always insisting that a student should make up his own mind.[34]

III. The Controversy and "Trial"

It was near the end of the Seminary's first session in Louisville that Dr. Boyce, and perhaps his other colleagues, began to be concerned about the teaching of Professor Toy. Apparently, at first some isolated reports had not too greatly disturbed Boyce, though he was not in agreement. For example, a student had gone to Dr. Boyce saying that Toy was teaching that the author of Psalm 16 "had no reference to the resurrection of Jesus, but that Peter said in Acts that it was a direct prophecy of the risen Christ." "Well," said Dr. Boyce, "as between Dr. Toy and Peter, you and I had better stick to Peter." [35] It was reported also that he was teaching that Daniel was written by an author in the second century B.C.[36] As the fuller implications of his teachings began to be known, Dr. Boyce became greatly concerned.

The agitation of Boyce was due not solely to his own opposition to the views being expressed by Toy, but quite as much to his fear that the teachings of such views in the Seminary would offend its supporters. The Seminary had been in a critical financial position ever since the Civil War; indeed, the move to Louisville had been made necessary by this fact. Just now its future was in the balance, and Dr. Boyce, in his position of president, felt the heavy weight of responsibility involved in trying to raise endowment funds and, as he saw it, to save the Seminary. He felt very fearful of what might result if the views of Toy became widely known. He did not believe that Baptists would support an institution in which such teachings were tolerated.

At the same time Boyce was "anxious to avoid anything that might look like an official inquisition." [37] It was at this point that Broadus, who had been a friend and colleague of Toy for six years, went as a kind of intermediary to lay before Toy the problem which the Seminary faced by virtue of his teaching. Toy believed strongly that his approach would remove most of the intellectual difficulties which students had with respect to the Scriptures and would actually serve to deepen faith. When it was insisted that most of the students were not prepared "for fitting examination of any such theoretical inquiries, and needed to be instructed in the Old Testament history as it stands," [38] he promised to try to do this.

When the next session opened, Toy tried honestly to keep his promise. However, it was impossible for him to fail to respond to student questions which were elicited by their knowledge of the ideas he had taught the previous session. It was not long before he confessed that he found it impossible to fulfill the request that had been made of him.[39]

Apparently, little public note had been taken of this developing controversy within the life of the Seminary; the Baptist papers of the South were uniformly silent concerning it. Perhaps the story would have had quite a different ending had it not been that the *Sunday School Times* carried Dr. Toy's weekly "Critical Notes" during the first half of 1878-79. In the issues of April 12 and 19, 1879, Dr. Toy dealt with Isaiah 42:1-10 and 53:1-12. He stated in effect that the Servant in these passages refers to Israel, though he added that there was a final complete fulfillment in Christ. Immediately (April 24), *The Christian Intelligencer,* a periodical of the Reformed Church in America, launched a frontal assault on Toy and the *Sunday School Times.*[40] While the *Sunday School Times* answered the *Intelligencer* and sought to justify Toy's position, some Baptist papers in the North took up the alarm.[41]

The Southern Baptist Convention was to meet in Atlanta in May, and there the Board of Trustees of the Seminary was also to have its annual session. Toy was elected a delegate to the Convention from the Broadway Baptist Church in Louisville of which he was a member.[42] In order to clarify the situation in which he found himself, Toy decided to take with him to Atlanta a document which would state his views, his argument that the teaching of these views was beneficial, and his resignation. Undoubtedly, he felt that by including his resignation in this document, he would bring the whole matter to a head.

There is good reason to believe that Toy was not of the opinion that the Board would accept his resignation. Undoubtedly, he knew that there was a chance that they might, but the likelihood is that he felt that he would receive vindication.[43] Toy's document, which included his letter of resignation to the Board, was a magnificent statement. At Dr. Boyce's insistence the Seminary had been founded upon the principle that the professors should be guarded in their orthodoxy by an Abstract of Principles which each should sign. This document, which was relatively generous in its doctrinal statements, had been employed from the beginning of the institution's history, and all the professors, including Dr. Toy, had signed it. Its statement with regard to the Scripture was that "the Scriptures of the Old and New Testament were given by inspiration of God, and are the only sufficient, certain, and authoritative rule of all saving knowledge and obedience." Dr. Toy maintained steadfastly that he fully accepted this first article of the Fundamental Principles of the Seminary, and that he taught "in accordance with, and not contrary to it." [44] He further stated that the Scriptures declare the fact of God's divine inspiration but they say nothing of the manner of his action. "Nothing is said of the mode of operation of the Divine Spirit, . . . of the relation of the divine influence to the ordinary workings of the human intellect. . . . Against facts, no theory can stand, and I prefer, therefore, to have no theory, but submit myself to the guidance of the actual words of Holy Scripture."

He went on to say that he believed

that the Bible is wholly divine and wholly human; the Scripture is the truth of God communicated by Him to the human soul, appropriated by it and then given out with free, human energy, as the sincere, real conviction of the soul. To undertake to say what must be the outward forms of God's revelation of himself to man, seems to me presumptuous.

He further stated that he believed that the writers of Scripture were men who had received messages from God and uttered them "under purely free, human conditions. The inspired man speaks his own language, not another man's, and writes under the conditions of his own age, not under those of some other age." He added:

I find that the geography, astronomy and other physical science of the sacred writers was that of their times. It is not that of our times, it is not that which seems to us correct, but it has nothing to do with their message of religious truth from God. . . . The message is not less divine to me because it was given in Hebrew and not in English, or because it is set in the framework of a primitive and incorrect geology. . . . If our heavenly Father sends a message by the stammering tongue of a man, I will not reject the message because of the stammering. . . .

The early history of Israel was for a long time not committed to writing but handed down by oral tradition, under which process it was subject to a more or less free expansion. In this expanded form it was received at a comparatively late time by the Prophets and Priests who put it into shape, and made it the vehicle of religious truth.

He applied the same principle to the New Testament. He said:

I will not lightly see a historical or other inaccuracy in the Gospels or the Acts, but if I find such, they do not for me affect the divine teachings of these books. The centre of the New Testament is Christ himself, salvation is in Him, and a historical error cannot affect the fact of His existence and His teachings.

He stated emphatically that he believed to teach these views was not only lawful in relation to the Abstract of Principles but that they were views which would "bring aid and firm standing-ground to many a perplexed mind and establish the truth of God on a firm foundation."

The Board was faced, in the question of whether or not to accept Toy's resignation, with a rather complicated set of problems. Toy had indicated that he was submitting to their judgment the question whether or not his view of inspiration was in conflict with the Abstract of Principles. Should they enter into the question seriously? It was obvious that Toy's views, even if not in technical conflict with the article on inspiration, were more advanced than those of the majority of Southern Baptists. Was this sufficient ground for his dismissal? If so, was this not limiting the Seminary in such a way as to make it simply an instrument to propagate the current preponderant view of Southern Baptists rather than an instrument of creative theological research and instruction? In the face of these issues the Board appointed a committee! Five members served, the chairman being James C. Furman, the president of Furman University, and an old friend and acquaintance of Toy. The committee met with Toy and had a further exchange of views. Their report, stated in part the following:

While deeply impressed with the Christian spirit of our beloved brother, they cannot but recognize, what he himself asserts, that there is a divergence in his views of inspiration from those held by our brethren in general. In view of this divergence your committee feel constrained to recommend to the Board the acceptance of Prof. Toy's resignation.[45]

Acting on the report of the committee the Board of Trustees accepted Toy's resignation with only two dissenting votes.[46]

Thus the committee and consequently the Board refused to enter into the question of Toy's orthodoxy or to consider whether or not he was teaching in harmony with the Abstract of Principles, and laid their acceptance of his resignation on the "divergence in his views of inspiration from those held by our brethren in general." That is to say, they determined that the Seminary would be an institution which was simply to reflect the current preponderant views of the denomination. It did not have the right to the type of freedom which would permit proper theological research and expression of views which differ from the majority. There is further evidence that this action was taken in large part because the Board felt that Toy's "remaining in the Seminary would hinder the raising of money for the endowment." [47]

That the Seminary would find it very difficult to become or remain an institution which could do fully the proper work of higher education including unfettered research and the expression of views arrived at as a result of critical analysis was questionable from its origin. At the insistence of Boyce the Seminary had been founded as an entity apart from the University. As a matter of fact, controversy had arisen over this matter because theological education in the South had previously been done in the college or university. Boyce further had been the one to propose that the doctrinal integrity of the faculty should be preserved by an Abstract of Principles.

The determination by the Board of Trustees to accept Toy's resignation was reached on Saturday afternoon. One of those who had voted to accept Toy's resignation was a former professor of Southern Seminary, Basil Manly, Jr. Manly had taught Toy Hebrew and had also been his colleague on the faculty. For the last eight years he had been serving as president of Georgetown College. In a letter to Charles Manly, Basil told that on Saturday night the three remaining members of the faculty, Boyce, Broadus, and Whitsitt, met to consider what should be done. They unanimously agreed to ask Manly to return to the Seminary faculty. Broadus told Manly of this decision on Sunday night. On Monday at the request of the pastor of the First Baptist Church, Atlanta, B. W. Gwin, who had not been present on Saturday, the whole Toy question was reconsidered, and he was heard again. This went on into Monday night. J. A. Chambliss, pastor of the Citadel Square Baptist Church in Charleston, South Carolina, joined with Gwin in protesting against the action of the Board as "precipitate and unwise." However, their motion to reconsider was laid on the table, they being the only ones out of the eighteen trustees to dissent.

The decision regarding Toy having been irrevocably made, the Board now elected Manly to Toy's position in order to be able to announce the vacancy and the fact that it had been filled at the same time. Boyce added that it was hoped that this would "lighten the shock and stir which would otherwise be made in the public mind." Manly did not delay his acceptance and promptly on Tuesday morning gave his affirmative answer.[48]

Toy accepted this decision gracefully and apparently did not hold bitterness in his heart. When it became known in the Convention that his resignation had been accepted, there were former students of his and other delegates who asked that the whole case be put before the Convention. However, Toy declined to enter into the controversy.[49]

Toy had also another immediate decision to make. James C. Furman, who had voted against Toy in the Board meeting, was himself in difficulty. Furman University, which he headed, was in great financial distress, and many were blaming Furman, at least in part. The Furman faculty resigned during the meeting of the Convention, and a committee of the Furman Board was seeking a way to continue the University. Within a few days of the Convention Toy was offered both a professorship at Furman and then the presidency. Though it was urged upon him, he declined both offers.[50]

IV. The Reaction to the Treatment of Toy

Undoubtedly, one of the most painful responses to the situation which had developed as far as Toy was concerned involved Miss Lottie Moon. Lottie had gone to China in 1873, joining her sister who was already there. When the sister's health failed in 1877, Lottie accompanied her home but returned almost immediately to China. In letters she wrote which were published in the *Religious Herald* in 1878, a note of loneliness crept in which called forth greetings from her old acquaintance, C. H. Toy. The result was a period of letter exchange between these two which went on for some months. The engagement which she had earlier refused she now accepted, and the two agreed to be married upon her return home on furlough. They were apparently planning to go to Japan as man and wife. However,

their wedding plans were never completed. Lottie began to hear
of the controversy surrounding her fiancée. She obtained books
which were representative of Toy's position which she studied.
She became violently opposed to his views, broke off the engagement, and never married.[51]

The reaction of Toy's colleagues to the resignation appeared to be one of real pain. Broadus wrote to his wife from
Atlanta, "Alas! the mournful deed is done. Toy's resignation
is accepted. . . . I learned that the Board were all in tears as
they voted."

"Poor bereaved three; we have lost our jewel of learning,
our beloved and noble brother, the pride of the Seminary. God
bless Toy, and God help us, sadly but steadfastly to do our
providential duty." [52]

When Toy returned to Louisville and was ready to leave,
Boyce and Broadus went with him to the railway station. While
they were standing alone in the waiting room, Boyce threw
his left arm about Toy's neck and lifting his right arm said,
"Oh, Toy, I would freely give that arm to be cut off if you
would be where you were five years ago, and stay there." [53]
It was William H. Whitsitt, however, who had been closest to
Toy. The two had been bachelor professors together and had
found suitable rooms and board together when the Seminary
moved to Louisville.[54] It is no wonder that Whitsitt felt that
what had happened was an academic calamity and a denominational blunder created by ignorance and lack of appreciation.
A friend who had been on the same train with Whitsitt as he
left the Atlanta Convention said, "He seemed like a man utterly
crushed and almost in despair." [55]

No doubt Whitsitt's distress was more than simply that
arising from a sense of personal loss. He too was a scholar who
had been taught to employ and respect the results of the
scientific historical method. After finishing his course in the
Seminary while it was in Greenville, he had gone to Germany
where he studied in the University of Berlin under Johann
Gustav Dreeper, professor of history, who deeply influenced

Whitsitt's scholarship.[56] Now he was seeing the Board of Trustees of his own seminary taking a step which could not but seriously hinder open, objective historical research as it related to theological matters.

He also had agonized over the future of his Baptist denomination. In 1874 he had gone so far in his thinking that he had written in his Journal, "I fear I shall be constrained to leave the Baptist Church. God help me!" [57] Though by September of 1875 he had "returned" with all his heart "to Baptist allegiance," [58] the treatment of Toy may have served to awaken some of his former anxieties.

It was in the summer of the year of Toy's resignation that Whitsitt worked in the British Museum over documents which soon were to bring him into conflict with his brethren. By the time the Seminary term was underway that fall (1879), Whitsitt was ill. He was given a leave of absence, and Manly taught the course in biblical introduction which Whitsitt had been scheduled to offer.[59]

After leaving Louisville Toy had spent a brief period in Virginia.[60] He then went to New York where without any definite plan for the future he continued his studies and writing. Soon he was contributing an occasional article for a newspaper and then began to work on the staff of *The Independent* as a literary editor.[61] He continued to serve in this capacity until the summer of 1880. He began his service at Harvard in September.

Now the significant thing about these dates is that on June 24, 1880, the first of four articles appeared in the *Independent* anonymously from the pen of Whitsitt. Surely it was not a simple coincidence that Toy was on the staff of *The Independent* when this first article was accepted. These articles (June 24, September 2, September 9, and October 7, 1880) outlined views which would later be developed in detail by Whitsitt. Essentially they asserted that immersion was not practiced by Baptists in England until 1641 and that Roger Williams, the first Baptist in America, was not immersed. This naturally flew in the face of the current opinion among Baptists since it effectively removed any possibility of a succession of Baptist Churches from New Testament times. Succession was a position dear to the hearts of the Landmarkers and had become widely accepted by others.

Whitsitt was not connected with these articles by Baptists in the South, but as early as 1883 his methods began to come under fire. Yet it was not until 1896 that the storm broke. Whitsitt signed an article in Johnson's *Encyclopedia* concerning the Baptists which clearly spelled out his views. He was now violently attacked. The Seminary, too, came under fire, especially so since Whitsitt had been elected president in 1895.

Again the issue was over the right of historical research, publication, and teaching, though admittedly it was confused by the unusual personality clashes and jealousies inherent in almost all controversies. Once again the pressure became so great that a resignation was sought and obtained. Whitsitt resigned both his professorship and his presidency.

While the friends who had persuaded Whitsitt to resign thought it to be for the good of the Seminary, some saw clearly the dangers. S. C. Mitchell wrote: "The Seminary is not set to teach tradition. Tradition is truth's last year's crop of leaves. . . . Better no Seminary than a Seminary in which truth cannot find a home." [62]

Whitsitt, like Toy, went home to Virginia (to teach in the University of Richmond) ; he died in 1911.

There were those in the South following the Toy episode who recognized the dangers involved in the method used dealing with his resignation. Indeed, some of his friends, many of them former students, carried on a prolonged battle in the Baptist papers during the months that followed. Manly, who felt himself to be in an especially delicate position,[63] was quite sensitive to the attempt of the loyal supporters of Toy to achieve some sort of positive action in Toy's behalf. He wrote to his sister in February, 1880, that the "Inspiration discussion" was dragging on, especially in the Baptist papers in South Carolina (*Courier*) and Virginia (*Herald*). He indicated concern over the fact that Toy and W. C. Lindsay, a Toy supporter, were "having it pretty much to themselves." While he did not want to get involved, he said, "If Whitsitt doesn't come back pretty soon, I shall go ahead and lecture on it here, in Biblical Introduction class." [64] He later wrote a theology text which refuted Toy's position and stated strongly a plenary-verbal view of inspiration.

Perhaps the strongest blast against the action of the trustees came from J. A. Chambliss, who had voted against accepting the resignation. He pointed out that the trustees never really dealt with the real question of whether Toy's views were "sensible and Christian." In effect what was done was to say that his views are not those to which Baptists are accustomed, "and therefore, much as we prize him, honor him, love him, he must go." [65] Chambliss was especially concerned that the trustees were making it a principle that a "Professor in the Seminary must not go outside or beyond the circles within which the mass of the people who sustain the Seminary find their opinions, however nebulous those opinions may be, or however shifting the limits that encircle them." [66] He added that there was a multitude of men who loved the Seminary ardently and who dreaded "the thought of its becoming a manufactory of theological music boxes, all shaped and pitched alike to give forth an invariable number of invariable tunes." [67]

That Chambliss was right in his judgment of the trustees' attitude toward the nature of the Seminary is born out by comments from another trustee on the Board action. T. H. Pritchard admitted that "the Board did not even pass judgment on the paper he (Toy) presented," but were simply concerned with the future of the Seminary. He added:

I do not regard Dr. Toy as denying the inspiration of the Scriptures. . . . The difference between him and me, and the Baptists generally, is not as to the fact, but as to the manner and extent of inspiration. . . . As a Christian or even a pastor Dr. Toy might hold the views he does. . . [but not as a Professor, as a Professor] he was . . . to represent Baptist views of truth.[68]

Paper after paper and article after article praised Toy's spirit, candor, and ability; yet time and time again the final phrase was similar to one which appeared in the *Religious Herald,* "It was evident that he could not be retained in his professorship." [69]

The Toy case became the subject of newspaper accounts and notices. The *Courier-Journal* of Louisville had an account (perhaps written by Broadus) which praised Toy for his community spirit and action and bemoaned his resignation.[70]

It was through newspaper accounts that President Eliot at Harvard first heard of Toy. Eliot had invited W. Robertson Smith, under attack by his communion for his teachings at the Free Church College, Aberdeen, to the chair of Hebrew and other oriental languages at Harvard. While he was inclined to accept it, Smith asked that the position be held open until June, 1880, when his own trial would be over. The Assembly in May did not condemn him, and Smith decided he should remain in Scotland. When Eliot replied to Smith's letter declining the appointment, he said that the "Governing Body had appointed an American heretic, whose views on Isaiah had offended the Baptist communion to which he had belonged." [71]

Toy began his work at Harvard in September, 1880, and soon proved himself to be one of the ablest of the professors in the Divinity School. He rapidly built up the Semitic department, adding greatly to the courses offered. He himself gave instruction from time to time in Hebrew, Aramaic, Arabic, Ethiopic, the Talmud, general Semitic grammar, history of Israel, religion of Israel, Old Testament introduction, quotations from the Old Testament, criticism of the Pentateuch and of Chronicles, and the Spanish Califate and the Bagdad Califate.[72]

The growth of the department was so rapid that Toy was able to bring in D. G. Lyon to help him in 1882. Lyon had been a devoted student of Toy in Louisville and had left when Toy resigned. He spent time in Germany completing his formal education. He was offered a position at Southern Seminary but declined it. Lyon in paying tribute to Toy's scholarship said that the only criticism he had ever heard of his knowledge "came from his laundress, who once said: 'Dr. Toy don't know nothing. He don't know how to sew on a button.' " [73]

Toy published extensively. Books, reviews, and articles appeared from his pen with regularity. In 1912 his students, colleagues, and friends presented him with a volume of essays, *Studies in the History of Religions* (New York: The Macmillan Company), edited by David Gordon Lyon and George F. Moore. The core of those who wrote were members of the Harvard Club for the Study of the History of Religions. Toy had founded the club in 1891.

He retired in 1909 but kept up his study and writing. He had married Nancy Saunders of Norfolk in 1888, and she survived his death, May 12, 1919. He was then 83 years of age. Toy wore a full beard, and his pictures remind one of another Virginian, Robert E. Lee. His major addiction was his pipe. Lyon, who lived with him for six years at Cambridge, declared that he "could go all day without food if he could but have his pipe." [74]

Toy on all counts was a gentleman. His acquaintances spoke of him as considerate, sweet tempered, charming, courteous, and sympathetic. He was also a man of integrity, candor, and a bold investigator and pioneer. George F. Moore said of him:

Professor Toy was one of the last survivors of the storm-and-stress period of Old Testament criticism in this country. His career as a teacher filled the years from the first rumors of the new criticism to a time when its revolutionary theories have become critical orthodoxy, and the ensuing historical reconstruction is taught in schoolbooks. . . . To this result Professor Toy contributed much.[75]

V. The Real Significance of the Toy Episode

While for Toy the immediate circumstances surrounding his resignation were distressing, the ultimate personal outcome was extremely favorable. Not only was he liberated from the necessity of laboring in the restrictive setting of the Seminary, but he was catapulted into the generous environment of a world-famous university. His contacts were enlarged, his opportunities for publication were increased, and his influence as a teacher was tremendously extended. His life was full and satisfying. He apparently held no bitterness toward his former associates or even those who had strongly opposed him. He remained affiliated with Baptists for several years after his move to Cambridge but later associated himself with the Unitarians. Yet he never was a protagonist for a particular denomination.

The situation which resulted for Southern Baptist theological education from the manner in which Toy's resignation was secured proved most unfortunate. It in effect proclaimed the policy that professors in Southern Baptist seminaries would be held accountable for teaching only those views accepted by the majority of Southern Baptists. This was a tighter rein than the Abstract of Principles. Indeed, Toy was not judged by them and constantly declared that he was teaching within their framework.

The Whitsitt case a few years later and subsequent similar resignations or dismissals have perpetuated the pattern. Able scholars have been produced in the Southern Baptist communion, but, for the most part, they have felt, perhaps often unconsciously, the necessity of restraint in teaching and in publication or have found it necessary to teach in institutions outside Southern Baptist control.

While Whitsitt was a historian, the pressures to conform to the accepted views have been strongest upon those men who have taught in the biblical fields. Southern Baptist scholars since Toy's day have had to be very cautious in their expression of even the most widely held results of the critical study of the Bible. Indeed, the waves set in motion by the Toy episode continued to disturb the cause of theological education among Southern Baptists.

APPENDIX

Toy's letter of Resignation to the Board of Trustees of the Southern Baptist Theological Seminary as reprinted in The Baptist Courier (South Carolina), November 27, 1879.

To the Board of Trustees of the Southern Baptist Theological Seminary.

Dear Brethren:—It having lately become apparent to me that my views of Inspiration differ considerably from those of the body of my brethren, I ask leave to lay my opinions on that subject before you, and submit them to your judgment.

At the outset I may say that I fully accept the first article of the Fundamental Principles of the Seminary; "the Scriptures of the Old and New Testament were given by inspiration of God, and are the only sufficient, certain and authoritative rule of all saving knowledge and obedience," and that I have always taught and do now teach in accordance with, and not contrary to it.

It is in the details of the subject that my divergence from the prevailing views in the denomination occurs. This divergence has gradually increased in connection with my studies, from year to year, till it has become perceptible to myself and others.

In looking for light on Inspiration, my resort has been, and is, to the Scriptures themselves alone, and I rest myself wholly on their testimony. It seems to me that while they declare the fact of Divine Inspiration, they say nothing of the manner of its action. We are told that men spake from God, borne along by the Holy Ghost, and that all Scripture is given by Inspiration of God, and is profitable for doctrine, for reproof, for correction, for instruction in righteousness, that the man of God may be complete, thoroughly furnished for every good work. The object of the Scriptures is here said to be an ethical, spiritual one. They were given man for his guidance and edification in religion, as our Lord also says: "Sanctify them in the truth; Thy word is truth."

As nothing is said of the mode of operation of the Divine Spirit, of the manner in which the divine saving truth is impressed on the mind, of the relation of the divine influence to the ordinary workings of the human intellect, we must, as to these points, consult the books of the Bible themselves and examine the facts. Against facts, no theory can stand, and I prefer, therefore, to have no theory, but submit myself to the guidance of the actual words of Holy Scripture.

As the result of my examination, I believe that the Bible is wholly divine and wholly human; the Scripture is the truth of God communicated by Him to the human soul, appropriated by it and then given out with free, human energy, as the sincere, real conviction of the soul. To undertake to say what must be the outward forms of God's revelation of himself to man, seems to me presumptuous. If rationalism be the decision of religious questions by human reason, then it appears to me to be rationalistic to say that a Divine revelation must conform to certain outward conditions; to insist, for example, that it must be written in a certain style, or that it *must* teach certain things in geography, or astronomy, or similar matters.

I hold all *a priori* reasoning here to be out of place, and all theories based on it to be worthless. Such procedure seems to me to be out of keeping with the simple, reverent spirit appropriate to him who comes to search into the truth of God. For this reason I am forced to discard the theories of some pious men as Fichte and Wordsworth, who have proceeded in this *a priori* way, and to keep myself to the facts given in the Bible itself.

These facts make on me the impression that the Scripture writers are men who have received messages from God and utter them under purely free, human conditions. The inspired man speaks his own language, not another man's, and writes under the conditions of his own age, not under those of some other age. His personality, his individuality, has the freest play, all under the control of the guiding Divine Spirit. In illustration of what I mean, I refer to I Cor. i. 14, 15, where Paul first says he had baptized nobody at Corinth but Crispus and Gaius; then, a while after, remembering himself, adds, that he had baptized also the household of Stephanas; and finally, coming to doubt his memory, declares that he don't [*sic*] know whether he had baptized any other person. Here, if we indulge in arithmetical criticism, is a flat contradiction, but if we see simply the free play of the writer's mind, under the ordinary conditions of human thought, there is no difficulty. If any one asks me how this perfectly free thought consists with Divine guidance, I answer that I can tell that no more than how supernatural Divine power co-exists with free action of the soul in conversion, or how I exist at all, or how, in general, the finite and the infinite can co-exist.

I find that the geography, astronomy and other physical science of the sacred writers was that of their times. It is not that of our times, it is not that which seems to us correct, but it has nothing to do with their message of religious truths from God. I do not feel authorized to impose on Divine revelation the condition that it shall accord with modern geography and geology, nor to say that I will not accept it except on this condition. It seems to me that geography has nothing to do with religion. The message is not less divine to me because it was given in Hebrew and not in English, or because it is set in the framework of a primitive and incorrect geology. When the Psalmist says (Ps. cxxi. 6.) : "The sun shall not smite thee by day, nor the moon by night," it does not matter to me whether the moon is injurious or not at night, for the obvious religious thought is independent of this outward form; or when discrepancies and inaccuracies occur in the historical narrative, this does not even invalidate the documents as historical records, much less does it affect them as expressions of religious truths. I am slow to admit discrepancies and inaccuracies, but if they show themselves I refer them to the human conditions of the writer, believing that his merely intellectual status, the mere amount of information possessed by him does not affect his spiritual relation to God, or the validity of his message as spiritual truth. If our heavenly Father sends a message by the stammering tongue of a man, I will not reject the message because of the stammering.

My position is the same when I find that political details have not fallen out in accordance with the form in which the prophets clothe their religious exhortations. If Hosea looked for a captivity of Ephraim in Egypt (Hos. ix. 3.), or Isaiah for political friendship between Assyria, Egypt and Israel (Isaiah xix. 23, 25) that is the mere clothing of their real thought. The prophets uttered everlasting truths which are embodied and fulfilled in Jesus Christ, and with which the geographical and political details have no essential connection. To them Israel was the centre and hope of the world, and the prospective possessor of all prosperity, and the spiritual gist of their teachings has been perpetuated in Christ, while the merely outward has passed away.

The prophets and priests were not only preachers of religion, but writers of religious history. The early history of Israel was for a long time not committed to writing but handed down by oral tradition, under which process it was subject to a more or less free expansion. In this expanded form it was received at a comparatively late time by the Prophets and Priests who put it into shape, and made it the vehicle of religious truth. All historical writing in Israel that has come down to us was of the nature of a sermon. It was composed not so much for the sake of facts, as for the lessons they taught. The idea of scientific history did not then exist—it was all pragmatic, that is, written for the purpose of inculcating a truth.—The traditional history is treated by the pious of Israel in the spirit of profound trust in God and regard for His law. I can no more demand historical science in the Scriptures than geological science. I regard them both as being outside of the domain of religion.

The same thing I hold in respect to the Levitical law, which grew up, as it seems to me, from generation to generation on a Mosaic basis, and could thus be called Mosaic.

In one word, I regard the Old Testament as the record of the whole circle of the experiences of Israel, the people whom God chose to be the depository of His truth, all whose life He so guided as to bring out of it lessons of instruction which He then caused to be written down for preservation. The nation lived out its life in a free, human way, yet under divine guidance, and its Prophets, Priests and Psalmist recorded the spiritual, religious history under the condition of their times. The divine truth is presented in a framework of relatively unessential things, as Christ in his Parables introduced accessories merely for the purpose of bringing out a principle, so that the Parable of the Ten Virgins, for example, may properly be said to be the framework or vehicle of religious truth. As a whole the Parable may in a sense be called a religious teaching, but speaking more precisely we should say that a part of it is such teaching, or that the teaching is contained in it.

What I have said of the outward form of the Old Testament applies, as I think, to the outward form of the New Testament. I will not lightly see a historical or other inaccuracy in the Gospels or the Acts, but if I find such, they do not for me affect the divine teachings of these books. The centre of the New Testament is

Christ himself, salvation is in Him, and a historical error cannot affect the fact of His existence and His teachings. The Apostles wrote out of their personal convictions of the reality of the truth of Christ. If Paul makes a slip of memory, as in the case above cited, that cannot affect his spiritual relation to Christ and to the Father, nor detract from his power as an inspired man. If his numerical statements do not always agree with those of the Old Testament, (as in Gal. iii. 17, compared with Exodus xiii. 40), that seems to me a matter of no consequence.

If the New Testament writers sometimes quote the Old Testament in the Greek Version, which does not correctly render the Hebrew, (as in Heb. x:5, quoted from Psa. xl:6.) that does not affect the main thought or the religious teaching. And it may be that in some cases my principles of exegesis lead me to a different interpretation of an Old Testament passage from that which I find given by some New Testament writer, as in Psa. xl:6, above mentioned; this again I look on as an incidental thing, of which the true religious teaching is independent. I should add that in the majority of cases I hold that the New Testament quotations correctly represent the sense of the Old Testament, and there is always a true spiritual feeling controlling them. I think that Peter's discourse, in Acts ii, gives the true spiritual sense of the passage in Joel, and so, many references of Old Testament passages to Christ throughout the New Testament. It ought also to be noticed that the ancient ideas of quotations were different from ours: ancient writers cite in a general way from memory for illustration, and permit themselves without remark such alterations as a modern writer would think it necessary to call attention to. This is to be regarded as a difference of habit arising from a difference of the times. The freeness of quotation in the Scripture writers does not, for example, affect their general honesty and truthfulness, nor their spiritual train of thought, nor their spiritual authority. It is only a human condition of the divine truth they utter. In these men the Spirit of God dwelt, and out of their writings comes a divine power. Recognizing in them a divine element, I cannot reject it because of what seems to me outward or non-spiritual limitation. I do not condition divine action, but accept it in the form in which I find it.

As to criticism (question of date and authorship) and exegesis, these stand by themselves, and have nothing to do with Inspiration.

The prophecy in Isa. xl-lxvi. is not less inspired if it be assigned to the period of the Babylonian Exile, and the "Servant of Jehovah" be regarded as referring primarily to Israel. These are questions of interpretation and historical research, in which, as it seems to me, the largest liberty must be allowed. If some of the Psalms should be put in the Maccabean period (B.C. 160), this is no reason for doubting their inspiration; God could as easily act on men in the year B.C. 160 as B.C. 400 or B.C. 700.

It is proper to add that the above statement of my views of Inspiration is the fullest that I have ever expressed. Some things I have not thought it expedient to state to my classes in the Seminary. At the same time I regard these views as helpful for Bible study. If at first they seem strange, I am convinced that they will appear more natural with further strict study of the text.

I beg leave to repeat that I am guided wholly by what seems to me the correct interpretation of the Scriptures themselves. If an error in my interpretation is pointed out, I shall straightway give it up. I cannot accept *a priori* reasoning, but I stake everything on the words of the Bible, and this course I believe to be for the furtherance of the truth of God.

And now, in conclusion, I wish to say distinctly and strongly that I consider the view above given to be not only lawful for me to teach as Professor in the Seminary, but one that will bring aid and firm standing-ground to many a perplexed mind and establish the truth of God on a firm foundation.

But that I may relieve the Board of all embarrassment in the matter, I tender my resignation as Professor in the Southern Baptist Theological Seminary.

Respectfully submitted,

May, 1879   C. H. Toy

NOTES

1. Words of President Eliot of Harvard, cited in J. S. Black and George Chrystal, *The Life of William Robertson Smith* (London: Adams and Charles Black, 1912), p. 375.
2. C. A. Briggs, *General Introduction to the Study of Holy Scripture* (New York: Charles Scribner's Sons, 1899), p. 286.

3. David C. Lyon, "Crawford Howell Toy," *The Harvard Theological Review,* XIII (Jan., 1920), 1-2. This study of Toy by Lyon is the most extensive presently available. A dissertation entitled, "Crawford Howell Toy, as an Interpreter of the Old Testament," is currently (Dec., 1964) under preparation at Southern Baptist Theological Seminary by Billy G. Hurt. Mr. Hurt furnished me with numerous references and permitted me to read his first chapter which has been completed. I am also indebted for references and help to Jerry Vardeman, Leo Crismon, and Morgan Patterson, all of the Southern Baptist Theological Seminary, Louisville, Kentucky.

4. Archibald Thomas Robertson, *Life and Letters of John Albert Broadus* (Philadelphia: American Baptist Publication Society, 1901), p. 111.

5. *Ibid.,* p. 121. Cf. Garnett Ryland, *The Baptists of Virginia* (Richmond, 1955), p. 292.

6. Hurt, "Crawford Howell Toy," p. 12. See p. 77.

7. *Ibid.,* p. 18; Lyon, "Crawford Howell Toy," p. 5.

8. Cf. Robertson, *Life and Letters of John Albert Broadus,* p. 78.

9. George F. Moore, "An Appreciation of Professor Toy," *The American Journal of Semitic Languages and Literature,* XXVI (Oct., 1919), 2; Lyon, "Crawford Howell Toy," p. 5.

10. Quoted in Robertson, *Life and Letters of John Albert Broadus,* p. 197.

11. J. S. Dill, *Lest We Forget* (Nashville: Baptist Sunday School Board, 1938), p. 43.

12. Moore, "An Appreciation of Professor Toy," p. 2.

13. Robertson, *Life and Letters of John Albert Broadus,* p. 232.

14. These may be seen on microfilm in the Library of Southern Baptist Theological Seminary.

15. Letter from Toy to Morton, Charlottesville, Feb. 28, 1859. Microfilm Publication No. 1424 in the Library of Southern Baptist Theological Seminary.

16. Robertson, *Life and Letters of John Albert Broadus,* pp. 173-74.

17. *Ibid.*

18. The date is given as June 10, 1860, by John Lipscomb Johnson, *Autobiographical Notes* (Privately printed, 1958), pp. 122-23.

19. Robertson, *Life and Letters of John Albert Broadus,* p. 180.

20. The erudition of Toy's inaugural was not lost on some of the brethren, and a North Carolina writer to *The Religious Herald* expressed it, "At last we are on a par with our brethren of other denominations, and our peculiar tenets will no longer be attributed to ignorance and narrow-mindedness." A letter signed W. H. Wilson, North Carolina, *The Religious Herald,* Mar. 31, 1870, p. 1.

21. C. H. Toy, "Private Letter to John A. Broadus," Norfolk, Aug. 20, 1861, p. 2.

22. Cited in Hurt, "Crawford Howell Toy," p. 25.

23. Dill, *Lest We Forget*, p. 43.
24. *Ibid.*, p. 44.
25. *Ibid.*, p. 45.
26. *Ibid.*, p. 54.
27. Newman became best known as a church historian serving as a principal editor of the *New Schaff-Herzog Encyclopedia of Religious Knowledge.*
28. Frederick Eby, *Newman, the Church Historian; A Study in Christian Personality* (Nashville: Broadman Press, 1946), pp. 27-29.
29. This and numerous other items related to Toy are contained in Pauline Lindsay, *Scrapbook Composed of Newspaper Clippings,* which is in the Library of Southern Baptist Theological Seminary.
30. Robertson, *Life and Letters of John Albert Broadus,* p. 260.
31. Toy, "A Bit of Personal Experience," in Lindsay, *Scrapbook,* p. 3.
32. *Ibid.*
33. Lyon, "Crawford Howell Toy," p. 6.
34. *Ibid.*
35. Dill, *Lest We Forget*, p. 45.
36. Lyon, "Crawford Howell Toy," p. 7.
37. Robertson, *Life and Letters of John Albert Broadus,* p. 262.
38. *Ibid.*
39. *Ibid.*
40. Lyon, "Crawford Howell Toy," p. 9, note 7.
41. *The Independent,* May 29, 1879, p. 14.
42. *History of Broadway Baptist Church* (Louisville, 1891), p. 68.
43. Lyon, "Crawford Howell Toy," p. 11.
44. *Toy's Letter of Resignation to the Board of Trustees* (original in the possession of the Library of Southern Baptist Theological Seminary). See the appendix to this chapter for a copy of this letter.
45. The manuscript of this report is in the Library of Southern Baptist Theological Seminary.
46. William A. Mueller, *A History of the Southern Baptist Theological Seminary* (Nashville: Broadman Press, 1959), p. 139.
47. W. O. Carver "Unpublished Notes," p. 26. Cited in Mueller, *A History of the Southern Baptist Theological Seminary,* p. 142.
48. Letter of Basil Manly, Jr. to Charles Manly, May 15, 1879. "The Letter-Copy Book of Basil Manly, Jr.," X. Cited in Joseph P. Cox, "A Study of the Life and Work of Basil Manly, Jr.," an unpublished dissertation, Southern Baptist Theological Seminary, 1954, pp. 281-82.
49. Lyon, "Crawford Howell Toy," pp. 9-10.
50. Harvey Toliver Cook, *The Life and Works of James Clement Furman* (Greenville, S.C., 1926), pp. 263, 274. Robert N. Daniel, *Furman University* (Greenville, S.C.: Furman University, 1951), p. 71.
51. Hurt, "Crawford Howell Toy," pp. 13-16. See also Una Roberts Lawrence, "Manuscript Materials Gathered in Connection with

Preparing and Publishing 'Lottie Moon' by Una Roberts Lawrence," n.d., Library of Southern Baptist Theological Seminary.

52. Robertson, *Life and Letters of John Albert Broadus*, p. 313.

53. *Ibid.*, 263-64.

54. "Memoirs of John R. Sampey, Persons and Institutions I have Loved," unpublished manuscript, Southern Baptist Theological Seminary, chap. 2, p. 1.

55. J. J. T. [Taylor], "William H. Whitsitt, B.D., L.L.D." *Religious Herald*, Mar. 2, 1911, p. 4.

56. W. H. Whitsitt, "The Whitsitt Controversy. 1896-1899," unpublished typescript on microfilm in the Library of Southern Baptist Theological Seminary, p. 18.

57. W. H. Whitsitt, "Journal," unpublished manuscript, Library of Southern Baptist Theological Seminary, p. 254.

58. *Ibid.*, p. 284.

59. Cox, "A Study of the Life and Work of Basil Manly, Jr.," pp. 291-92.

60. The Broadway Baptist Church in Louisville, of which he was a member, granted him a letter of dismissal at Norfolk, Virginia, Sept. 17, 1879. *History of Broadway Baptist Church*, p. 69.

61. Lyon, "Crawford Howell Toy," p. 12. His wife said his work on this paper included writing the "funnies." Jan Toy Coolidge, "Crawford Howell Toy, 1836-1919," unpublished manuscript, cited in Hurt, "Crawford Howell Toy," p. 36.

62. S. C. Mitchell, *After Whitsitt, What?* (Louisville: Chas. T. Dearing, 1899), p. 12.

63. Manly wrote Lulie Manly, May 13, 1879: "If I agree with him, I shall be censured for unsoundness, if I differ, I shall be thought to be actuated by prejudice or narrow views, clinging to orthodoxy rather than Truth." Cited in Cox, "A Study of the Life and Work of Basil Manly, Jr.," p. 283.

64. Cited in Cox, "A Study of the Life and Work of Basil Manly, Jr.," p. 292.

65. Lindsay "Scrapbook," p. 67. Most, if not all, of the articles appearing in the *Courier* and *Herald* with respect to this controversy are displayed in this scrapbook. These include several letters from Toy written from New York.

66. *Ibid.*

67. *Ibid.*, pp. 67, 68.

68. *Ibid.*, p. 68.

69. *Ibid.*, p. 69.

70. The article was reprinted in the *Western Recorder*, May 22, 1879, p. 4. Toy had been a founder of the Conversation Club in Louisville. A colleague in this work, Bishop T. U. Dudley, wrote a poem, "A Christmas Squib," about Toy's leaving:

And Toy, our founder, preacher, scholar, sage
Who knew all learning, whatsoe'er its age,
Who dreamed in Arabic, and smoked in Greek,
And read the Zend-Avesta once a week;
As bold as paladin, as shy as girl
As bright as diamond, pure as any pearl;
Alas! he too is gone, nor shares our feast,
H. Modern Magus, he went to the East
His learning grew too heavy for his station;
He fell to Boston just by generation.

Conversation Club (Louisville, 1935), p. 60.

71. Black and Chrystal, *The Life of William Robertson Smith,* p. 375.
    Cf. Moore, "An Appreciation of Professor Toy," p. 5.
72. Lyon, "Crawford Howell Toy," pp. 14-15.
73. *Ibid.,* p. 17.
74. *Ibid.*
75. Moore, "An Appreciation of Professor Toy," p. 17.

3. Charles Augustus Briggs Heresy at Union

MAX GRAY ROGERS

Presbyterianism, like other segments of American Protestantism in the late nineteenth century, was predominantly influenced by biblical evangelicalism. In the 1880's American Presbyterianism came under the influence of a rather peculiar form of scholasticism known as Princeton theology. Characteristic of this position were the views of verbal inspiration and textual inerrancy. Juxtaposed to this position was the growing acceptance of the school of thought which advocated the critical historical methodology in biblical interpretation. These two forces became major adversaries in a power struggle which climaxed in the last decade of the nineteenth century. The man most closely identified with the rise of the critical method of biblical study was Charles Augustus Briggs.

Born in New York City on January 15, 1841, Briggs attended the University of Virginia where he was converted to the Christian faith in the fall of 1858. After serving three months with the New York 7th Regiment in the Civil War, he entered the Union Theological Seminary in October, 1861. His studies at Union were interrupted in the fall of 1863 by the illness of his father; young Charles was forced to assume the management of his father's barrel works, then the largest in this country. In pursuit of these duties he made several excursions into Virginia. Amid the widespread misery of the last war years, he renewed some of his earlier acquaintances from college days.

On October 19, 1865, Charles married Julie Valentine of Trenton, New Jersey, and New York City. He had given much thought to study abroad. After his father's recuperation Charles and Julie sailed for Germany in the summer of 1866. The next three years were spent at the University of Berlin under Isaac August Dorner, E. W. Hengstenberg, Emil Roediger, and H. G. A. Ewald. Though he had gone to Germany with definite predilections toward the conservative approach to biblical interpretation, his studies under Hengstenberg convinced him that he was "defending a lost cause." [1]

To Professor Henry Boynton Smith, under whom he had studied at Union, Briggs wrote:

> In exegesis there is a very great want in America. Here every great theologian is an Exegete. They are too much influenced by rationalism as we would say in America, and this is perhaps because they have thought more deeply and candidly upon the subjects and seen the difficulties and tried to grapple with them. Whereas we have overlooked them or passed them by without examination; but in spite of their *coldness* in handling Scripture, it is more *satisfactory* to the student than a devotional spirit without *thought*.[2]

After only five months in Germany he wrote to an uncle: "I cannot doubt but what I have been blessed with a new—divine light. I feel a different man from what I was five months ago. The Bible is lit up with a new light." [3]

Briggs abandoned the study of the Pentateuch after only one semester under Hengstenberg, and it was not until his last year abroad that he resumed this work under Professor Heinrich Georg Augustus Ewald of Göttingen.

The primary value of the historical critical methodology as Briggs saw it lay in the construction of a comprehensive biblical theology. Biblical theology as a discipline could provide a unity for the theological statements of the various biblical authors. He described his chief aims as "(1) a more consistent and thorough doctrine of justification and sanctification suitable to the demands of the times, (2) in order to this a thorough study of Biblical Theology, and in order to this a practical acquaintance with the original Scriptures and with the cognate languages." [4] The first of these aims revealed the influence of Professor Dorner, whose view of progressive sanctification gave rise to Briggs' own modification of that position.

Due to the state of his parents' health, Briggs returned home in July, 1869. Shortly thereafter he published what was possibly the earliest article on biblical theology in this country in which he said: "Biblical Theology has for its range . . . the entire Scripture. It seeks to reach and realize the unity of Scripture amidst the manifold forms of its presentation." [5]

On June 30, 1870, he was ordained and installed in the First Presbyterian Church of Roselle, New Jersey. This proved to be the only parish he ever served, for in January, 1874, he assumed the duties of provisional professor at Union Theological Seminary. This was the beginning of an association of almost forty years—one that was to affect profoundly the destinies of both the man and the institution.

After serving two years as provisional professor at Union, Briggs was elected Davenport Professor of Hebrew and Cognate Languages. In his inaugural, delivered on September 21, 1876, he urged that the use of reasonable scientific methods in biblical study in no way endangered the supernatural character of revelation. "So long as the word of God is honored, and its decisions regarded as final, what matters it if a certain book be detached from the name of one holy man and ascribed to another, or classed among those with unknown authors?" [6]

By the end of the decade Briggs was instrumental in the founding of the *Presbyterian Review,* a joint venture between the faculties of Princeton and Union Seminaries which functioned from 1880 to 1889. Under the coeditorship of Briggs and Professor A. A. Hodge of Princeton, the *Review* quickly became the most thorough and comprehensive journal of religion of its time. This joint undertaking, however, tended to increase the strain between these respective institutions on the question of biblical interpretation. In the early years of this endeavor the issues of biblical criticism were brought to the fore by the heresy trial of Professor W. Robertson Smith in Scotland. The American opponents of this methodology insisted that the matter be discussed in the *Presbyterian Review*. And so, with some reluctance, an eventful series of eight articles was decided upon, with each editor selecting four contributors.[7] Hodge represented the negative viewpoint and Briggs, the affirmative.

In the first article of that series, entitled "Inspiration," [8] Hodge was joined by Professor B. B. Warfield.[9] This article, more than any other single statement, embodied the formulation of "Princeton theology." In his portion of the article Hodge defined inspiration as "the superintendence by God of the writers in the entire process of their writing, which accounts for nothing whatever but the absolute infallibility of the record in which the revelation, once generated, appears in the original autograph." [10] Hodge asserted that

the historical faith of the Church has always been, that all the affirmations of Scripture of all kinds, whether of spiritual doctrine or duty, or of physical or historical fact, or of psychological or philosophical principle, are without error, when the *ipsissima verba* of the original autographs are ascertained and interpreted in their natural and intended sense.[11]

Warfield in his turn insisted: "A proved error in Scripture contradicts not only our doctrine but the Scripture claims and, therefore, its inspiration in making those claims." [12] Thus for a doctrine which, according to Hodge,[13] had no priority for the Princeton men, inspiration emerged as the single point upon which their entire theological system rested.

In the second article of the series Briggs rejected both the dogma of verbal inspiration and the idea of an original auto-graph.[14] Instead he endorsed the view of plenary inspiration, which acknowledged the presence of errors and inconsistencies in the Bible, yet accepted it as the infallible rule of faith and practice. *"Verbal* Inspiration is doubtless a more precise and emphatic definition, than *plenary* Inspiration; but this very emphasis and precision imperil the doctrine of Inspiration itself by bringing it into conflict with a vast array of objections along the whole line of Scripture and History." [15]

Such was the reaction to that series that in January, 1882, Hodge wrote Briggs: "I shall unite with you in doing all I can to prevent controversy in Newspapers and otherwise on the matter of Biblical Criticism until the series in our Review is finished." [16] Dr. Hodge resigned in October of that year, and Dr. Francis L. Patton assumed the duties of coeditor.

Controversy flared anew in 1885 with the appearance of the American edition of the Revised Version of the Old Testament. Princeton's Professor William Henry Green, as editor of that project, had refused to incorporate into the translation any of the findings and conclusions of biblical criticism. Briggs was severe in his criticism of the work, noting "it is doubtful whether they have not done more harm than good in their attempt to give English readers an idea of Hebrew poetry." [17] The heated exchange that ensued between Green and Briggs had the effect of further emphasizing Briggs' identity with the critical methodology.

In 1886 the pace of Briggs' written work increased with the appearance of *Messianic Prophecy*[18]; previously he had published *Biblical Study: Its Principles, Methods and History*[19] in 1883 and *American Presbyterianism*[20] in 1885.

The amicable association which had existed between Briggs and Patton as coeditors came to an end in 1888 with the designation of the latter as the next president of Princeton College. Dr. B. B. Warfield was selected to succeed Patton; and Briggs was pleased with this choice. But his initial confidence was of short duration. Dr. Warfield soon began exerting pressure upon Briggs in matters which the latter considered his own prerogative.[21]

The strain which quickly developed in this relationship was complicated by the action of the General Assembly of 1889. At that time overtures were sent to all presbyteries posing the question: "Do you desire a revision of the Confession of Faith? If so, in what respects, and to what extent?"[22] Briggs later described the results in this way: "These questions greatly agitated the whole Presbyterian Church. Three parties sprang into existence: One in favor of revision; one opposed to revision; and a third in favor of a new and simple consensus creed. . . . Union Seminary led the party of revision; Princeton the anti-revision party."[23]

At first Briggs opposed the revision movement as "premature and impracticable."[24] In an article in the October issue of the *Review,* he argued that "the statements of the Calvinistic system in the Westminster symbols are the most cautious, firm, and carefully guarded that can be found, and I would not trust any set of divines now living to revise them or improve them."[25] In lieu of revision Briggs preferred "simply to emend the strictness of the formula of subscription."[26] As the controversy grew in intensity, he joined the ranks of the revisionists. As he described it, "seeing that the movement was an earnest and powerful one, and that it was necessary for me to take sides, I could not refrain from joining the party of progress."[27]

The revision issue directly affected the relationship of the coeditors of the *Review.* According to a previous agreement, it was Briggs' turn to review the action of the Assembly of 1889. Warfield, however, insisted upon inserting a note of his own regarding the issue of revision. When Briggs refused to allow this, an exchange erupted between the two that resulted in Warfield's resignation.[28] A conference followed in which the resignation was declined and an agreement reached whereby both parties submitted articles on revision in the October *Review.* The calm which followed this compromise was short-lived. In September Warfield again pressed Briggs in the execution of editorial duties.[29] This was more than the latter could bear, and on September 22 Briggs submitted his resignation. The Union faculty thereupon voted to discontinue the *Review*. The issue of higher criticism coupled with that of revision proved too great a strain, and the one remaining link between these parties was severed.

Only one week prior to his resignation Briggs brought out a defense of the revision movement, entitled *Whither? A Theological Question for the Times*.[30] In this work he stated that his examination of Westminster theology had affirmed "the fact that modern Presbyterianism had departed from the Westminster Standards, all along the line." [31] He demonstrated a thorough understanding of the basic lines of thought behind Princeton theology, pointing out the weaknesses and dangers of this approach to the Christian faith.

The major weakness of Princeton theology lay in the essential role it attributed to verbal inspiration and textual inerrancy. As for the contention for inerrant original autographs, Briggs noted:

It is admitted that there are errors in the present text of Scripture, but it is claimed that there could have been no errors in the original documents. But how do we know this: We have not the originals and can never get at them. . . . It is sheer assumption to claim that the original documents were inerrant. No one can be persuaded to believe in the inerrancy of Scripture, except by *a priori* considerations from the elaboration of the doctrine of verbal inspiration.[32]

Among those portions of the Confession of Faith most in need of revision, Briggs cited the fourth chapter which dealt with creation. He noted that the discoveries of modern science had long since precluded any creation period of six days of twenty-four hours. "All the profound discoveries of modern science in geology, astronomy, chemistry, biology, and archaeology, have opened up new problems for the doctrine of creation that were not in the minds of the Westminster divines." [33]

Whither? met with a vigorous reaction upon publication. It was hailed by many as a penetrating evaluation of the revision issue; yet it was not without its critics. In any event it tended to identify Briggs as a leading proponent of the movement. A debate was soon arranged in which Briggs was invited to represent the party favoring revision. He later described it in this way:

The Presbyterian Union of New York invited Dr. Patton and myself to represent the two sides of the question before them December 2, 1889. This debate drew the fire of the entire anti-revision party on me. The very next evening, December 3rd, *The Mail and Express* published a bitter editorial attack on Union Seminary and on me, inspired by the anti-revisionists; and this attack continued in a most shameful way from that date onward.[34]

Only weeks after the debate Briggs edited a collection of papers entitled *How Shall We Revise?*[35] In the lead article[36] of that collection, he took the position that in place of amending the Confession, a wiser solution would be to formulate "a new and simple creed."[37] By this proposal he intended "a creed that will express the faith, life, and devotion of the present time, born of our experience and needs."[38] This creed would serve only to supplement the Confession, keeping in strict accord with it in "all the essential and necessary articles."[39] This would provide a degree of flexibility between strict and loose subscription to the Standards and thus, in a large measure, relieve the cause of the revision controversy.

While this issue continued to rage, another episode involving Briggs came to light. John McComb, an entering student at Union Seminary in 1890, soon found himself at odds with the teachings he encountered in Briggs' classes. He offered his support to Colonel Elliott F. Shepard, editor of the ultra-conservative newspaper, *The Mail and Express,* agreeing to provide the latter with lecture notes from Briggs' classes. Throughout the fall of 1890 scathing attacks upon Briggs and the seminary appeared in the press. When the identity of the student collaborator was learned, quite by accident, McComb was dismissed from the seminary.[40]

During the decade of the 1880's Briggs' name had gained considerable attention on two counts: his insistence upon some reasonable form of biblical criticism and his support of the revision movement. By the end of that decade the conservative faction of the church had come to regard him with suspicion and misgiving. As the situation became more crucial, Union's Board of Directors on November 11, 1890, transferred him to the newly established Edward Robinson Chair of Biblical Theology. Briggs was delighted with this move. In his letter of acceptance to the Board, he wrote: "Biblical Theology is, at the present time, the vantage ground for the solution of those important problems in religion, doctrine and morals that are compelling the attention of the men of our times." [41]

Briggs initially planned to develop his inaugural address around the subject matter of biblical geography in honor of the man for whom the chair was named. However, Charles Butler, President of Union's Board and donor of the chair, insisted that Briggs speak on a more timely topic of the day, one that would deal directly with the major issues such as revision and biblical criticism. Briggs warned him that the results would only serve to increase the hostility of the ultra-conservatives; but Butler remained persistent.[42] Briggs later described the circumstances leading up to the address in this way:

Yielding to his advice, which was reinforced by the faculty and other members of the board, the theme selected was the *Authority of Holy Scripture.* The aim of the address was to maintain and to assert in the strongest terms the divine authority of Holy Scripture in connection with a full recognition of the results of modern Biblical criticism and modern thought in all departments. No position was taken in that address which had not previously been taken in articles in the *Presbyterian Review* and in printed books many months before. The limits of the discourse required the condensation of a vast amount of material and the concentration of a very great many points of difference, which in the nature of the

case were exceedingly disagreeable to the ultra conservative section of the Church, and the situation exacted of the speaker that his
rhetoric should be fired to some degree of passion in view of the
defense of himself and the cause that he represented, after more
than a year of unjust attack.[43]

The inaugural address[44] was delivered in the Seminary's
Adams Chapel on January 20, 1891. In his opening remarks
Briggs touched upon a basic fear in the religious mind of that
day: "The progress of criticism in our day has so undermined
and destroyed the pillars of authority upon which former generations were wont to rest that agnosticism seems to many
minds the inevitable result of scientific investigation." [45] He
sounded the keynote of his address by assuring his listeners that
God had revealed his presence and authority to men of all ages;
this had been accomplished historically through "three great
fountains of divine authority—the Bible, the Church and the
Reason." [46]

Next Briggs enumerated six barriers which had greatly im-
peded men in their approach to the Scriptures. First he listed
Superstition, under which he equated Mariolatry, hagiolatry,
and bibliolatry. Then came *Verbal Inspiration* and the *Authen-
ticity of the Scriptures.* As for the latter "barrier," he said: "The
great mass of the Old Testament was written by authors whose
names or connection with their writings are lost in oblivion. If
this is destroying the Bible, the Bible is destroyed already." [47]
Next he posited *Inerrancy* and the *Violation of the Laws of
Nature,* which lay in the claim that a miracle by definition must
violate the basic laws of nature. Such a position was not only an
affront to modern science, but it tended to obscure the purpose
and intent of any extraordinary act. Finally, there was the barrier of *Minute Prediction.* Here emphasis was placed upon
"predictive prophecy" so as to make it "a sort of history before
the time." [48] Predictions were often unfulfilled; many had been
withdrawn or reversed by God. Predictive prophecy was always
secondary to man's salvation. God's actions in history had al-

ways been redemptive; to emphasize the significance of prediction at the expense of redemption was only to distort the fundamental lesson of Scripture.

Within his discussion of the role of redemption Briggs
emphasized the role of the middle state between death and resurrection. Careful to deny the doctrines of purgatory and second
probation, he insisted that redemption could not be limited to
this world. He conceived of biblical redemption as a process
which extended beyond earthly life through the period which
preceded the second advent and final judgment. In this middle
state between justification, which occurred at the time of death
through the Holy Spirit, and the final judgment, each individual
was prepared for judgment through progressive sanctification.
Briggs rejected the concept of a judgment immediately following death. "The bugbear of a judgment immediately after death,
and the illusion of a magical transformation in the dying hour
should be banished from the world." [49] No one could be fully
prepared for judgment at the time of death. Though faith in
Christ was a prerequisite, this was only a very early stage of
redemption; everyone was in need of sanctification beyond
death.[50]

Under the topic of biblical ethics Briggs proposed that a
moral development had taken place throughout Israel's history,
culminating in the Messiah, Jesus of Nazareth. Of the earliest
Old Testament figures, he said:

The ancient worthies, Noah and Abraham, Jacob and Judah,
David and Solomon, were in a low stage of moral advancement.
Doubtless it is true, that we would not receive such men into our
families, if they lived among us and did such things now as they
did then. We might be obliged to send them to prison, lest they
should defile the community with their example. But they do not
live now; they lived in an early age of the world, when the divine
exposition of sin was not so searching, and the divine law of righteousness was not so evident. They were not great sinners to their
age; they were the saints of God.[51]

On the following morning coverage of the address appeared in many major newspapers. The reaction surpassed anything Briggs had expected. The religious press quickly took up positions in the fray. The *New York Evangelist* had this to say:

> If it were the object of the recent Inaugural Address to make a sensation, it has certainly succeeded. All the religious papers treat of it at length, and all, with the single exception of the *Christian Union,* in a tone of severe condemnation. Listening to the heavy blows from every quarter, it sounds like an Anvil Chorus from one end of the country to the other.[52]

Within three months the religious and secular press had fanned the flames of religious conservatism and insecurity to white heat. With overtures from five presbyteries protesting the inaugural already before the General Assembly, the Presbytery of New York, at its monthly meeting in April, appointed a committee of seven to examine the address and decide if any action should be taken. At the time Briggs was confined to bed with the grippe and not present when the committee was appointed. Due to extended illness and his resentment of the Presbytery's action in his absence, Briggs refused an invitation to appear before the investigating committee.[53]

At the next monthly meeting on May 12 the Presbytery heard two reports from its committee. The majority report, signed by four members, cited three points wherein the inaugural ran counter to the Confession of Faith: (1) equating the Bible, the church, and the reason as coordinate fountains of divine authority; (2) rejecting the inerrancy of the original autographs of Holy Scripture; (3) holding that progressive sanctification after death was both biblical and church doctrine.[54]

The minority report urged that no action be taken regarding the address, noting "that charges based upon this address cannot be successfully sustained, and that such a trial for heresy would be a cause of immeasurable disturbance to the Church." [55]
It was late in the day when a vote was taken on the reports.

Many who favored the minority report were absent at the time, thinking that no vote would be called for that day. A number of those who had departed early were Briggs' strongest supporters.[56] The majority report carried by a vote of 44 to 30.[57]

This action greatly distressed Briggs. Three days later he penned these words to his colleague, Francis Brown, then in Europe:

I have no confidence whatever that my friends will stand by me. They say that they will. But I doubt whether I shall be willing to pay the cost. They tell me that the Faculty have prepared a paper. But there seems to be a division of opinion in the Board. I know not what the upshot will be. A crisis may come in a few days. It may be better than I think. But it is plain to me that my friends blame me for the situation, and I have no confidence in them or in their judgment in the case. It is probable that the General Assembly will veto my appointment and I doubt whether the Directors will resist their veto. The Presbytery acted so shamefully towards me that I was sorely tempted to renounce their jurisdiction and go over to the New York Association. I do not see how I can ever feel at home in the Presbytery again, even if I should win the battle next winter.[58]

The text of the faculty statement appeared in the press on the following day. Though expressing regret at the general tone of the inaugural, the statement left no doubt of the faculty's support of his views.[59]

On May 17 Moderator George L. Shearer in an adjourned meeting of the Presbytery of New York named a committee of five "to arrange and prepare the necessary proceedings appropriate in the case of Prof. Briggs." [60] Three of these five members were also members of the investigating committee who had signed that committee's majority report. To their number was added the Reverend Robert F. Sample and Colonel John J. McCook, a prominent New York attorney and elder in the Church.[61]

As the situation continued to deteriorate, Union's Board of Directors formulated a series of eight questions which covered the major points at issue. Briggs answered these categorically.

Question 1. Do you consider the Bible, the Church, and the Reason as co-ordinate sources of authority? Answer. No. Or, do you believe the Scriptures of the Old and New Testament to be the only infallible rule of faith and practice? Answer. Yes.

Question 2. When you use the word "reason" do you include the conscience and the religious feelings? Answer. Yes.

Question 3. Would you accept the following as a satisfactory definition of inspiration: "Inspiration is such a divine direction as to secure an infallible record of God's revelation in respect to both fact and doctrine?" Answer. Yes.

Question 4. Do you believe the Bible to be inerrant in all matters concerning faith and practice, and in everything in which it is a revelation from God or a vehicle of divine truth, and that there are no errors that disturb its infallibility in these matters or in its records of the historic events and institutions with which they are inseparably connected? Answer. Yes.

Question 5. Do you believe that the miracles recorded in Scripture are due to an extraordinary exercise of divine energy either directly or mediately through holy men? Answer. Yes.

Question 6. Do you hold what is commonly known as the doctrine of a second probation? Do you believe in Purgatory? Answer. No.

Question 7. Do you believe that the issues of this life are final and that a man who dies impenitent will have no further opportunity of salvation? Answer. Yes.

Question 8. Is your theory of progressive sanctification such that it will permit you to say that you believe that when a man dies in the faith he enters the middle state regenerated, justified and sinless? Answer. Yes.[62]

The Board of Directors thereupon adopted a resolution on May 19 affirming their confidence in and support of Briggs. This resolution, together with that of the faculty, served to unite the Seminary behind Briggs only two days before the General Assembly of 1891 convened in Detroit.

II

Princeton leadership within the One Hundred and Third General Assembly was reflected at the outset in the election of Professor William Henry Green as Moderator. The *New York Tribune* gave the following description:

This is pre-eminently a conservative Assembly; more, it is a Princeton Assembly. The Moderator is a Princeton man, the senior professor in that seminary; the State Clerk is a Princeton man, having been for a long time librarian of that institution; the chairman of the Standing Committee on Theological Seminaries, Dr. Patton, is president of Princeton College, and it is to this committee that the report of Union Seminary is to be submitted. Friends and opponents of Dr. Briggs are already forming their opinions as to what action this committee will report in regard to the New York professor.[63]

Noting that sixty-three presbyteries had overtured the Assembly concerning the Briggs address, the Committee on Theological Seminaries began its report on May 27 by raising the possibility of the Assembly's veto of Briggs' appointment.[64] Chairman Francis L. Patton insisted that the Assembly did possess the right of approval over any and all faculty elections; the Briggs transfer was no exception. Union Seminary's Board, however, took the position that Briggs had been "elected" to their faculty years before and the Assembly had not disapproved then. The recent change in his status did not constitute an "election" but merely a "transfer" in duties; this action lay entirely at the discretion of the Directors.

The problem of interpretation was reflected in portions of the Committee's report. Referring to the agreement of 1870, Chairman Patton conceded: "While your committee are of the opinion that the compact in question did not contemplate the distinction between the election of a person to be professor and the appointment of one already a professor to the work of a certain department of instruction, it cannot be denied that such a distinction exists." [65] The report concluded with the recommendations that Briggs' transfer be vetoed by the Assembly and that a committee be appointed to confer with the Union Directors regarding relations between that institution and the Assembly.[66]

In the debate over the recommendations which followed, efforts were made to postpone a final decision on the question of the veto. But Chairman Francis Patton and John J. McCook argued persistently in favor of immediate action. Said Patton: "I tell you it is in the interest of freedom; it is in the interest of a proper freedom that you should not allow that it is possible to postpone the veto. You have to do it now, or not at all. Very well. Now, then, you have the right to veto, and if you veto, you must veto now." [67] The two recommendations of the Committee were adopted decisively, 447 to 60.[68]

The Board was particularly annoyed with two aspects of the Committee's action. First, those directors who were present at Detroit were given no opportunity to explain their view of Brigg's transfer; even the prepared questions which Briggs had answered went unnoticed. Second, the recommendation that the transfer be vetoed was put forth without any reasons being given. This action called for a verdict without a hearing; and all the while, legal procedures were under way in the Presbytery of New York. The Committee's action had a twofold effect: (1) it directly prejudiced Briggs' case before the Presbytery; (2) the competence of Union's Board was seriously impugned. On June 4 the Board voted 22 to 2 not to heed the Assembly's veto of Briggs' transfer.

The first of the meetings between Union's Board and the Assembly's Committee of Conference took place on October 28 and 29. Papers were exchanged by the two parties, with each side maintaining its earlier position.

On October 5 the New York Presbytery's Committee in charge of preparing the case against Briggs returned two charges of heresy:

(1) With teaching doctrines which conflict irreconcilably with
and are contrary to the cardinal doctrines taught in the Holy
Scriptures and contained in the Standards of the Presbyterian
Church, that the Scriptures of the Old and New Testaments are
the only infallible rule of faith and practice; (2) with teaching
a doctrine of the character, state and sanctification of believers after
death, which irreconcilably conflicts with and is contrary to the
Holy Scriptures and the Standards of the Presbyterian Church.[69]

These were the charges which Briggs set about to answer
on the morning of November 4, when the Presbytery convened
in the Scotch Presbyterian Church on Fourteenth Street near
Sixth Avenue. He relied heavily upon criteria which the
General Assembly of 1824 had set forth in the Craighead Case:

All charges for heresy should be as definite as possible. The article
or articles of faith impugned should be specified, and the words
supposed to be heretical shown to be in repugnance to these articles;
whether the reference is made directly to the Scripture as a standard of orthodoxy; or to the Confession of Faith, which our Church
holds to be a summary of the doctrines of Scripture. (Craighead
Case, 1824, p. 121.)[70]

In keeping with these principles Briggs argued that the first
charge alleged "more than one offense" and failed to "set forth
the alleged offense." [71] This charge was so vague that it contained "any and every reason" for condemnation. The second
charge, while less vague than the first, did not define which
doctrine of the Standards and Holy Scripture had been violated.
He argued:

It will be necessary for the prosecution to prove (1) that immediate sanctification at death is taught in the Scriptures and the
Standards; (2) that it is a cardinal doctrine of the Westminster
Confession; and (3) that the two doctrines are in irreconcilable
conflict with each other, ere the Presbytery would be justified in
condemning me.[72]

Briggs' attack upon the charges was devastating. And the committee quickly found itself in an awkward situation. Axiomatic in his response to the two charges and eight specifications was this portion of the Craighead decision:

That a man cannot fairly be convicted of heresy, for using expressions that may be so interpreted as to involve heretical doctrines, if they may also admit to a more favorable construction: Because, no one can tell in what sense an ambiguous expression is used, but the speaker or writer, and he has a right to explain himself; and in such cases, candor requires that a court should favor the accused, by putting on his words the more favorable, rather than the less favorable construction. Another principle is, that no man can rightly be convicted of heresy by inference or implication; that is, we must not charge an accused person with holding those consequences which may legitimately flow from his assertions. Many men are grossly inconsistent with themselves; and while it is right, in argument, to overthrow false opinions, by tracing them in their connections and consequences, it is not right to charge any man with an opinion which he disavows.—Craighead Case: "Minutes of the Assembly," 1824, p. 122.[73]

At the conclusion of Briggs' response an effort was made to dismiss the charges and discharge the committee. This attempt led to one of the most debated points of the proceedings: Was the committee presenting the charges only a functionary of the Presbytery, or was this committee the representative of the Presbyterian Church and, as such, an original party in the case? This was a crucial question. Should the committee be only a functionary of the Presbytery, its existence would cease with the dismissal of the charges. But should it be declared the representative of the Presbyterian Church and an original party in the case, then the committee's existence would continue wholly independent of the Presbytery which created it.[74] In the latter instance an unfavorable verdict could be appealed to a higher court.

In the furor which erupted between the members over this

point, Henry van Dyke [75] and Francis Brown argued that the committee was only an instrument of the Presbytery and could be discharged by it. With some hesitation Moderator John C. Bliss ruled that the function of the committee had been that of a prosecuting committee and it should formally be declared the representative of the Presbyterian Church. Brown immediately appealed the decision, but the moderator was sustained by a vote of 64 to 57.[76]

John J. McCook on behalf of the prosecuting committee then assured the Presbytery that should the charges be dismissed, the committee would appeal. A motion for dismissal, plus three amendments, was then presented to the Presbytery in this form:

Resolved, That the Presbytery of New York, having listened to the paper of the Rev. Charles A. Briggs, D.D., in the case of the Presbyterian Church in the United States of America against him, as to the sufficiency of the charges and speculations in form and legal effect, and without approving of the positions stated in his inaugural address, at the same time desiring earnestly the peace and quiet of the Church, and in view of the declarations made by Dr. Briggs touching his loyalty to the Holy Scriptures and the Westminster Standards, and of his disclaimers of interpretations put on some of his words, deems it best to dismiss the case, and hereby does so dismiss it.[77]

The motion was carried by a vote of 94 to 39.[78] Thereupon, the prosecuting committee gave notice of an appeal to the Synod of New York.

An article by Union's Professor Philip Schaff appeared in the January issue of *The Forum* in which he defended Briggs' views. Schaff wrote:

In Germany Dr. Briggs would be classed with the conservative and orthodox rather than with radicals and rationalists. He is, in fact, a Calvinist in everything except the questions of higher criticism, where he adopts the opinions of the school of Ewald and Wellhausen, though not without some modifications, and with a distinct disavowal of rationalism.[79]

Negotiations between Union's Board and the Assembly's Committee of Conference were resumed on January 20, 1892. In rejecting the Committee's position the Board made this proposal: "We sincerely believe that both parties to the agreement of 1870 should equally desire its abrogation, alike for the sake of the Church, and for the sake of the seminaries." [80] This constituted the first formal suggestion that the agreement be dissolved.

Throughout the early months of 1892 the forthcoming General Assembly gained considerable attention. The surge of conservative power was felt in the New York Presbytery at its April meeting. Of the fourteen commissioners elected to the Assembly by that body, thirteen were known conservatives, including four of the five members of the prosecuting committee. The fifth member of that committee, its chairman, was scheduled to present his committee's appeal before the Assembly. Thus the entire committee had official status before the Assembly. Union's President Thomas S. Hastings had hoped to have Francis Brown elected a delegate. But his overwhelming defeat was seen by some as an intentional rebuff to Hastings and the seminary.

When the General Assembly of 1892 convened on May 19 at Portland, Oregon, conservative predominance was very much in evidence. However, under Moderator William C. Young there was a more equitable representation in the appointments to the standing committees.

In the report of Union Seminary to the Assembly, Briggs' transfer was explained in this way:

A professor can be elected in this institution only in accordance with our laws, and according to those laws Dr. Briggs was not elected. His inauguration was a ceremonial technically unnecessary, but designed only to honor publicly the generosity of the founder of the Chair of Biblical Theology in which department Dr. Briggs has been teaching for ten years.[81]

The report concluded with a memorial to the Assembly in which the Seminary Board requested the abrogation of the Compact of 1870. The Assembly's reply to this request was postponed until the appeal of the prosecuting committee could be considered.

On May 24 the Assembly's Judicial Committee brought in two reports. The majority report found the appeal in proper order, thus recognizing the prosecuting committee as an original party in the case. The minority report, while recognizing the appeal, objected to its being brought before the Assembly. This report recommended that the appellants be advised to take their appeal to the Synod of New York, instead of bypassing that body.[82] In the debate upon these reports[83] Chairman Birch of the appellants cited section 102 of the Book of Discipline, noting that appeals were "generally to be taken to the judicatory immediately superior to that appealed from." Birch insisted that the term "generally" in itself allowed for exceptions. Characteristic of the reasons submitted by the chairman for considering this case an exception was this: "This case involves the very fundamental truths of Christianity, and especially the doctrines of the Presbyterian Church. We cannot disguise the fact . . . that the history of the Christian Church records no more exciting and important controversy than that which is before this court." [84]

In his turn Briggs pointed out the highly unusual nature of this appeal. Only twice before had the General Assembly recognized appeals which had bypassed the Synod. In both cases the appeals had been brought by defendants, not prosecutors. Only one of those appeals was entertained by the Assembly. There was no precedent whatsoever for such an appeal by a prosecutor. The prosecution could not incur injury through the delay of regular procedure, whereas a condemned defendant could. "The law of appeals does not allow exceptions in the interest of prosecutors," argued Briggs, "but solely in the interest of defendants, and even these must give exceptional reasons." [85]

Following a period of confusion on the floor, the Assembly voted to table the minority report, 385 to 122.[86] The majority report which recommended the appeal be entertained was then moved and carried. Both sides presented their arguments for and against sustaining the appeal. Members of the Presbytery of New York as well as commissioners to the Assembly were next permitted five minutes each in which to express their views on the matter. Before calling for a vote on May 28 Moderator Young made the following ruling regarding the outcome of the vote: "In my view, the power of this Assembly is limited to sending it [the Briggs case] back to the presbytery." [87] Accordingly, should the vote be to sustain the appeal, the entire case would be remanded to the Presbytery of New York for a full trial. The vote was to sustain, 429 to 87.[88]

The evening of May 30 saw the Assembly return to the question of its relationship to Union Seminary. Resolutions were adopted by which the Assembly (1) declined to break the compact of 1870, and (2) called for the appointment of a committee of arbitration to interpret the question of "transfer" within the compact. The second portion of this action was especially irritating to Union's Directors.[89]

On the day of adjournment an overture was introduced before and adopted by the Assembly which came to be known as the "Portland Deliverance." This move was clearly intended to promote the Hodge-Warfield theory of verbal inspiration as Presbyterian dogma: "Our Church holds that the inspired Word as it came from God is without error." [90] This continued in part:

The assertion of the contrary cannot but shake the confidence of the people in the sacred books. All who enter office in our Church solemnly profess to receive them as the only infallible rule of faith and practice. If they change their belief on this point, Christian honor demands that they should withdraw from our ministry. They have no right to use the pulpit or the chair of the professor for the dissemination of their errors until they are dealt with by the slow process of discipline.[91]

Obviously directed at Briggs, this overture proved to be an accurate indication of the conservative trend which was developing in the Presbyterian Church.

III

Meeting on October 13, Union's Board adopted by 19 to 1 a resolution, (1) rescinding the Assembly's veto power over faculty appointments, (2) terminating the compact of 1870, (3) and at the same time professing loyalty for the government and doctrine of the Presbyterian Church.[92] The charter of the Seminary placed the complete control of the institution in the care of the Directors. Accordingly, the right of veto over faculty appointments could not legally be delegated to any other party. Therefore, the Directors concluded that they had no choice in light of the charter but to terminate unilaterally the compact.

Francis Brown appeared before the Synod of New York on October 21 to press his complaint against the status of the prosecuting committee. A motion was passed by the Synod, (1) recognizing the complaint as being in order, but (2) indicating that any action by the Synod would be inappropriate in light of the Assembly's stand.[93] This was precisely what Briggs had warned the Assembly would happen, should the appeal be entertained. He had pointed out:

If the General Assembly, without the consideration of these fundamental questions which are not before your venerable body, and which cannot legally come before you at this time, if you should recognize these appellants, you decide by indirection three questions of vast importance pending before the Synod of New York, which only that Synod has jurisdiction to decide under present circumstances. You might damage the complainants in their rights before the Synod. You would compel the Synod either to disregard the rights of the complainants and refuse them a hearing because the case had been already decided by the Assembly, or you would force the Synod to disregard the action of the Assembly in order to protect the complainants in their rights. The Synod would be placed in a cruel dilemma.[94]

Placed in that dilemma, the Synod yielded to the Assembly. The complainants' rights to a fair and impartial hearing were destroyed, and the status of the prosecuting committee was virtually guaranteed.

On the ninth of November the Presbytery of New York met to consider preliminary matters involved in the forthcoming trial. At that time the prosecuting committee presented its amended charges and specifications. The two original charges of the previous year were expanded to eight. These read as follows:

The Presbyterian Church in the United States of America charges the Rev. Charles A. Briggs, D.D., being a Minister of the said Church and a member of the Presbytery of New York,

1.—with teaching that the Reason is a fountain of divine authority which may and does savingly enlighten men, even such men as reject the Scriptures as the authoritative proclamation of the will of God and reject also the way of salvation through the mediation and sacrifice of the Son of God as revealed therein; which is contrary to the essential doctrine of the Holy Scripture and of the Standards of the Church, that the Holy Scripture is most necessary, and the rule of faith and practice.

2.—with teaching that the Church is a fountain of divine authority which, apart from the Holy Scripture, may and does savingly enlighten men; which is contrary to the essential doctrine of the Holy Scripture and of the Standards of the said Church, that the Holy Scripture is most necessary and the rule of faith and practice.

3.—with teaching that errors may have existed in the original text of the Holy Scripture, as it came from its authors, which is contrary to the essential doctrine taught in the Holy Scripture and in the Standards of the said Church, that the Holy Scripture is the Word of God written, immediately inspired, and the rule of faith and practice.

4.—with teaching that many of the Old Testament predictions
    have been reversed by history, and that the great body of Messianic prediction has not been and cannot be fulfilled, which is contrary to the essential doctrine of Holy Scripture and of the Standards of the said Church, that God is true, omniscient and unchangeable.

5.—with teaching that Moses is not the author of the Pentateuch,
    which is contrary to direct statements of Holy Scripture and to the essential doctrines of the Standards of the said Church, that the Holy Scripture evidences itself to be the word of God by the consent of all the parts, and that the infallible rule of interpretation of Scripture is the Scripture itself.

6.—with teaching that Isaiah is not the author of half of the book
    that bears his name, which is contrary to direct statements of Holy Scripture and to the essential doctrines of the Standards of the said Church that the Holy Scripture evidences itself to be the word of God by the consent of all the parts, and that the infallible rule of interpretation of Scripture is the Scripture itself.

7.—with teaching that the processes of redemption extend to
    the world to come in the case of many who die in sin; which is contrary to the essential doctrine of Holy Scripture and the Standards of the said Church, that the processes of redemption are limited to this world.

8.—with teaching that Sanctification is not complete at death,
    which is contrary to the essential doctrine of Holy Scripture and of the Standards of the said Church that the souls of believers are at their death at once made perfect in holiness.[95]

One newspaper gave this description of the opening scene of the trial on November 28:

The floor of the church was filled with the members of the presbytery and friends who came early to secure seats from which they could hear to advantage. The galleries were filled, scores of the fair sex being present and seemingly as eager to catch every word and as quick to note the force of the points made as though they could enforce their views with a vote. Mrs. Briggs and Mrs. Birch occupied their reserved seats opposite each other in the galleries near the pulpit.[96]

In his initial reply to the amended charges Briggs raised many objections. Of the charges, he considered only the eighth to be sufficient in form and legal effect. Of the remaining seven, he expressed willingness to waive his objections to one, two, three, five and six on the condition that a separate vote be taken on each alleged violation of doctrine.[97]

As for charges four and seven, Briggs insisted they were thoroughly unacceptable to him. "They charge me with teaching doctrines which I have expressly disclaimed." [98] Charge four attributed the views of Kuenen, regarding the fulfillment of predictive prophecy, directly to Briggs. The context of the inaugural from which this charge was taken clearly indicated that Briggs had rejected the position of Kuenen. This charge constituted a misquotation of the defendant's inaugural. Turning to charge seven, Briggs noted that in the categorical questions prepared by Union's Board, he had denied any belief in the doctrine of a future probation.[99] He demanded that these charges be withdrawn. Following extended debate, the Presbytery voted to dismiss both of the contested charges, with the prosecuting committee vigorously protesting.[100] Briggs pleaded not guilty to the remaining six charges.

The prosecution began its presentation on December 5, and the sessions which followed were marked with repeated skirmishes. Chairman Birch and John J. McCook closely followed the text of the charges and specifications in their opening statements. The defense opened on December 13, with Briggs deriding both the charges against him and the prosecution's presentation. Of McCook's effort, he said:

Its subtle analyses of hypothetical premises, its simple-minded substitution of inferences from the language of the defendant for
that language itself, . . . the cool assumption of its logic and the
condensed heat of its rhetoric, all remind us of the intellectual
processes of a scholastic theologian rather than a lawyer.[101]

At the outset of his argument Briggs raised this significant
issue. Regarding questions on which the Confession of Faith
had taken no position, a believer could freely hold a private
opinion as "extra-confessional" doctrine as long as that opinion
could be supported "from Holy Scripture or from the experience of mankind, or from any other valid reasons." [102]

In answering the first charge Briggs denied having exalted
the reason above Holy Scripture. As he used the term, the
"reason" combined both the conscience and the religious feeling.
The reason was the human capacity to understand the Holy
Spirit speaking through Scripture. "I claim that the Reason
is a great fountain of divine authority and yet not a rule of
faith and practice." [103] The appreciation for the role of the
reason had greatly increased since the seventeenth century. The
Westminster Confession was inadequate in its attention to this
area. Therefore, a believer was justified at this point in passing beyond the Confession into the area of "extra-confessional"
opinion. He described the reason as God's greatest gift to man
—"the holy of holies of human nature." [104]

Turning to the second charge, Briggs reaffirmed his view
that the church as the kingdom of Christ was indeed a fountain
of divine authority. "If this Presbytery is ready to declare that
the Presbyterian Church has no divine authority, I will at
once renounce your jurisdiction." [105] Like the reason, the
church was not a rule of faith and practice. Yet the church
did serve to channel God's divine authority through its divine-
ly appointed institutions.

The third charge had its basis in the Princeton doctrine of
inspiration. Briggs did not hesitate to scorn verbal inspiration
and its logical conclusion, textual inerrancy. He drew freely

from church history to illustrate that errors had long been recognized in Scripture. Describing his own position as the plenary doctrine of inspiration, he said: "You cannot exact of me that I shall say there are no errors in Holy Scripture, for the reason that the Confession does not assert this and I am not bound to your views of consistency or inconsistency— but only to the Confession and to my own judgment." [106] Briggs pointed out that such errors as did exist in no way impaired the infallibility of Scripture in matters of faith and practice. God had used "the human reason and all the faculties of imperfect human nature. He used the voice and hands of imperfect men. He allowed the sacred writings to be edited and re-edited, arranged and rearranged again by imperfect scribes. It is impossible that such imperfect instrumentalities should attain perfect results." [107] The difficulty lay not with a few inconsequential errors in Scripture, but in the minds of the prosecuting committee who included verbal inspiration in their doctrine of inspiration as had Chairman Birch in his opening statement: "God is the arranger of its clauses, the chooser of its terms, and the speller of its words so that the text in its letters, words, or clauses is just as divine as the thought." [108]

As for his own position, Briggs assured the Presbytery that he believed the Holy Scriptures to be the only infallible rule of faith and practice. Citing chapter one, section eight, of the Confession, he made this qualification:

The Scriptures are the final appeal in religious controversies; matters of faith and practice, not for questions of science. Those who have resorted to the Bible to prove that the sun moved round the earth, that the earth could not be circumnavigated, that the universe was created in six days of twenty-four hours, and the like, have surely gone beyond the range of the Westminster Confession, which specifies controversies of religion.[109]

The next two of the amended charges, five and six, had to do respectively with the Mosaic authorship of the Pentateuch and the authorship of the book of Isaiah. As a part of his defense at this point, Briggs had prepared for the Presbytery a pamphlet entitled "Who Wrote the Pentateuch?" [110] In this he traced the history of higher criticism to its present development. Drawing from writings ranging from Irenaeus to Luther, Briggs urged that the church had never taught that Moses was the author of the Pentateuch. As for the book of Isaiah, one need only compare the literary styles, theologies, and historical situations reflected in its various chapters to realize that this book was the product of several centuries and not the work of a single man. The notion that a writing could be an infallible rule of faith and practice only if it came from well-known prophets and apostles was a recent bit of nonsense brought forth by the Princeton theologians to support their doctrine of inspiration. This position could find support neither in the Bible nor in the Westminster Standard.[111]

The last of the amended charges accused Briggs of teaching that sanctification was not complete at death. Of the charges which he faced, none was as difficult to overcome as this.[112] He argued that the Standards did not teach that the souls of believers were made perfect in holiness immediately, in a moment of time, upon death. Instead, he insisted that upon death the souls of believers entered the middle state wherein each soul was made perfect in holiness over a period of time through progressive sanctification.[113] This, he maintained, was the teaching of the Standards. The most difficult statement in the Standards with which to reconcile this position was Question 86 in the Larger Catechism:

Question: What is the communion in glory with Christ, which the members of the invisible church enjoy immediately after death?

Answer: The communion in glory with Christ, which the members of the invisible church enjoy immediately after death, is in that their souls are then made perfect in holiness, and received into the highest heavens, where they behold the face of God in light and glory; waiting for the full redemption of their bodies, which even in death continue united with Christ, and the rest in their graves as in their beds, till the last day they be again united with their souls.

Briggs held that "immediately after death" in this context referred to "the whole state which begins immediately after death" and extends to the resurrection and judgment, rather than to "the moment of time that begins that state." [114] He granted, in elaborating upon the undefined middle state, that he was going beyond the formulation of the Confession. But he saw this as the region of extraconfessional opinion which he was entitled to pursue. This was in no way a violation of the Confession.

By his definition sanctification was far more than simply being cleansed of sin. "Christian sanctification is vastly higher, grander, and more glorious than this. According to the Westminster Confession, it is not merely cleansing from sin and rising to a higher grade of Christian life and experience, 'it is being more and more strengthened in all saving graces, to the practice of true holiness.' " [115] This required ample time for completion. This practice "must be the exercise and work of man, under the influence of the divine Spirit." [116] Through this training process, which continued until the second advent and the resurrection, the soul could gradually achieve "Christ-likeness and perfect purity and holiness." [117] For Briggs the greatest part of the church's ministry occurred in the middle state "in training the departed babes and pious heathen in the holiness and blessedness of the heavenly state." [118]

Progressive sanctification played two important roles for Briggs. First, it filled the middle state with "an attractive, industrious, holy life, a progress in grace, in knowledge, in holiness, in all perfections." [119] And second, it provided for the education of each soul. Briggs emphasized this educational aspect of sanctification as indispensable for all believers. "Even if they commit no positive sin they do not reach positive perfection until their sanctification has been completed in the attainment of the complete likeness of Christ." [120] He saw this doctrine as being capable of uniting all facets of a Christian world view.

December 29 and 30 were spent in voting on the charges in their several items. When the count was completed, the moderator announced that Briggs stood acquitted on each charge. The margin of acquittal ranged from 73—49 to 67—61. The defendant received his major support from the ministers who strongly resisted each charge. The elders, however, barely sustained three of the six charges and split their votes evenly on another.[121]

A committee including the Reverend Henry van Dyke presented their report to the Presbytery on January 9. Noting the principles laid down in the Craighead case, the report brought forth the following verdict:

Therefore, without expressing approval of the critical or theological views embodied in the Inaugural Address, or the manner in which they have been expressed and illustrated, the Presbytery pronounces the Rev. Charles A. Briggs, D.D., fully acquitted of the offences alleged against him, the several Charges and Specifications accepted for probation having been "not sustained." [122]

The report continued by suggesting "that the grave issues involved in this case will be more wisely and justly determined by calm investigation and fraternal discussion than by judicial arraignment and process." [123] Indicative of the committee's effort at reconciliation is the following paragraph of that report:

In view of the present disquietude in the Presbyterian Church, and of the obligation resting upon all Christians to walk in charity and to have tender concern for the consciences of their brethren, the Presbytery earnestly counsels its members to avoid, on the one hand, hasty or over-confident statement of private opinion on points concerning which profound and reverent students of God's word are not yet agreed, and, on the other hand, suspicions and charges of false teaching which are not clearly capable of proof.[124]

With the prosecuting committee taking "exception to the final judgment in this case . . . and to each and every part thereof," [125] the turbulent nature of the trial continued to the final rap of the gavel.

If the prosecuting committee were unhappy with the results, so was the defendant. Briggs felt that his acquittal was undermined by the opening clause of the verdict: "Without expressing approval of the critical or theological views embodied in the Inaugural Address, or the manner in which they have been expressed and illustrated." [126] He wished to appeal the verdict to the Synod, but other opinion prevailed. On January 4 President Thomas S. Hastings wrote him:

> I agree with you that you are entitled to a clear verdict. But I hope you will not maintain an aggressive spirit. You have already gained much for the cause you represent. The Board of Directors has stood by you under great pressure and now is a unit. The Presbytery has once dismissed the case against you, and now has acquitted you by a majority in which is the whole strength of the Presbytery. These are great gains. It seems to me more and more as I reflect upon the matter, that it would be a dreadful mistake to sacrifice any of these gains by an unwillingness to concede anything to the friends who have so nobly stood by you. Some of them you know cannot agree with all your positions and honestly feel that they have in a measure compromised themselves by advocating your cause. Do they not deserve some consideration? You know that I am not among that number.[127]

At the same time other efforts were being made to preserve the peace. In January Henry van Dyke penned these words to J. J. Lampe of the prosecuting committee:

> You are a member of the Committee of Prosecution in the case which has just been tried in the Presbytery of New York. You have doubtless observed the verdict of the Presbytery in that case has been framed with the utmost care; first, to avoid committing the members of the Presbytery to a personal agreement with the theories of the defendant or the manner in which they have been

expressed; second, to do full justice to the Committee of which you are a member and to refrain from any assertion of the Presbytery's authority to control your future action.

As a member of the committee which framed this judgment I wish to say to you frankly that our desire in framing it was to make peace. I appeal to you personally to cooperate with us in that desire.[128]

On January 18 the prosecution filed notice of an appeal to the General Assembly of 1893.

A memorial entitled *A Plea for Peace and Work* [129] appeared under the date of February 17. Sponsored by a group of prominent ministers, including Henry van Dyke, this memorial contained the signatures of 235 of the leading ministers in the Presbyterian Church. On February 18 Colonel Elliott F. Shepard, editor of the ultraconservative newspaper *The Mail and Express,* in denouncing the memorial, published a letter which allegedly had accompanied the memorial as it was circulated for signatures. Among the more obvious parts of the letter were these words:

As a matter of policy, the Union professors are keeping out of direct participation in this movement, but fortunately there are a number of us who are ready and glad to contribute much of our time to carrying out their wishes.—

If we can, by urging the demand for peace and liberty, attract attention away from the real issues involved in the Briggs case, we may prevent adverse action at Washington in May, and we then ought to control, as Professor F. Brown feels confident we will, the assembly of 1894.

The matter has been carried on very quietly and secretly, so as to keep it out of the papers until early March, when it will strike the church like a thunder clap, and have a tremendous effect when it is known that the city pastors of the rich and influential churches have been committed to us.[130]

Henry van Dyke denied having seen this letter prior to its appearance in *The Mail and Express;* he noted that he had personally handled all the mail involving the memorial. In the *Interior* he wrote:

We have indeed fallen upon evil times in our church, when the reporters of secular newspapers are used to originate slanders and the columns of religious newspapers to copy them. The very violence of such methods of resistance is a testimony to the strength of the "Plea for Peace"; and the character of its signers is a guarantee for its candor, its fairness, and its firmness.[131]

Also on February 18 the *New York Sun* reported that Briggs and his old friend and ally Henry Preserved Smith of Lane Seminary were planning to bolt from the Presbyterian Church and form a new church.[132] With an appeal due before the Assembly in three months, no rumor could have been more damaging to Briggs and his supporters. Briggs had long since refused to be interviewed by the press on such subjects as this, and his refusal to reply only served to enhance the rumor. Smith, however, quickly issued a denial through the Associated Press.[133]

This alleged conspiracy together with the fabricated letter of *The Mail and Express* did substantially reduce whatever influence the memorial might have had; this was a significant victory for the ultraconservatives. One observer later described the situation as one in which every single trick known in the political game was used.[134]

IV

No part of the proceedings against Briggs was as revealing of the thinking of the prosecuting committee as their appeal to the Assembly of 1893. The intensity of personal antagonism reached its peak and largely obscured the theological issues involved. This was true to such a degree that the theological position of the prosecuting committee could no longer be identified strictly with Princeton theology. In fact the Princeton leadership which had been so evident in the Assembly of 1891, had been pushed from the scene in 1893 by a vigorous ultraconservative force which had oriented itself about the Princeton doctrine of inspiration. It was most unfortunate for the Presbyterian Church that the Princeton men did not openly espouse a more moderate position against this surge. This reluctance on their part surprised no one; but it allowed the church to be dominated by a strong ultraconservative influence throughout the remainder of that decade.

The General Assembly of 1893 convened on May 18 in Washington's New York Avenue Presbyterian Church to hear retiring Moderator W. C. Young strike the keynote of the Assembly with an attack upon higher criticism. The conservative trend was further reflected in the election of Prof. Willis G. Craig of McCormick Seminary as moderator.

The appeal was brought before the Assembly on May 23 in the form of two reports from the Judicial Committee. The majority report (1) recognized the prosecuting committee and (2) found the appeal in proper order. It went on to recommend (3) that the appeal be entertained and the case be issued. Finally the report proposed this resolution: "That the appeal from the decision and final judgment of the Presbytery of New York in the case of Prof. Charles A. Briggs, D.D., is hereby entertained and it is ordered that the case proceed to trial in accordance with the provisions of the Book of Discipline." [135]

The obvious injustice of recommending that the appeal be entertained and the case issued was pointed out in the minority report. This report concurred with the majority in recognizing the status of the prosecution and the order of the appeal; but it noted that in recommending the appeal be entertained and the case issued, the majority report clearly prejudiced the case before the Assembly at a time when the parties had not yet been heard. This recommendation also committed the members of the Judicial Committee to the position of entertaining the appeal prior to the hearing.[136] Without making any corrections to the majority report Moderator Craig opened the case on the following afternoon.

The church quickly took on the atmosphere of a courtroom.

The pulpit and space in front were reserved for the officers of the Assembly, parties to the case, chairmen of the various committees in connection with the meeting of the Assembly, ex-Moderators, and Elders over eighty years old. The last five pews in the body of the church were given over to visitors, clergymen preferred, and the gallery to the ladies, who were not admitted to the main floor. Every bit of available seating and standing room was occupied.[137]

Professor Henry P. Smith sat with the Briggs family in their reserved seats in the gallery.

Chairman G. W. F. Birch opened the proceedings for his prosecuting committee with an attempt to explain why his committee had bypassed the Synod of New York in their appeal. This was due to the fact that the errors involved in the defendant's teachings were errors of discipline and doctrine. Most significant in Birch's complaint was the wording of the verdict of acquittal. He argued:

We are here to invoke this Supreme Court to put an end to the dissension and disputation which the New York Presbytery vainly endeavored to silence first by the dismissal of the case against Dr. Briggs on November 4th, 1891, and second by the acquittal of Dr. Briggs on January 9th, 1893, qualifying both the said dismissal and the said acquittal by the positive disclaimer of any approval of the controverted statements of the Inaugural Address, as to critical or theological views, and the manner of expression.[138]

That portion of the verdict which Birch cited as the Presbytery's failure to end the strife, ironically enough, had been composed out of a sole effort to achieve peace within the Presbytery.[139]

After reminding the Assembly that the only question before the house in this hearing was that of entertaining the appeal, not sustaining it, Briggs replied to Birch's complaint:

What matters it that the Presbytery acquit Dr. Briggs "without expressing approval of the critical or theological views embodied in the Inaugural Address, or the manner in which they have been expressed or illustrated"? This reservation of approval is not a part of the final judgment even if it is embraced within the limits of the same paragraph. The final judgment is simply and alone the acquittal with its reasons.[140]

This modification could not legally be an object of appeal. And such irrelevant matter should be stricken from the appeal.[141]

This appeal from a verdict of acquittal placed the appellee's ecclesiastical life in jeopardy a second time. Though the physical loss of life or limb was not threatened, other commitments were. Briggs assured the Assembly:

To injure a minister in his ministry is therefore far more cruel to him than to cut off his limbs. To depose him, and so cut off his ecclesiastical life, is a far greater penalty than to deprive him of his physical life. Will the Presbyterian Church commit an act of cruelty and wrong worse than that prohibited in the constitution of our country?[142]

Arguing as his own counsel, Briggs noted that the prosecution had greatly exaggerated the scope of his teachings. His acquittal in no way endorsed the validity of his doctrines; this simply exonerated him of heresy.

The doctrines of Dr. Briggs stand or fall by themselves, without any endorsement of the Presbytery, and without any responsibility of the Presbytery, or the Presbyterian Church for them. It is a common mistake that the Presbyterian Church is responsible for all doctrines of its ministers. The Presbyterian Church is responsible for its constitution and its constitutional rules, and for them alone. It cannot exact more of its ministers.[143]

The prosecution was obviously attempting to use a heresy trial in order to obtain new definitions of dogma.[144]

In reviewing the history of his case, Briggs reminded the Assembly that a complaint was then before the Synod of New York with respect to the status of the prosecuting committee. Regarding that committee's bypassing of the Synod, he said this:

The defendant has reason to believe that the appellants fear to bring their case before the Synod of New York. They have reason to dread lest their appeal against the verdict of acquittal will not be entertained by the Synod. The defendant has great confidence in the Synod of New York that it will do him justice, and that its decision will be just and right. It is his constitutional right to go before the Synod. His city of refuge against these prosecutors is the Synod of New York. The General Assembly has no constitutional right to obstruct him from seeking refuge with the Synod. He casts himself into the arms of the Synod of New York, in the confidence that the Synod will shield him from any injustice and wrong that may be done him. He claims the jurisdiction of the Synod, and denies that the Assembly has any present jurisdiction of the case. What right have you under the constitution to deprive him of this right? What precedent have you to justify you in refusing him this right? What principle of equity can you plead for such a violation of individual rights? You would do a wrong unparalleled in the history of Presbyterianism, a wrong which could be equalled only in the annals of the inquisition.[145]

Showing the strain of exhaustion, he concluded his argument by reaffirming his belief in Holy Scripture as the only infallible rule of faith and practice. He said:

I beg leave to affirm that I hold to the entire system of doctrine set forth in the Westminster Confession, and anything that I may have said that at all conflicts with this statement is due to the misinterpretations which have been put upon the language which I have uttered. I will not say that those misinterpretations are always intentional. I shall not exonerate myself from some possible blame in lack of clearness in the enunciation of them. But I beg leave to affirm the truth, that I have made no statement that at all conflicts with the affirmations that I have made before you.[146]

In his closing statement McCook summarized a number of preliminary questions which had been determined by the Assembly of 1892. The appellee had argued well against the actions of the previous Assembly, and McCook found it neces-

sary to defend, among other things, the status of his committee. As he presented his argument, McCook was able to
evoke the sympathy of the commissioners on several issues.
Despite his shallowness in theological training, he was a per-
suasive speaker, adept at turning a phrase. To those equally in-
ept in the finer points of theological thought, he seemed quite
convincing. This, together with the fact that the defense had
no chance to reply, especially enhanced his presentation.

McCook reminded the commissioners at one point: "Keep in
mind the only thing that these proceedings are based upon is
the Inaugural Address." [147] The irony of this can be seen in a
description later written by a minister who attended every
session: "Strange as it may seem, though all the charges against
Dr. Briggs were based upon his inaugural address, not a copy
of that address was to be found in the Assembly. A commissioner proposed to have copies of it introduced, that the
quotations might be read in their connection, but the Assembly paid no heed to the proposal." [148]

Drawing frequently upon the arguments his committee had
used before the previous Assembly, McCook attempted to defend
the direct appeal to the Assembly in this way. Should the appeal be taken to the Synod, in any event it would come before
the next Assembly. Then all thirty-one presbyteries of the
New York Synod would be excluded from voting in the decision. But by appealing directly to the Assembly, only one
presbytery in the Synod would be excluded: the Presbytery
of New York which had already acquitted the defendant. On
the surface this appeared to be a noble gesture, and it undoubtedly influenced the commissioners. Yet this had nothing to do
with the legality of entertaining the appeal.

From the appellants' past performance Briggs had anticipated this argument in his statement:

It is true that there is an apparent unfairness in excluding fifteen
per cent of the Church from the court of last resort. But if the
Synod should be excluded will it injure the appellants or the

appellee? The appellee is willing to trust his Synod and to run the risk. He is the one who is most deeply concerned. He is the only one who risks his ecclesiastical life. If he is willing to take the risk, why should the appellants be so anxious to avoid it? [149]

For the most part this was lost upon the Assembly.

McCook closed his remarks on this matter with this misleading bit of advice: "If this court should, in its wise discretion, think that this matter should go to the Synod, the first steps toward that result must be to entertain this appeal. You cannot act or take any act in disposing of this matter until you have first voted to entertain the appeal." [150]

In conclusion, five "special reasons" were offered as to why this direct appeal should be entertained. Characteristic of these was the second reason which McCook presented: "The case is fully ripe for final judgment by this Assembly." [151] He explained

that the questions involved have been before the Church for more than two years, and have been discussed both by the secular and the religious press . . . ; there is good reason for concluding that the brethren are well informed on the subjects involved in the case. Like the children of Issachar, the members of this Assembly have "understanding of the times, to know what Israel ought to do." [152]

This reference to coverage in the secular and religious press was particularly noteworthy in view of the vast amount of abuse that had been heaped upon Briggs since his inaugural. Of the numerous weeklies that comprised the religious press, only the *New York Evangelist* demonstrated any real grasp of the issues involved. The secular press did little more than parrot the same half-truths of its religious counterpart. This sort of irresponsible journalism had led Henry P. Smith to write earlier:

It is perhaps too much to expect an editor to rate justly the evils of abuse of the power of the press. As a matter of fact, trial by newspaper is superseding trial by Presbytery. The most unjust suspicion, entertained by the most narrow mind in the church, is entertained in this court. The charge is published and carries sentence with it. The unfortunate victim is allowed to protest, but at the worst advantage. Public opinion has already decided—too often without inquiry, without reflection, and without charity. It would seem to be time to exhort to some sort of caution in making accusations of unsoundness.[153]

The tactics of McCook were again evident in this line of argumentation:

So earnest is the attempt to keep this case from coming before the Assembly for decision, that the disruption of the Church is threatened if the Assembly should entertain and issue it. But this threat argues on the one hand, conscious weakness on the part of those who make it, and on the other, a deliberate intention to unduly influence the Assembly so as to prevent it from giving an honest expression of opinion.[154]

Though this argument had no basis in fact, nonetheless, it was damaging.

It was late on the evening of May 25 when McCook concluded. One spectator said of the hearing: "It was interesting to me to find that Dr. Briggs and his friends seemed to me to have quite the best of the argument upon the question as to whether the case should be tried there and then, or sent to the Synod of New York." [155] One newspaper reported: "The speaker never appeared to better advantage in any of the judicial proceedings to which he has been subjected during the last two years or more." [156]

After a prolonged period of discussion among the commissioners, a resolution was offered on the floor of the Assembly to the effect that the appeal be entertained and the case brought to trial. An amendment referring the appeal to the Synod was tabled. The resolution was carried by a vote of 405 to 145. The majority report was then adopted and the Judicial Committee were instructed to prepare the case for trial.[157] This overwhelming defeat thoroughly discouraged Briggs. As had been the case immediately following his acquittal, only the persuasion of close friends prevented his withdrawal from the Presbyterian Church.[158] Charles Butler, the venerable president of Union's Board wrote him: "The interests of the Seminary and the Presbyterian Church and the cause of truth require you to remain in the Church & stand fast—unless like Luther, you are driven out." [159]

On the day following the vote the conservative leadership remained hard at work. Ex-Moderator W. C. Young presented a recommendation pertaining to the "Portland Deliverance." Regarding the inerrancy of the Bible, the report urged "that the said deliverance enunciates no new doctrine, but rather interprets and gives expression to what has ever been cherished and believed in as a fundamental truth, and which is expressly taught in our Standards." [160]

On May 29, the day designated for the opening of the trial, rain fell in Washington. But despite this, every seat was taken at an early hour.[161] With the Assembly again constituted in its judicial capacity, McCook delivered a few brief remarks for the appellants and then gave way to the Rev. Joseph J. Lampe who presented the opening argument.[162]

Before turning to Lampe's statement, a brief examination should be given to the appeal. The five grounds listed were: irregularity in the proceedings of said Presbytery of New York; receiving improper testimony; declining to receive important testimony; manifestation of prejudice in the conduct of the case; mistake or injustice in the decision. Of the thirty-four specifications listed, three had to do with the Presbytery's striking out charges four and seven. Five others were concerned with the Moderator's ruling that Briggs need not be sworn as a witness while explaining the language he had used; five more cited the introduction into the Official Report of written testimony by the defense which was not read aloud on the floor of the Presbytery (despite the fact that the prosecution was granted the same privilege and J. J. Lampe had used it).[163] The majority of the specifications were simply repetitions listed under the various grounds.

Characteristic of the prosecution's thinking was the second specification under the fifth ground of the appeal:

> In this, that the said final judgment of the said Presbytery was not warranted by the law and the evidence, because the Court had decided that the Charges were sufficient in form and legal effect; that is, it had already substantially determined that if the accused had taught the doctrine with which he was charged, he was guilty of an offence. The several allegations were proved by extracts from the Inaugural Address cited in the several Specifications, and said extracts were admitted as authentical by the accused, and were not retracted by him. The proof was therefore complete. Said accused also introduced his own writings as evidence, which writings, so introduced, contained the extracts recited by the Prosecuting Committee in the several specifications. If the accused had brought evidence to show that he had made no such utterances as were contained in the specifications, then and then only should he have been 'fully acquitted.' The indictment had been found in order. The evidence was unchallenged and the judgment should have been 'guilty as charged.' [164]

By this line of reasoning Briggs' writings were capable of only one meaning: that which the prosecution understood. No meaning could be attributed to the defendant's words other than that which the prosecuting committee assigned. Briggs' only recourse would have been to disclaim those statements which the prosecution had questioned. Any support the defendant might adduce for his views from the Scriptures and the Standards was virtually irrelevant. Such fallacious thinking was in evidence throughout the arguments of the committee. Illustrative of this was a statement made by Chairman Birch in his opening address: "The position that a man cannot be convicted of heresy upon an inference, even though it be a necessary inference, is a false one, and that was not the principle upon which the General Assembly of 1824 based its decision in the Craighead case." He continued: "The use of the Craighead case in this matter is an *Evasion* of the *Facts,* and what lawyers would call confession and avoidance—a subterfuge on the part of the inferior court to evade its clear duty." [165] The glaring inaccuracy of this interpretation only served to indicate the prosecuting committee's determination to gain a conviction at any cost.

Opening with a defense of the grounds and specifications of the appeal, Lampe soon moved to other topics. He scorned the eight questions which Briggs had answered for Union's Board, pointing out that "all but one of the questions are susceptible of more than one meaning." [166] For one who found it so difficult to comprehend "more than one meaning" in Briggs' inaugural, this indicated a marked improvement, once the subject matter was changed.

The plaintiff then turned to the amended charges on which Briggs had been acquitted. His discussion of the first two charges is reflected in this statement:

The Bible, the Church and the Reason, then, are equal in being great fountains of divine authority. The quality of divinity, and the right of divine authority belong alike to all three; and, as such, each can be to man an infallible guide to life, and speak to him with eternal and immutable certainty, for he can yield to each implicit obedience, rest on each with loving certainty and build with joyous confidence." [167]

Lampe seemed to labor under this misconception of the expression, "fountains of divine authority." He repeatedly interpreted this to mean three original, independent, and equal sources. Briggs had regularly disclaimed this view, explaining that God was the only original source of divine authority. For the appellee the Bible, the church, and the reason only channeled this authority to man; and of the three, only the Bible was an infallible rule of faith and practice. An observer described this part of Lampe's statement with these words: "This is, at the outset, a remarkable distortion of the views of Dr. Briggs, arising from a refusal to accept his explanation of the meaning of a single word, and a consequent failure to understand the scope of his argument." [168]

Under the fifth charge, Lampe argued at length for the Mosaic authorship of the Pentateuch. "If this claim be not true," he urged, "then the Pentateuch is neither genuine nor authentic, and it must be untrustworthy. If the Pentateuch's claim of Mosaic authorship be false, and the work originated piece by piece during the centuries after the death of Moses, the document as it has come to us is a fraud, and no dependence can be placed upon it." [169]

Next, the plaintiff directed attention to the fourth and seventh of the amended charges. Briggs quickly challenged the appellants' right to discuss these charges since the Presbytery had rejected them. Moderator Craig ruled that Lampe might proceed. And this caused a good deal of excitement on the floor in which the moderator's decision was appealed, but sustained.[170] Under the fourth charge, Lampe summed up Kuenen's position as a "denial of the reality of predictive prophecy, the inspiration of the prophets and the presence of the supernatural in the Bible." [171] He then attributed Kuenen's views directly to the defendant and climaxed on this note: "It is the Bible and Christ against Dr. Briggs." [172] With this review of the charges Lampe concluded his remarks.

As Briggs began his defense, he remarked: "The Presbytery of New York must be a very inconsiderate and wicked body if it could make so many blunders and do such grave injustice to these five innocent presbyters whom it appointed to 'arrange and prepare the necessary proceedings appropriate in the case of Dr. Briggs.' " [173] In view of the repetition of specifications he decided to deal with the objections in the chronological order of their occurrence. He turned first to the two rejected charges which the appellants had been permitted to introduce. Of charge seven he said: "I have distinctly disclaimed that there is any regeneration after death for those who die unregenerate, or that there is any beginning of the Christian life after death. My doctrine of redemption after death concerns alone, in all the

statements that I have made respecting it, those who die as
believers, those who enter the future life as born again under the
influence of the Holy Spirit in this world." [174] Regarding the
doctrine of second probation, he quickly added: "Would that I
could teach such a comfortable doctrine; and if the time ever
comes that I can, I will gladly lay down my ministry in the
Presbyterian Church and go forth to teach the hope of salvation of some of those who apparently have died without regeneration in this world. But I do not hold that belief now: I
cannot." [175]

As for the fourth charge which attributed Kuenen's view of
prophecy to Briggs, the defendant read a passage from his book,
Messianic Prophecy,[176] embodying these words: "Kuenen has
taken advantage of the errors of the scholastic theory and
interpretation of predictive prophecy, and has dealt Hebrew
prediction the severest blows it has ever received. We shall
parry these blows of Kuenen by showing that they have destroyed the scholastic theory, but they have not in the slightest
degree injured Hebrew prediction as such." [177] He further assured the Assembly: "I am opposing Kuenen and endeavoring
to state the evangelical position on which the whole system of
the Messianic prophecy of the Old Testament can be defended, and then I go to the Old Testament predictions and
point them forward to fulfillment by Jesus Christ in history." [178]
A commissioner asked him if he still held this opinion. He
replied: "I hold the same views precisely. I have not changed a
particle." [179]

The effectiveness of Briggs' performance can be seen in his
handling of the first objection, which combined five specifications having to do with the "unsworn" evidence offered by the
defense. He insisted this objection was invalid:

Dr. Briggs, acting as counsel for the defendant, read extracts from
printed documents which were sufficiently verified by the submission of the documents themselves to the Presbytery, which documents were not challenged by the prosecution. The defendant was

not a witness. He gave no oral testimony and therefore was not required to be sworn as a witness." [180]

Briggs countered by pointing out that the prosecution's evidence was also purely documentary. He said:

If it be necessary that documentary evidence should be sworn to be valid, then the prosecution have no valid evidence. They ask you to receive their unsworn documentary evidence as valid and to reject the unsworn documentary evidence of the defendant as invalid. Their documentary evidence consists chiefly of the writings of the defendant. Are unsworn extracts from the writings of the defendant to be accepted as valid evidence against him, and unsworn extracts from his writings to be rejected as invalid evidence for him? [181]

Though his presentation was convincing and lucid, the strain of three sessions per day began to show among the commissioners. While the appellee was reviewing the charges against him, one commissioner moved for a recess, noting that half a dozen commissioners near him were fast asleep. Briggs, however, was allowed to continue.[182]

At the end of his first day one newspaper reported: "Dr. Briggs has made a better impression at Washington than either at New-York or Portland, but he has never risen so high as in his address today." [183] Concerning Briggs' comment in which he had wished that he might believe in second probation, the article continued: "The very audacity of the man within a few hours of a verdict of which there can be no doubt, judging from the vote of last week, added a deeper interest to the occasion." [184] The following sessions Briggs devoted to an examination of those doctrines which he believed and taught. In this he relied heavily upon the arguments he had used before the Presbytery. He concluded his seven-hour presentation in the afternoon of May 30.

The closing argument by J. J. McCook was brief. One who heard it gave this description: "I listened to the closing argument of Colonel McCook, in which he did not attempt to refute the statements and arguments of Dr. Briggs, but contented himself mainly with reiterating statements which to an unbiased onlooker, the address of Dr. Briggs had wholly disproved." [185] He continued: "From this time onwards I found myself no longer neutral as an onlooker. I was, both by conviction as to the merits of the case, and from a sense of fairness, on the side of the accused." [186]

With the long hours of debate at an end it was only a matter of time before the vote. The workhorse of the conservative leadership, ex-Moderator W. C. Young, was again in action. For the second time in two consecutive days he submitted a recommendation dealing with the Portland Deliverance.[187] In addition to this, an appropriately timed article appeared in *The New York Times* that very morning:

It is learned from authentic sources that Prof. Briggs, now on trial at Washington on the charge of heresy, has been corresponding with E. D. Morris of Lane Seminary concerning the best method of forming a new church. Dr. Briggs wants to raise the banner of a new theology.

Prof. Morris has replied to the letter, attempting to discourage the scheme. He told Dr. Briggs that very few Presbyterian ministers would desert to a new standard. The movement has not been squelched, however, as it is known that four well known liberal Presbyterians of Cincinnati have gone to Washington with the avowed intention of assisting Dr. Briggs' new church project.[188]

The period of discussion which ensued on the floor of the Assembly carried over into the following day. While this was taking place, President Thomas Hastings penned these words to the president of Union's Board:

One thing impresses me very much & I think our Directors should bear it in mind, namely, that the position which our Seminary has taken as toward the General Assembly has angered the enemies of Dr. Briggs and aggravated their opposition to him to a degree which makes him personally a sufferer on our account. I do not know that I make my meaning quite clear but my thought is that Dr. Briggs would have received more impartial consideration from the court if our Seminary had not made them intensely angry. I hope our Directors will feel this as an important element in the case. What the verdict will be I cannot divine.[189]

The discussion ended late in the evening of May 31, and the vote was taken. Of the 499 commissioners voting, 383 favored sustaining the appeal in its entirety or in part; 116 were opposed.[190]

A Committee of Judgment was appointed the following morning. When approached by this committee, Briggs refused to retract any of the positions he had taken before the Assembly.[191] The committee's report, in addition to noting that the Presbytery of New York had "erred in striking out said amended charges four and seven," [192] brought in a recommendation to

suspend Charles A. Briggs, the said Appellee, from the office of a minister in the Presbyterian Church in the United States of America, until such time as he shall give satisfactory evidence of repentance to the General Assembly of the Presbyterian Church in the United States of America, for the violation by him of the said ordination vow as herein and heretofore found.[193]

The recommendation was adopted *viva voce.*

This sentence became the object of a protest which was signed by sixty-three commissioners and filed later the same day.[194] Also adopted by the Assembly was a report regarding its relations with Union Seminary which read in part:

Because, then, of the strange and unwarranted action of the directors in retaining Dr. Briggs after his appointment had been disapproved by the Assembly; . . . and because of the attempt of the board on its own motion and against the expressed desire of the Assembly to abrogate the compact of 1870, the Assembly disavows all responsibility for the teaching of Union Seminary, and declines to receive any report from its board until satisfactory relations are established.[195]

Next, ex-Moderator Young appeared once more with his committee's recommendation, this time for the formal action of the Assembly. It read in part:

This General Assembly reaffirms the doctrine of the deliverance of the Assembly of 1892 touching the inspiration of Holy Scripture, namely, that the original Scriptures of the Old and New Testaments, being immediately inspired of God, were without error, and in so doing declares that the said deliverance enunciates no new doctrine and imposes no new test of orthodoxy, but interprets and gives expression to what has always been the belief of the Church taught in the Westminster Confession of Faith.[196]

After this was adopted Dr. Herrick Johnson formally protested this pronouncement, listing among the five grounds of this protest: "Because it is setting up an imaginary Bible as a test of orthodoxy" and "Because it is disparaging the Bible we have and endangering its authority under the presssure of a prevalent hostile criticism." [197]

Shortly thereafter, Young again came forward with the following supplement to his previous recommendation: Resolved "That the Bible as we now have it, in its various translations and versions, when freed from all errors and mistakes of translators, copyists, and printers, is the very Word of God, and consequently wholly without error." [198] The cloud of ultraconservatism which had hung menacingly upon the Presbyterian horizon in recent years settled over Washington on that first day of June, 1893. And its darkness was not to be easily dispelled.

Perhaps during that long day, Briggs remembered the words he had received from his uncle, Marvin Briggs, in the first days of the Assembly: "Let the mocking be all done by the chief priests & Scribes of the Washington Assembly. They will stone you if they can; but their children will build your sepulchre." [199]

V

Looking back upon this period of his life from the vantage point of later years, Charles Augustus Briggs remained convinced that the struggle he had endured was the result of "bitter feelings engendered by the revision controversy." [200] He gave this explanation:

It was organized and carried on as an anti-revision conspiracy by a very small body of active and unscrupulous partisans, who used *The Mail and Express* and affiliated organs and also an extensive pamphlet literature, and expended a large sum of money in order to fire the Presbyterian Church against the Higher Criticism and to persuade them that the Bible and the evangelical faith were in peril. In fact, the Presbyterian Church was deliberately thrown into a panic about the Bible in order to defeat the revision movement and to discredit Union Seminary. I was only an incident in this warfare. Circumstances made me the convenient target on which to concentrate the attack. In all respects this conspiracy was successful. The revision movement was defeated; Union Seminary was discredited; and I was suspended from the ministry of the Presbyterian Church.[201]

The years of his life which followed this ordeal were full ones. In 1899 he was received into the priesthood of the Episcopal Church, thus becoming the first non-Presbyterian member of the Union Seminary faculty. His energies were devoted largely to matters other than higher criticism. The trials had already done more to disseminate his views on that subject in two years than he could have done in his lifetime. The predominant concern of these later years was Christian unity. No doubt, much of the ecumenical concern which has remained the hallmark of Union Seminary can be traced to his influence.

Soon after Briggs' death on June 8, 1913, Henry Preserved Smith, then librarian at Union, well summarized the irony of those charges of heresy: "It would hardly be too much to say that, judged by the historic faith of the church, Dr. Briggs was the last of the line of orthodox theologians. That the conservative party has not discovered this and realized what a loss their church suffered is one of the strangest facts of our time." [202]

NOTES

1. C. A. Briggs, *The Higher Criticism of the Hexateuch* (New York: Charles Scribner's Sons, 1892), p. 62.
2. The chief source of information for the life of Charles Augustus Briggs is the collection of his private papers and correspondence which has been housed in the library of Union Theological Seminary in New York since 1947. The person responsible for this collection was Briggs' eldest daughter, Emilie Grace Briggs. In amassing this material Miss Briggs gathered bits of biographical information and all available correspondence which she copied by hand into twelve bound volumes. Professor Lefferts A. Loetscher, in his previous use of the collection, has identified the transcribed material as the Briggs Transcript, or B.T. The same abbreviation will be used in this study. Reference will be made according to volume (one through twelve), page, and arabic numerals which refer to the serial numbers of the transcribed letters.
   Here then the reference reads: B.T., III, 419, #320, Jan. 24, 1867, Briggs to Smith.
3. B.T., I, 34, #317a, Jan. 8, 1867 (?).
4. Emilie Grace Briggs, "A Sketch of Dr. Charles Augustus Briggs," *The Alumni Bulletin,* published quarterly by the faculty of the University of Virginia, V (Feb., 1899), 94. This letter was written in Nov., 1868, to Professor H. B. Smith.
5. C. A. Briggs, "Biblical Theology with Especial Reference to the New Testament," *The American Presbyterian Review,* New Series, II (Jan., 1870), 120.
6. Briggs, "Exegetical Theology, especially in the Old Testament," an address on the occasion of his Inauguration as Davenport Professor of Hebrew and Cognate Languages in the Union Theological Seminary, New York City, on Sept. 21, 1876 (New York: Rogers and Sherwood, 1876), p. 15.
7. G. L. Prentiss, *The Union Theological Seminary, Its Design and Another Decade of Its History* (Asbury Park, N.J.: M., W., & C. Pennypacker, 1899), p. 329.
8. A. A. Hodge, and B. B. Warfield, "Inspiration," *Presbtyerian Review,* II (April, 1891), 225-60.
9. At that time Dr. Warfield was teaching at Western Theological Seminary; however, in 1887 he joined the Princeton faculty.
10. *Ibid.,* pp. 225-26.

11. *Ibid.,* p. 238.
12. *Ibid.,* p. 245.
13. *Ibid.,* p. 227.
14. Briggs, "Critical Theories of the Sacred Scriptures in Relation to Their Inspiration," *Presbyterian Review,* II (July, 1881), 550-79.
15. *Ibid.,* p. 551.
16. B.T., VI, 111-13, #1719, Dec. 27, 1882.
17. Briggs, "The Revised English Version of the Old Testament," *Presbyterian Review,* VI (July, 1885), 507.
18. (New York: Charles Scribner's Sons, 1886).
19. (New York: Charles Scribner's Sons, 1883).
20. Briggs, *American Presbyterianism: Its Origin and Early History together with an Appendix of Letters and Documents* (New York: Charles Scribner's Sons, 1885).
21. B.T., VII, 465, #3668, May 7, 1889, Warfield to Briggs.
22. Prentiss, *Union Theological Seminary,* p. 330.
23. *Ibid.*
24. *Ibid.*
25. Briggs, "The General Assembly of the Presbyterian Church in the United States of America," *Presbyterian Review,* X (Oct., 1889), p. 467.
26. *Ibid.,* p. 470.
27. Prentiss, *Union Theological Seminary,* p. 330.
28. B.T., VII, 470-72, #3673, June 7, 1889, Briggs to Paxton.
29. B.T., VII, 491, #3714, Sept. 21, 1889, Warfield to Briggs.
30. (New York: Charles Scribner's Sons, 1889).
31. *Ibid.,* p. viii.
32. *Ibid.,* p. 68.
33. *Ibid.,* p. 105.
34. Prentiss, *Union Theological Seminary,* pp. 330-31.
35. (New York: Charles Scribner's Sons, 1890).
36. Briggs, "The Advance Towards Revision," in *How Shall We Revise?,* pp. 1-33.
37. *Ibid.,* p. 28.
38. *Ibid.*
39. *Ibid.*
40. William Adams Brown Scrapbook of newspaper clippings, the library of Union Theological Seminary, (TX73/B85/U5), I, 31; the clipping is from the *New York Sun,* Feb. 15, 1891, "Student McComb Put Out."
41. Prentiss, *Union Theological Seminary,* p. 535.
42. *Ibid.,* p. 332.
43. *Ibid.*
44. Briggs, *The Authority of Holy Scripture: An Inaugural Address* (New York: Charles Scribner's Sons, 1891).
45. *Ibid.,* p. 24.

46. *Ibid.*
47. *Ibid.,* p. 33.
48. *Ibid.,* p. 38.
49. *Ibid.,* p. 54.
50. *Ibid.*
51. *Ibid.,* p. 56.
52. William Adams Brown Scrapbook, I, 44, from the *New York Evangelist,* Feb. 9, 1891, "The Anvil Chorus on Professor Briggs" (editorial).
53. John J. McCook, *The Appeal in the Briggs Heresy Case* (New York: John C. Rankin Co., 1893), p. 203.
54. *One Hundred and Fourth General Assembly, Record of the Case: From the Minutes of the Presbytery of New York,* pp. 32-49. The majority report was signed by George W. F. Birch, J. F. Forbes, J. J. Lampe, and J. J. Stevenson.
55. *One Hundred and Fourth General Assembly,* p. 55.
56. *The Case Against Professor Briggs* (a collection of the official papers in the case against Professor Briggs) in three parts, Part I (New York: Charles Scribner's Sons, 1892), p. 133.
57. *One Hundred and Fourth General Assembly,* p. 58.
58. B. T., VIII, 174, #4098, May 15, 1891, Briggs to F. Brown.
59. Prentiss, *Union Theological Seminary,* pp. 545-50. The only faculty member who did not support this statement was Dr. W. G. T. Shedd, professor of systematic theology; Professor Shedd opposed Briggs' views throughout the controversy.
60. *One Hundred and Fourth General Assembly,* p. 165.
61. *Ibid.,* p. 58. The three members carried over from the investigating committee included Chairman G. W. F. Birch, the Rev. J. J. Lampe and Professor J. J. Stevenson, professor of geology at New York University.
62. Prentiss, *Union Theological Seminary,* p. 544.
63. *Ibid.,* p. 93, quoted from the *New York Tribune,* May 22, 1891.
64. Shortly after the reunion of the Old School and New School Churches in 1870, a compromise had been reached in regard to the ecclesiastical control to be exerted over all seminaries. The Old School seminaries had been subjected to strict control, whereas the New School Church had granted its seminaries far more autonomy. So in an effort to achieve some measure of balance, the Old School seminaries were granted the right to elect their professors; but the Assembly retained the privilege of veto over such appointments. The New School seminaries then also granted to the Assembly, for the first time, the right of veto over their appointments of professors. The opponents of Briggs were seeking to evoke the Assembly's right of veto in order to block his transfer of chairs at Union Seminary.
65. Prentiss, *Union Theological Seminary,* pp. 98-99.
66. *Ibid.,* p. 99.

67. *Ibid.,* p. 124.
68. *Ibid.,* p. 122.
69. *One Hundred and Fourth General Assembly,* pp. 70-71, 107.
70. *Ibid.,* p. 119.
71. *Ibid.*
72. *Ibid.,* pp. 127-28.
73. Briggs, *Authority of Holy Scripture,* third edition, p. 145.
74. According to section 11 of the Book of Discipline, a prosecuting committee appointed to represent the Presbyterian Church (U. S. A.) would be an original party in the case and would be responsible for conducting its prosecution in all courts, independent of the Presbytery that created it. The question under contention was whether or not the Presbytery's committee had been formally designated a "prosecuting committee." Professor Francis Brown correctly held that the committee had not been so designated; and the record of May 12, 1891, supported his argument: "On motion it was resolved that a committee be appointed to arrange and prepare the *necessary proceedings appropriate* in the case of Prof. Briggs." (*One Hundred and Fourth General Assembly,* p. 165.)
75. Henry van Dyke was then pastor of the Brick Presbyterian Church in New York City; later he enjoyed a long and outstanding literary career.
76. *One Hundred and Fourth General Assembly,* p. 172.
77. Briggs, *Authority of Holy Scripture,* third edition, p. 161.
78. *One Hundred and Fourth General Assembly,* p. 247.
79. Philip Schaff, "Other Heresy Trials and the Briggs Case," *The Forum,* XII (Jan., 1892), p. 626.
80. Prentiss, *Union Theological Seminary,* p. 178.
81. *The Tribune Monthly,* IV (May, 1892), "The General Assembly of 1892," p. 29.
82. *Ibid.,* "Fourth Day," p. 31.
83. Each side was allowed one and one-half hours for the presentation of arguments. The prosecution was permitted to divide its time equally between opening and closing statements; and Briggs was required to use his time in one statement placed between those of the prosecution.
84. *The Tribune Monthly,* "The Joint Argument," p. 47.
85. *The Case Against Professor Briggs,* Part I, p. 90.
86. *Ibid.,* p. 123.
87. *The Tribune Monthly,* "The Voting," p. 82.
88. *Ibid.*
89. Prentiss, *Union Theological Seminary,* pp. 264-71, 280. This proposal of arbitration came as a surprise to the directors of Union Seminary. Such a proposal had been made by the Committee of Conference at the January meeting between the two bodies. Dr. Hastings and Mr. Wm. A. Booth, acting as a committee of two,

requested the Committee to withdraw the proposal, explaining that should the Seminary accept arbitration involving the Briggs case, Dr. Briggs would certainly resign, Dr. Francis Brown would likely resign, and there would be a breakup of the faculty. Arbitration would also be a blow to Charles Butler, through whose generosity Briggs' transfer and inaugural had been made possible. And should the Board reject arbitration, once it were proposed, this would place the Seminary at a genuine disadvantage before the Church. The Committee complied with Hastings' request and withdrew the proposal. However, in the minutes of the Committee of Conference, it was noted that Dr. Wm. H. Roberts and Mr. J. J. McCook "reserved the right to act independently upon such portions of the paper as were not satisfactory to them." (Prentiss, p. 269.) Dr. Wm. H. Roberts, secretary of the Committee of Conference and Stated Clerk of the Assembly, was one of the six members who submitted the report urging arbitration; and it was he who introduced the formal resolution on the floor of the Assembly.

90. *The Tribune Monthly,* "Tenth Day," p. 90.
91. *Ibid.*
92. Prentiss, *Union Theological Seminary,* pp. 282-83.
93. *The Case Against Professor Briggs,* Part II, p. 28.
94. *Ibid.,* Part I, p. 95.
95. *One Hundred and Fifth General Assembly:* the Presbyterian Church in the United States of America against the Rev. Charles A. Briggs, D.D., Notice of Appeal, pp. 44-73.
96. Emilie Grace Briggs newspaper clippings, uncatalogued, in the Union Seminary Library; the clipping has no identification other than the date, Nov. 29, 1892.
97. Briggs contended that no less than nine violations of doctrine were alleged in the charges:
    (1) That Holy Scripture is most necessary.
    (2) That Holy Scripture is the rule of faith and practice.
    (3) That Holy Scripture is the word of God written.
    (4) That Holy Scripture is immediately inspired.
    (5) That God is true, omniscient, and unchangeable.
    (6) That Holy Scripture evidences itself to be the word of God by the consent of all the parts.
    (7) That the infallible rule of interpretation of Scripture is the Scripture itself.
    (8) That the processes of redemption are limited to this world.
    (9) That the souls of believers are at their death at once made perfect in holiness.
98. *The Case Against Professor Briggs,* Part II, p. 63.
99. *Ibid.,* p. 65; questions 6 and 7.
100. *One Hundred and Fifth General Assembly,* p. 79.

101. *The Defense of Professor Briggs before the Presbytery of New York, December 13, 14, 15, and 19, 1892* (New York: Charles Scribner's Sons, 1893), p. viii.
102. *Ibid.*, p. 35.
103. *Ibid.*, p. 44.
104. *Ibid.*, p. 45.
105. *Ibid.*, p. 70.
106. *Ibid.*, p. 87.
107. *Ibid.*, p. 89.
108. *Ibid.*, p. 96.
109. *Ibid.*, p. 97.
110. Original copy placed before the Presbytery of New York being an argument on Charge IV in printed form, December 15, 1892. This was later published as *The Higher Criticism of the Hexateuch* (New York: Jenkins, Printer, 1892. Third edition, April 3, 1897; New York: Charles Scribner's Sons, 1897).
111. *Ibid.*, p. 122.
112. The prosecuting committee supported their charge with the following excerpts from the Standards: Confession of Faith, Chap. XXXII, Section 1; the Larger Catechism, Question 86; the Shorter Catechism, Question 37.
113. *Ibid.*, p. 153.
114. *Ibid.*
115. *Ibid.*, p. 159.
116. *Ibid.*, p. 160.
117. *Ibid.*, p. 175.
118. *Ibid.*, p. 179.
119. *Ibid.*, p. 180.
120. *Ibid.*, p. 168.
121. *One Hundred and Fifth General Assembly*, p. 162.
122. *Ibid.*, p. 161.
123. *Ibid.*, p. 162.
124. *Ibid.*, p. 163.
125. *Ibid.*, p. 164.
126. *Ibid.*, p. 161.
127. B. T., VIII, 447, #4705.
128. Tertius van Dyke, *Henry van Dyke: a Biography* (New York: Harper & Brothers, 1935), p. 135.
129. This statement plus the 235 signatures occupies 4 pages. No publishing data is given, save the title and date (Feb. 17, 1893).
130. Thomas S. Hastings Scrapbook, Union Seminary Library (Cage TX73/B85/P), VII, 12.
131. *Ibid.*, p. 19.
132. *Ibid.*, p. 6.
133. B. T., VIII, 447, #4766, Feb. 21, 1893, H. P. Smith to Briggs.
134. William Adams Brown, *A Teacher and His Times* (New York: Charles Scribner's Sons, 1940), p. 157.

135. *The Case Against Professor Briggs,* Part III, p. 128.
136. *Ibid.,* pp. 131-32.
137. *The New York Times,* May 24, 1893, "Plea Made by Professor Briggs," p. 9, col. 1.
138. McCook, *The Appeal in the Briggs Heresy Case,* p. 178.
139. Van Dyke, *Henry van Dyke,* p. 133.
140. *The Case Against Professor Briggs,* Part III, p. 40.
141. *Ibid.,* pp. 40-45.
142. *Ibid.,* p. 54.
143. *Ibid.,* p. 64.
144. *Ibid.,* p. 66.
145. *Ibid.,* pp. 105-6.
146. *Ibid.,* pp. 125-26.
147. McCook, *The Appeal in the Briggs Heresy Case,* p. 238.
148. Robert J. Laidlaw, *The Trial of Dr. Briggs Before the General Assembly; A Calm Review of the Case by a Stranger who attended all the sessions of the court* (New York: Anson D. F. Randolph and Company, 1893), p. 29.
149. *The Case Against Professor Briggs,* Part III, p. 113.
150. McCook, *The Appeal in the Briggs Heresy Case,* p. 247.
151. *Ibid.,* p. 253.
152. *Ibid.*
153. "Dr Lowrie and the Seminaries," the *Presbyterian,* LII (Sept. 23, 1882), 9.
154. McCook, *The Appeal in The Briggs Heresy Case,* p. 255.
155. Laidlaw, *The Trial of Dr. Briggs,* p. 34.
156. *The Tribune Monthly,* V (May, 1893), "Sixth Day," May 24, 1893, p. 34.
157. *The Case Against Professor Briggs,* Part III, pp. 136-37.
158. B. T., IX, 10, 12, #4837, 4840.
159. *Ibid.,* IX, 15, #4843.
160. *The Tribune Monthly,* "Ninth Day," p. 54.
161. *Ibid.,* "Tenth Day," p. 58.
162. *Ibid.*
163. *The Case Against Professor Briggs,* Part III, pp. 174-76.
164. *Ibid.,* p. 29.
165. McCook, *The Appeal in the Briggs Heresy Case,* p. 184.
166. *One Hundred and Fifth General Assembly,* The Argument of Joseph J. Lampe, D.D., p. 25.
167. *Ibid.,* p. 29.
168. Laidlaw, *The Trial of Dr. Briggs,* p. 40.
169. *One Hundred and Fifth General Assembly,* Lampe, p. 54.
170. *The Tribune Monthly,* "Tenth Day," pp. 59-60.
171. *One Hundred and Fifth General Assembly,* Lampe, p. 66.
172. *Ibid.,* p. 70.
173. *The Case Against Professor Briggs,* Part III, p. 140.
174. *Ibid.,* pp. 147-48.

175. *Ibid.*, p. 149.
176. (New York: Charles Scribner's Sons, 1886).
177. *The Case Against Professor Briggs,* Part III, p. 149.
178. *Ibid.*, p. 151.
179. *Ibid.*, p. 153.
180. *Ibid.*, p. 164.
181. *Ibid.*, p. 166.
182. Laidlaw, *The Trial of Dr. Briggs,* p. 28; *Tribune Monthly,* "Tenth Day," p. 60.
183. *Tribune Monthly,* "Tenth Day," p. 60.
184. *Ibid.*
185. Laidlaw, *The Trial of Dr. Briggs,* p. 36.
186. *Ibid.*, p. 37.
187. *The Tribune Monthly,* May 30, 1893, "Eleventh Day," p. 68.
188. *The New York Times,* XLII, 13031, "Will Dr. Briggs Secede?" May 30, 1893, p. 3, col. 2.
189. B. T., IX, 7-8, #4854, May 31, 1893, Hastings to Charles Butler.
190. *The Case Against Professor Briggs,* Part III, p. 304.
191. McCook, *The Appeal in the Briggs Heresy Case,* pp. 374-75.
192. *Ibid.*, p. 376.
193. *Ibid.*, p. 377.
194. *The Case Against Professor Briggs,* Part III, pp. 310-11.
195. Prentiss, *Union Theological Seminary,* pp. 291-92.
196. *The Tribune Monthly,* June 1, 1893, "Inspiration of the Scriptures," p. 114.
197. *Ibid.*
198. *Ibid.*
199. B. T., IX, 3, #4821, May 20, 1893.
200. Prentiss, *Union Theological Seminary,* p. 333.
201. *Ibid.*
202. "Charles Augustus Briggs," *American Journal of Theology,* XVII (Oct., 1913), 502.

4. Borden Parker Bowne
Heresy at Boston

HARMON L. SMITH

Irony seems to surround the lives of great men. Perhaps it envelops the lives of all of us but only impresses itself forcefully when important figures prove the rule. It may be that this is the sole unexceptional fact about the life of Borden Parker Bowne.

He was born at a time when the new winds of sectionalism and individualism were blowing across the young American nation. Andrew Jackson had inaugurated a new democracy during his term as president, rapid changes were occurring in the economic life of the country, and demographic patterns were being altered by westward expansion. New and strange sects were arising, reforms and new thoughts were developing, and established churches were being victimized by internal strife. The Presbyterians engaged in controversy which eventuated in schism in 1837-38; Lyman Beecher, the distinguished president of Lane Seminary, was charged with heresy in 1835; New York's Union Theological Seminary was founded in 1836 by the liberal wing of the General Assembly; from 1835 to the Civil War the Protestant Episcopal Church was torn with strife; the conservative Missouri Synod of the Lutheran Church was formed in 1846; Mormonism was gaining strength steadily; the American Anti-Slavery Society was formed in 1833; the Southern Baptist Convention was organized in 1845;

and in 1844 a Plan of Separation was drawn up at the General Conference of The Methodist Episcopal Church, resulting in the division of this communion north and south.

It was in this setting that Borden Parker Bowne was born during the bleak winter of 1847 on January 14. His father, Joseph, was a justice of the peace in Leonardville, New Jersey, and a strong abolitionist "when it cost something to speak against slavery." [1] His mother, Margaret, was described by Bishop McConnell as "a character of straight-forward simplicity with a marked vein of mystic piety." [2] Boyhood on the family farm apparently impressed young Bowne greatly. He often referred to this time for illustrations in his lectures on philosophy and visited the home place as frequently as he could, even after his sixtieth birthday.

When he was seventeen, Bowne went to live with friends in Brooklyn and worked for a time as a teamster. He matriculated at New York University in September, 1867, and was licensed to preach just one month later at the Navesink Church. Two weeks before his twenty-first birthday, on December 29, 1867, he preached his first sermon from Genesis 4:9 on the subject, "Am I My Brother's Keeper?" He received the B.A. degree from N.Y.U. in January of 1871, was elected Phi Beta Kappa, and named valedictorian of his class. Later he was the recipient of two additional degrees from N.Y.U.: the M.A. in 1876 and the L.L.D. in 1909. In 1872 he entered the New York East Conference of The Methodist Episcopal Church, was ordained deacon, and appointed to the church in Whitestone, Long Island. After one year in this parish he had opportunity to travel and study in Europe, and it was not until 1878 that he rejoined the Conference and was ordained Elder. While in Europe Bowne studied chiefly in Paris, Halle, and Göttingen, but the greatest impact upon his thought was occasioned by his work with Hermann Lotze. [3]

Bowne was called to Boston University in 1876 and remained there until his death on April 1, 1910. His tenure at Boston was marked by brilliant teaching, prolific publication (he is credited with having written 17 books and over 130 articles), and a liberalizing and maturing influence upon Methodist theology. His legacy to American religion and culture is reinforced by the great number of ministers and teachers whose own effectiveness is a measure of Bowne's greatness, and by a vigorous philosophical and theological school of thought whose impact is still felt throughout The Methodist Church and, in perhaps less obvious form, in the academic community.

Six years before his death, in April of 1904, he was indicted by a fellow Methodist minister for heresy and tried before a "Select Number" of the New York East Conference. His lifetime, at both terminals, was thus marked by ecclesiastical controversy and it is perhaps a further irony that, of all the happenings within those sixty-three years, his trial and vindication have been treated least of all.

In the now more than six decades since Borden Parker Bowne was tried for heresy, only scant attention has been given to the anatomy of the trial itself. Because Bowne's indictment and acquittal constitute the last significant investigation by The Methodist Church into the alleged heresy of one of its ministers, it deserves a more thorough treatment. This essay is an attempt to bring together fugitive and sometimes unrelated references and citations in order to reconstruct in some substantial way the facts relating to the trial.[4]

The search for data relating to the trial has been arduous and often frustrating, and some of the bibliographical problems deserve brief mention before setting forth the primary elements of the trial itself.

There have been and continue to be apparently permanent *lacunae* in the materials available for reference. Most notable among these is the absence of any record of the trial transcript. James M. Buckley, editor of *The Christian Advocate,* has reported that "the time consumed in the trial was sixteen hours. . . . The stenographic report would make a book of two hundred and forty pages." [5] But at present the whereabouts of such a document is unknown. It was thought, at one time, that a trunk containing the archives of the New York East Conference of The Methodist Episcopal Church might contain the trial record. Two extensive searches by the secretary of the Conference have proved that this was a fruitless lead.

Two publications do, however, contain excerpts of the recorded testimony. The oldest is to be found in *The Methodist Review* for May, 1922, where fourteen pages of the transcript are reproduced.[6] Together with this material, the editor, George Elliott, included a brief recapitulation of the circumstances surrounding the trial, the charges against Bowne, and the action of the Conference. The greater portion of the article is given to excerpts from the trial transcript, and these deal mainly with the first three of the five specifications of heresy against Bowne.

Seven years later, Francis John McConnell published his biography of Bowne and reproduced the excerpts from *The Methodist Review* in a chapter titled, "The Defender of Biblical Research."[7] McConnell also set the larger stage for Bowne's controversies with certain elements within The Methodist Episcopal Church by describing the dismissal of Professor Hinckley G. Mitchell from the department of Old Testament in the Boston University School of Theology. Mitchell's tenure was initially jeopardized in 1895 and later in 1900. In the first conflict the authorities ruled that Mitchell had not exceeded the limits of his legitimate academic freedom in giving instruction in the new "higher criticism" of the Bible.

To complicate matters, in those days the appointment of faculty to the Boston University School of Theology was reviewed every five years by the bishops of The Methodist Episcopal Church, at least two of whom had to give formal sanction. When Mitchell was attacked again in 1900, Bowne feared that the bishops would fail to give the necessary approval for Mitchell's continuance unless he were supported. McConnell states that "two or three" of the bishops were "rabidly anti-Mitchell" anyway and that this, together with the diffidence of his colleagues, suggested the likelihood of the case going against

him by default.[8] Bowne did actively engage himself in galvaniz-
ing support for Mitchell, but the victory was short-lived. In
1905, the year following Bowne's vindication of heresy charges.
Mitchell's appointment was not renewed. At the time of
Mitchell's dismissal Bowne was in the Orient and thus unin-
volved. There is no textual evidence to show that Bowne's trial
in 1904 was in any way related to his defense of Mitchell in
1900, though it is difficult not to suppose that the same group
which opposed Mitchell also found objection to Bowne. The
central issue with the Mitchell case was with the nature of biblical revelation—an issue which also appears in the charges
against Bowne and of which more will be said later.

Mitchell's case excited considerable interest within both the
church and the literary world. Descriptions of the events perti-
nent to his dismissal, together with editorial comment, may be
found in "The Case of Professor H. G. Mitchell." [9] and in "Professor Mitchell's Case." [10] The substance of both these articles
reflects the judgment that the trustees of Boston University and
the bishops of The Methodist Episcopal Church acted precipi-
tately and without sufficient cause, *The Independent* describes
the action as one of "moral inability" after stating, "Really, this
is startling." Ecclesiastical opinion was concurrently being expressed in the *Western Christian Advocate* (Cincinnati), *Zion's
Herald* (Boston), *The Christian Advocate* (New York), the
Congregationalist (Boston), and the Protestant Episcopal
Churchman (New York). One of the more significant es-
timates of the Mitchell case came from the pen of George Albert Coe, then John Evans Professor of Moral and Intellectual
Philosophy at Northwestern University. Coe provides one of
the better accounts of the issues and polity involved in the case
and gives strong support to Mitchell. He concludes his article
with the hope that the decision might be reversed and realistically adds: "But if they should not do so, still, under God's guidance, the slow process of history will prune the branch that bears
fruit and take away the branch that bears it not." [11]

Undoubtedly, the most significant development to eventuate

from this affair was the action of the Judiciary Committee of
the 1908 General Conference, which relieved the bishops of responsibility for the orthodoxy of professors in the church's
theological schools.[12]

Withal, the most perplexing hiatus in the Bowne case remains that occasioned by the absence of anything but a mere
remnant of the official trial transcript. One exceedingly interesting consequence of the search through the archives trunk
is worthy of mention and continues to tantalize the scholar's
imagination. It is generally unknown that the plaintiff in the
case against Bowne, George A. Cooke, brought charges on
three different occasions. The first set of allegations resulted
in the trial which is the subject of this essay. Failing to gain
a conviction on the first set of specifications, Cooke introduced
new charges against Bowne on Friday, April 8, 1904, at the
same Annual Conference. Four years later, in the New York
East Annual Conference of 1908, Cooke again presented
charges.[13] Of these three actions against Bowne, there is record
(beyond that included in the Conference *Minutes*) *only* of
the second set of charges and the Conference's decision. The
presence of the record of these charges is not, however, significant except as it contributes to the mystery of the missing trial
transcript. The Conference disposed summarily of these charges
by adopting the recommendation of a committee of three,
headed by G. E. Reed, which had been given responsibility for
consideration of the charges. Their report that "there is nothing
in the charges presented demanding the consideration of the
Conference, and therefore, respectfully move that the said
charges be not entertained" [14] was promptly sustained by the
Conference. And absence of the record of the third action may
be explained by the fact that the Conference refused to entertain it "by a unanimous rising vote."

James M. Buckley has stated, however, that the stenographic
report of the proceedings in which Bowne was tried for the
first action "would make a book of two hundred and forty
pages." [15] That record of this deliberation should be missing

is itself provocative; but that record of the *second* action should be found in the Conference archives is doubly consternating. Suspicion that the trial transcript may have been removed is given added credence by the fact that it was of such considerable size and that it was certainly available eighteen years after the trial when Elliott excerpted portions for his article in *The Methodist Review*. The absence of this document, it would appear at this juncture, is likely to remain an unsolved mystery.

The final remarkable fact relating to the dearth of bibliography is that very little remains of Bowne's personal papers. His widow saw fit to destroy most of these effects. In fact, even Bowne's personal library was distributed among several colleges, universities, and theological schools. So there is at present nowhere extant a substantial collection of Bowne materials.

What follows, then, by way of reconstructing the particular elements in Bowne's heresy trial of 1904, is gleaned from a number of disparate sources. While *The Methodist Review* for May-June, 1922, affords the most adequate indication of the actual proceedings, we must look elsewhere for the specific character of the indictments lodged against Bowne. This has been accomplished by cross-matching references from (1) Buckley's editorial in the April 14, 1904, issue of *The Christian Advocate*, (2) a pamphlet published by George A. Cooke,[16] (3) the *Minutes* of the Conference, (4) the excerpts from the trial transcript which appeared in *The Methodist Review*, and (5) Bowne's own writings. This is an admittedly provisional and somewhat experimental procedure, but it is arguably a legitimate method for reconstruction, given the paucity of data. To such a reconstruction we now turn.[17]

Buckley reports that the trial was conducted on two successive days of two sessions each, embracing a total of sixteen hours. Three hours were consumed discussing procedural matters, ten hours in examination of the defendant, two hours for summation, one and one-half hours in an address by the complainant, forty-five minutes by counsel for the defense, and twenty-five additional minutes by the complainant. The "Select Number" then considered and recorded its verdict of each specification.[18]

The procedures governing the trial of ministerial members of Methodist Conferences were determined by paragraphs 222-35, inclusive, of the 1900 edition of *The Doctrines and Discipline of the Methodist Episcopal Church*. Under these rubrics the presiding officer of the Conference, the duly appointed Bishop, might elect any one of three methods for trying the case.[19] The entire trial might be conducted openly before the entire Conference "in full session"; it might be handled by having one of the Elders of the Conference receive all the evidence, collate and correct it, and present it to the Conference for disposition; or, finally, a "Select Number" of not less than nine nor more than fifteen members of the Conference might be appointed to "have full power to consider and determine the case according to the rules which govern Annual Conferences in such proceedings." Bishop Cyrus D. Foss, who presided at the 1904 session of the New York East Conference, elected the third of these alternative methods and appointed Frank Mason North as chairman. The other members of the trial commission consisted of J. E. Adams, D. W. Couch, John Rippere, F. B. Upham, Herbert Welch, J. O. Wilson, A. H. Wyatt, F. L. Strickland, G. P. Mains, C. H. Buck, S. O. Curtice, D. G. Downey, C. L. Godell, J. W. Johnston, and W. V. Kelley. Kelley was later replaced, without explanation but before the proceedings began, by W. N. Rice. Under the rules of the *Discipline* the finding of the "Select Number" was final and not remandable to the Conference for approval. Apart from these specified procedures, the conduct of the trial itself provided for the same general conditions as appropriate to criminal or civil court, e.g., the accused has the right to be faced by his accuser, specifications of the charges are to be made known to the accused and his counsel, witnesses may be called to appear before the tribunal, counsel must be appointed for both prosecution and defense.

The etiology of Bowne's trial remains ambiguous, owing chiefly to the absence of the official trial transcript. Nevertheless, certain judgments are reasonably assured by existing documents. Buckley states that charges were initially sent to Dr. Charles S. Wing, who was Presiding Elder of the Brooklyn District North of the New York East Conference, "several months before the assembling of the Conference." These charges, however, were found to be defective for some unstated reason and were thus resubmitted to Wing on February 26, 1904, approximately five weeks prior to the date of the Conference.[20]

Moreover, it can be established that Bowne was aware of the charges of George A. Cooke as early as December 26, 1903. In a letter written on that date to his friend, James Mudge, Bowne ventured this assessment of the situation:

Cooke is, certainly, a curious study. From all accounts he is certainly standing alone at present. . . . Both Mallalieu and Townsend [Mallalieu is unknown to me; Townsend is probably L. T. Townsend, Boston University emeritus professor] have advised him, lately, to recall his charges; but he seems bent upon going to New York, and in that case he will certainly come back sadder and, perhaps, wiser.

Is there, or should there not be, some penalty for such a gratuitous and conceited performance as this of Cooke's? His charges are utterly baseless and in addition he has indecently rushed into print to the no small disgrace of the Church. It would seem that some penalty should be provided for such folly. Otherwise, I don't see what is to prevent anyone sufficiently ignorant and shameless from attacking anyone whatever. So far as I am personally concerned I do not regret his attack at all and am in no way disturbed by it, but it seems too bad to have the Church humiliated in this way.[21]

It would appear that the publication to which Bowne refers when he speaks of Cooke's having "rushed into print" is the pamphlet, *The Present and the Future of Methodism: An Examination of the Teaching of Prof. Borden P. Bowne.* Although this document is undated, it is certain that it appeared sometime between April of 1902 and April of 1904.[22]

On the first day of the Conference formal charges were presented to the Conference by Charles S. Wing, on behalf of George A. Cooke, a member of the New England Conference.[23] Specifically, Bowne was charged with teaching:

1. Doctrines which are contrary to the Articles of Religion of the Methodist Episcopal Church.

2. Doctrines which are contrary to the established standards of doctrine of the Methodist Episcopal Church.

First Specification. He denies the Trinitarian conception of the Deity and also the moral attributes of the Deity as set forth in the first and fourth Articles of Religion of the Methodist Episcopal Church. . . .

Second Specification. His teaching on miracles is such as to weaken if not destroy faith in large portions of the Old and New Testaments. His views on the inspiration of Scripture are contrary to the teachings of the Scriptures themselves, contrary to article five of the Articles of Religion of the Methodist Episcopal Church, and tend to destroy faith in the authority of the Bible in matters of faith and practice. . . .

Third Specification. He denies the Doctrine of the Atonement as set forth in the second and twentieth Articles of Religion of the Methodist Episcopal Church and as taught by our established standards of doctrine. . . .

Fourth Specification. He teaches such views of the divine government and of the future of souls as to destroy the force of Christ's teaching about the future punishment of the wicked and the future reward of the righteous. . . .

Fifth Specification. He teaches views on the subject of Sin and Salvation, on Repentance, Justification, Regeneration, and Assurance of Salvation through the Witness of the Spirit that do not represent the views of the Methodist Episcopal Church as expressed in our standard works of theology.[24]

We must now take these specifications *seriatim,* cite the passages quoted from Bowne's works as proof of his guilt together with references to the Articles of Religion, and recapitulate in this way the anatomy of the trial proper.

The First Specification

It was alleged in the first specification that Bowne denied the doctrine of the Trinity and the moral attributes of the Deity as these are described in the first and fourth Articles of Religion. These Articles assert that there is "but one living and true God" in whose unity "there are three persons, of one substance, power, and eternity" and that the Holy Ghost "is of one substance, majesty, and glory with the Father and the Son." [25] According to Buckley,[26] pages 453-56 of *Metaphysics,*[27] and pages 173-75, 237, and 240 of *Philosophy of Theism* [28] were cited as corroborative evidence. It is probable, however, that Buckley (and perhaps Cooke also) was careless in citing the title of the second book and that Bowne's volume on *Theism* is in fact the one cited in the specification.[29]

We have no document from Cooke's own hand which isolates the particular character of the heresy with which he charged Bowne.[30] We must, therefore, hypothecate the specific objection on the basis of these sections in *Theism, Metaphysics,* and the record of Bowne's testimony in *The Methodist Review.* In a chapter in *Theism* on "The Metaphysical Attributes of the World-Ground," and a subsection headed "Unity," Bowne discussed the necessity for affirming unity as the first of the metaphysical attributes of a thing. He spoke here as a philosopher, though he affirmed that "our speculative conception of the world-ground begins to approximate to the religious conception of God." [31]

The key sentences are probably the following:

When, then, we say that a thing is a unit, we mean first of all that it is not compounded, and does not admit of division. Hence the doctrine of the unity of the world-ground is first of all a denial of composition and divisibility.[32]

[The] necessary result of thinking only under mechanical conditions [is that] when we begin with plurality, we never escape it, for mechanical necessity cannot differentiate itself. . . . This puzzle can be solved only by leaving the mechanical realm for that of free intellect.[33]

[Further], free intelligence by its originating activity can posit plurality distinct from its own unity, and by its self-consciousness can maintain its unity and identity over against the changing plurality. Here the one is manifold without being many. Here unity gives birth to plurality without destroying itself. Here the identical changes and yet abides.[34]

The thought of many gods, each of which should live in a world by himself, or rather, in a universe of his own, is a pure fancy due to the abstracting and hypostasizing tendency of the mind.[35]

In *Metaphysics* the key passages deal with the question whether "the nature of an object in perception" has "an ontological, or only phenomenal reality?" [36] The discussion on the pages cited, 452-56, is not conclusive, though Bowne had earlier ended a chapter on epistemology by affirming that things do exist in some form in external reality and that therefore we perceive the "outer world" only as it is revealed to us through sensations.[37] More to the point than Buckley's citation seems to be Bowne's judgment at the end of the chapter which embraces these pages. The finite mind, he argued, confronts genuine difficulties.

On the one hand, it cannot view itself as the independent generator of its objects; and, on the other hand, it cannot admit any existence which is essentially unrelated to thought. *The only solution of the problem lies in the theistic conception. . . .* In no other conception can the mind find relief from an untenable idealism on the one hand, or from a suicidal doctrine of the unknowable on the other, or rather from a dreary and endless oscillation between them.[38]

Because the precise intention of Cooke's charge is not clear from the available sources, it will suffice to allow Bowne to interpret for us what apparently was at stake. He states, first, that he was "arguing in a general way some points in epistemology, etc." and that the proposition adduced as evidence "would prove me guilty of stealing horses just as quickly as they prove me guilty of Unitarianism." [39] Later, during examination by G. P. Mains, Bowne disavowed any intention on his part, in these volumes, to discuss theology:

G. P. Mains: When writing these matters did you have any thought of the Trinity and the moral attributes of Deity?
Professor Bowne: Not in the slightest.
G. P. Mains: In other words, you were not engaged in theological questions?
Professor Bowne: Not in the least.[40]

When J. W. Johnston pressed for elaboration on Mains' questions, Bowne responded that "not the slightest theological bearing is discussed here." [41] Defense Counsel J. M. Buckley then asked Bowne to comment specifically. Bowne replied,

There *is* a Trinitarian argument. I am a Trinitarian of the Trinitarians. I published a sermon in Zion's Herald on the Incarnation, in which I set forth that our Lord had existed before his incarnation. That sermon was published not very long ago. I am a Trinitarian of the Trinitarians. . . . All this argument, which was meant as Trinitarian, and which is Trinitarian, is brought here as proof that I am a Unitarian.[42]

This, one is constrained to say, was not a substantive answer; but then, if the contemporaries who reported that the trial was popularly viewed "in the light of a joke" and "with a degree of amusement" are correct,[43] perhaps Bowne had no reason to do more essentially, than protest his innocence! Elliott, at least, later supported Bowne's defense of himself. Commenting upon the absence of lengthy citations from Bowne's works from the trial excerpts which he published, Elliott argued that they were unnecessary, "for these very able speculations in the philosophic realm have nothing more to do with the concrete values of religious faith than the theory of logarithms with the Declaration of Independence." [44]

Despite the almost frivolous character of the remark by Elliott and the nonsubstantive form of Bowne's own protestations of innocence, the evidence does not support the charge that Bowne was a Unitarian. In the volumes cited by the specification there is no discussion of the Trinity. Instead, Bowne was preoccupied with the questions of cosmology, ontology, epistemology, and psychology. These matters would, no doubt, tend to shape one's doctrine of the Trinity, but *how* this would be accomplished is not the subject of inquiry in either *Metaphysics* or *Theism*. Moreover, one could survey all the writings of Bowne and remain unconvinced that such a charge, on its face, warranted sustained investigation.

It would be correct to argue that the *emphasis* in Bowne's work lay upon the unity of God, but fairness to Bowne would also require it to be said that this emphasis was sponsored by an interest to make it impossible for one to think of God at all except by thinking of him at once as Father, Son, and Spirit. Cooke was surely acquainted with Bowne's pamphlets on *The Christian Revelation* (1898), *The Christian Life* (1899), and *The Atonement* (1900), all of which constitute variations upon this central theme. Since we are deprived of the particulars of Cooke's allegation and since Bowne's writing is so extensive and lucid, what was precisely at stake in this specification will continue to be somewhat a mystery. There is, however, less ambiguity with respect to the issues in the second and third specifications, and to these we now turn.

The Second Specification

According to the earliest record of the trial proceedings, "Probably the longest time in the trial was consumed in consideration of Professor Bowne's attitude on the Doctrine of Sacred Scripture." [45] This is understandable when one considers that all the other doctrines specified in the indictment directly derive from the primal notions of inspiration and authority of Scripture. And it also probably explains why subsequent discussion, in Elliott's article, of the third, fourth, and fifth specifications is very meagre.

The second charge, specifically, held that Bowne's teaching on miracles tended "to weaken if not destroy faith in large portions of the Old and New Testaments" and that his views on the inspiration of the Bible contradict the Bible itself and article five of the Articles of Religion.[46] According to Buckley,[47] pages 10-11, 40, 41, 42, 57, 61, 65, 70, 79, 80, and 106 of *The Christian Revelation* were offered in support of this specification.[48] These pages describe, essentially, a perspective or point of view which informs Bowne's understanding of the character of authentic revelation. The fundamental question relating to a doctrine of revelation, then, he regarded as methodological, i.e., it is concerned not with the reality of the revelation but with the "manner of conceiving it." [49]

Bowne argued that what is needed is some guiding principle for interpretation. The Christian revelation, he said, "is not the Bible, though it is in the Bible. It consists essentially in certain ways of thinking about God, his character, his purpose in our creation, and his relation to us." [50] The Christian revelation, therefore, cannot be reduced to abstract speculative theology any more than it can be thought to consist of a text in ethics or anything other than a self-revelation of God himself. In sum, the character of revelation is not constituted as truth *about* God but rather as encounter with the very God himself.[51]

When Cooke introduced comments on *The Christian Revelation* in his pamphlet, *The Present and the Future of Methodism,* he observed that "Prof. Bowne criticises the conservative and orthodox doctrine of Holy Scripture." [52] There is little doubt that Cooke meant by "conservative and orthodox doctrine" the notions of biblical inerrancy and divine dictation. In support of this allegation five passages were quoted from *The Christian Revelation.*[53] None of these exactly corresponds textually to the sparse citations that Elliott provides in his excerpts from the trial transcript. Nevertheless, the two sets of references do unquestionably complement each other to give us a reasonable picture of the issues at stake. Cooke himself, in fact, stated his own problem thus: "How are we to know that we have the Christian idea of God and man, and their mutual relations, if the Bible is not reliable?" [54]

Elliott did not miss the opportunity to identify Cooke with a larger movement within American Protestantism at the time. In his introductory remarks, which precede the excerpts of testimony relating to the second specification, he pointed out that Bowne was attempting to save "to the modern mind the fundamentals of Christian truth." Immediately thereafter, he added: "But he [Bowne] would not mean by 'Fundamentals' what is now being propagated by some fossil survivors of seventeenth century Protestant scholasticism and who are trying to load up the Christian consciousness with a lot of extra-confessional stuff." [55]

The first and last quotations cited by Cooke in his pamphlet will suffice to state what he supposed to be Bowne's heterodoxy:

(1) We have no longer a dictated and an infallible book, but we have the record of the self-revelation of God in history and in the thought and feeling of holy men. With this change, the intellectual scandals and incredibilities which infest the former view [i.e., of Biblical literalism and Scriptural inerrancy] have vanished, and in their place has come a blessed and a growing insight into what God is and what he means, which is our great and chief source of hope and inspiration. [56]

(2) The only persons who will experience any sense of loss in this view are the dealers in proof-texts and detailed information concerning the Divine plan and government. [57]

In his testimony before the "Select Number" Bowne reaffirmed his belief that "the Bible has not come through such dictation," and added:

We cannot separate the authority of the Bible from the authority
of the church and the authority of the Christian Conference
[consciousness?] that would set up one as independent of the
other. . . . We have the authority of the church and the Bible,
the authority of the religious community, all the work of God, including great conflicts, vital functions, but there is no possibility
of separation. I do not believe, for instance, that any church would
long consent to accept statements in the Bible which were agreed
upon as distinctly contradictory to reason and conscience. On the
other hand, I do not believe that reason and conscience would very
long support themselves without the use of the Bible. I do not think
that either one of them would support themselves without the
Christian community in which the Christian life were going on.[58]

While these references well enough portray Bowne's general
position, they do not do so as substantively as one found somewhat earlier in *The Christian Revelation,* where he states that

We have supposed ourselves bound to maintain the infallibility
of the Bible, to find a revelation in every detail, and to defend the
divineness of all that is attributed to God. In truth, the revelation
consists in what we have learned concerning God, his character,
and his purposes; and the revelation is mainly made by a great historical movement. Of this movement the Bible is at once the
product and the historical and literary record. The truth of the
revelation depends on the general truth of the history, and not
at all on the infallibility of the record. But we identify the record
and the revelation, and make ourselves additional difficulties by a
hard-and-fast theory of our own invention concerning the inspiration of the record. In this way the Bible itself has often been made
an obstacle to the acceptance of the revelation.[59]

The church itself is witness to this truth, existing before it had
a Bible and continuing because of the truth expressed in Scripture, not because of some doctrine of inspiration and authority.[60]

What is chiefly at stake, then, is whether the general truthfulness of the biblical record accords with history and ex-

perience. If the Bible helps men to God, its religious use is justified; but as a book it is functional only, and not to be worshiped or glorified for its own sake.[61] But this, of course, is to bring one back to the primacy of the hermeneutical question; and here, in anticipating the work of Rudolf Bultmann and others, Bowne indicates again how he is far ahead of his own time. "There are a few persons who say that they take the Bible just as it reads; but that only means that they take their interpretation for the Bible." [62] "There is no such thing as a hard-and-fast interpretation of such language. What we find in it will depend very much on ourselves, and on the presuppositions which we bring with us." [63] Just as in the *Metaphysics* Bowne had wanted to distinguish between phenomenal and noumenal categories, or object and idea, so here he seems also to be arguing that idea can never be exhausted by any concrete and objective expression of itself. Jesus, he says, was certainly "the objective manifestation" of consummate revelation, but "the revelation of that revelation is still going on." [64] The truth of Jesus as Christ thus transcends any propositional formulation because it is intensely "personal" and neither mechanistic nor naturalistic. It is, above all, for this reason that "this revelation can never be put into a book, so that any one who can read may discern it; it is possible only to and in the prepared heart." [65]

The same logic applies to other phenomena which are supposed to be miraculous. One of the passages cited as evidence of his aberrant teaching on miracles advanced the claim that

When we come to the distinctly miraculous, to that which breaks with the natural order and reveals the presence of a supernatural power, we may still look for some of the familiar natural continuities. Miracles which break with all law would be nothing intelligible. We can understand them as signs whereby sense-bound minds are made aware of a divine power and purpose which they would otherwise miss, in their subjection to the mechanical movement of nature; but we cannot suppose them wrought at random and without any reference to the antecedents and environment.[66]

In defense of these statements Bowne argued before the "Select Number":

While we believe in a good deal that is supernatural without affirming that it is miraculous, we believe in the divine presence in our lives, but we do not mean by that that we have angels or anything of that kind coming and directing us. . . . I believe that all the processes of nature are supernatural. They obey the divine will and are carried on with the ever-living will in which we live, and move, and have our being. I do not think everything is miraculous. . . . It [the distinctly miraculous] would be no more divine than the outgoings of the world; no more dependent upon God than the sparrow which does not fall without the Father.[67]

And when A. C. Eggleston asked whether he really believed this, Bowne replied, "I am a crass supernaturalist." [68]

But Bowne was a supernaturalist of a special stripe. What was intended, it cannot be doubted, was only a statement of faith affirming the divine causality and meaning of the world and its process. Science, Bowne would have insisted, has its own integrity in determining the method by which that causality proceeds. And the question asked by religion and science are, in this sense, distinguished and separate.

In the end Bowne did not deny the possibility of miracle but inclined to view it mainly as phenomenal experience which is rationally inexplicable. The theist has no problem with miracle because he can see it faithfully as an expression of divine activity; that is, the theist can interpret apparently miraculous phenomena noumenally. Miracle, nevertheless, cannot be made the precondition of faith nor its validation. Indeed, the genuinely miraculous can be identified as such only by a faithful interpretation of its phenomenological occurrence.

In a not dissimilar way revelation is communicated as "nothing mechanically given or rigidly fixed" but as the "working of the Holy Spirit upon the minds and hearts of holy men." [69] God, in other words, reveals himself through *human* and *personal* agency. He speaks through men to men; and, as history unfolds itself, that speech seems increasingly to make itself more intelligible to us. "In the human world," Bowne says, "God is less a *with-worker* than a *through-worker*, but he works nevertheless to will and to work of his good pleasure." [70]

Perhaps the most lucid, and one thinks the most moving, of Bowne's statements on revelation is the following, which appears fairly early in his essay:

Here [in the Christian revelation] we have, not indeed a God whom we understand, but one whom we can trust while we do not understand. I do not think that Christianity removes many, if any, of the intellectual difficulties we feel in contemplating life and the world; it rather outflanks them by a revelation of God which makes it possible to trust and love him, notwithstanding the mystery of his ways, and which assures us that all good things are safe, and are moving on and up. . . . The great significance of the Christian revelation, then, does not lie in its contribution to ethics or to speculative theology . . . but rather in this, that back of the mystery and uncertainty of our own lives, back of the apparent aimlessness of much history, and back of the woe and horror of much more, it reveals God, the almighty Friend and Lover of men, the Chief of burden-bearers, and the Leader of all in self-sacrifice. Over the seething chaos there broods a Spirit divine; and from everlasting to everlasting there stretches a broad bow of promise and of light.[71]

If the "Select Number" labored under further doubt, it was doubtless relieved by the concluding testimony under this specification. Buckley reports that Bowne was asked:

"Do you believe that the ideas of God the Father, His Son our Saviour and Lord, the inspiring and sanctifying Spirit, the forgiveness of sins, the kingdom of God upon earth, and the life everlasting, have come with abiding power and definiteness and fullness into the world's thought and life only along the line of God's revelation of Himself through the prophets and through His Son?" He answered, "All these I steadfastly believe." He was asked . . . also, how he thought "a knowledge of God's gracious purpose toward men is to be found?" He answered, "Only by consulting His word and works." And, whether "the Scriptures were written by men who were moved and enlightened by the Holy Spirit?" He answered that they were.[72]

Bowne's views were undoubtedly advanced and liberal for his time, but none of the documents submitted in evidence against him shows him to be at variance with article five of the Articles of Religion. All that is demonstrated is a hermeneutical conflict, and this in no way jeopardizes the authority of Scripture but only a particular approach toward its interpretation. With this matter decided the trial moved to a consideration of the third specification.

The Third Specification

The charges on the doctrine of the Atonement were "wholly based on extracts from Professor Bowne's little book, *The Atonement,* in which he criticizes substitutionary, commercial and governmental theories as being based on excessive literalism in exegesis." [73] Pages 22, 26, 31, 33-34, 48-49, 102, 105, and 115 were cited as *exempla* and articles two and twenty of the Articles of Religion were listed as references for refutation of Bowne's teaching. These articles have to do with incarnation and oblation and the following phrases were probably thought to be critical:

To reconcile his Father to us, and to be a sacrifice, not only for original guilt, but also for the actual sins of men (Art. II); The offering of Christ, once made, is that perfect redemption, propitiation, and satisfaction for all the sins of the whole world . . . and there is none other satisfaction for sin but that alone (Art. XX).[74]

It is plainly apparent, from both the excerpt of trial testimony which Elliott provides[75] and the quotations in Cooke's pamphlet,[76] that the charge focused on Bowne's repudiation of substitutionary and penal theories of the Atonement. Early in his book Bowne was at pains to have it understood that what he proposed to discuss was not the *fact* of the Atonement but only the *theory* of it.[77] Cooke, however, was not to be placated. Thus, in his first extended remark upon Bowne's work, he wrote:

No doubt Prof. Bowne is honest in his belief that the traditional and orthodox theories of the atonement have a blighting effect upon the human mind, else he would not attack them in such a savage manner. If half what he says about them is true they ought not to be tolerated anywhere, and the book from whence they came ought to be burned and forgotten. How he can remain in a church that plainly professes these theories, in its articles of Religion, is passing strange.[78]

Elliott argued that it is very doubtful whether any specific theory of the Atonement is "definitely set forth" in the Articles of Religion.[79] It may be that Elliott's zeal to defend Bowne obscured his critical reading of Article XX, where Methodist interpretation traditionally has been in terms of a substitutionary theory. Moreover, reference to John Wesley's sermons would further support the contention that, at this point, Bowne was diverging from accepted Methodist teaching.[80] Nevertheless, it was the question of the appropriate theory, and not the fact, of the Atonement that dominated this portion of the trial.

Elliott's excerpt opens with an *apologia* from Bowne for the writing of this and similar volumes. They were, he said, intended to assist young people, particularly college students, in their understanding and not at all written for the instruction of theologians.[81] Moreover, never was the question of the fact of the Atonement raised but the entire undertaking was rather premised upon the rational need to construct some kind of systematic framework expressive of the meaning of the fact. His task, then, was to give

an interpretation of the atonement which is in entire harmony with the Scriptures, more in harmony with the present type of Christian thought, with all the enlightenment there has come to it in the illumination of the Spirit and of experience, more in harmony than the theories which have hitherto obtained among us.[82]

Bowne rejected the older views of substitution and ransom, first of all, because the Bible itself does not offer a "single and consistent" notion.[83] Even Paul, he argued before the "Select Number," gives no constant and uniform view.[84] Bowne contended that the major factor which accounts for this situation lies in the nature of biblical language. "The failure to understand the instrumental and adumbrative nature of language led to the fancy that every bold and striking metaphor was a literal fact." [85] Any viable principle of interpretation must therefore transcend the mere literalness of the Bible; the letter kills, but the Spirit makes alive. Again, phenomenal and noumenal categories, objective and ideational reality, must be distinguished because we cannot allow the record and the revelation to be confused.[86]

To illustrate his point during the trial, Bowne responded to a question put by Dr. Couch, saying:

I myself use the Scripture terminology with great freedom. I have no difficulty with using such a hymn as "There is a fountain filled with blood." I can sing it with great zeal, but after you have said that, how do you interpret it? It is an adumbration with a great meaning behind it. We try to get the meaning into the minds of men. . . . I do not butt against analogy. I am after meanings.[87]

In the second of five "conclusions" which he appended to *The Atonement,* Bowne succinctly stated the principle in this way:

We must note the instrumental and undogmatic character of Scripture language on this subject [i.e., Atonement], and the resulting necessity of taking it in a free and living way rather than as the language of a dogma or a statute. A person who reads the Scriptures with no aid but the dictionary, and without knowledge of ancient life and custom, and without diligently comparing Scripture with Scripture, will certainly go astray in this matter.[88]

His second fundamental reason for repudiating substitutionary and penal theories was that they contained "two incommensurable notions," one of which assumed the sacrificial figures of the Old Testament as normative and the other of which adopted the notion of the imputation of merit to the justified believer. Apart from the error of these views when taken singly, Bowne thought them "entirely disparate when taken literally" and wholly incapable of being "united in one homogeneous thought." [89] Moreover, Bowne argued that a "moral view," in contradistinction to forensic views, would insist strongly on justification *sola gratia*. The substance of his reasoning was that "any value . . . which the world of finite spirits may have depends primarily and essentially, not on the merit and worth of their service, but on the Divine love. . . . All we can do is to love and trust and obey; and the love of God does all the rest." [90]

Bowne's claim was that no quasinaturalistic rite can save us, not even Christ's atonement when it is interpreted and celebrated so woodenly as to become a merely mechanical transaction. "The faith that saves is no mere assent of the understanding; it is the practical surrender of ourselves to the revealed grace and will of God, according to the commands and promises of our Lord." [91] This same strain of simple, unadorned piety informs the closing paragraph in *The Atonement*.

For practical purposes all we need is to become the disciples of our Lord, trusting in his promises and the Father whom he revealed. With this practical discipleship we shall receive all the benefits of the Savior's work without any theory; and without this discipleship we are lost, whatever our theory.[92]

We have no record of statements from the prosecution; but, if Cooke's pamphlet be any indication, the argument was probably *ad hominem* for the most part. Commenting upon a quotation from Bowne, Cooke wrote: "It hardly seems possible that a Christian gentleman could drop his argument to such a level. He must have forgotten himself, and written these words in a moment of carelessness." [93] Or again, referring to Bowne's article in *The Methodist Review* for May, 1898,[94] Cooke ventured the following:

It seems to me that if his theology were preached and his theories of church government were seriously adopted, the Christian church would soon end its career in moral collapse. . . . I do not know any genuinely spiritual members of the church that are asking for the removal of paragraph 248 from the discipline.[95]

Cooke could have pursued a more vigorous course here, and had he done so it would be difficult to conceive how the "Select Number" could fail to convict Bowne on this charge. Of all the specifications, it is in his teaching on the Atonement that he appears most vulnerable. Traditional Methodist theory of the Atonement has been substitutionary and penal in character; and however much the theological climate may have changed in the half-century since Bowne, at the time of his trial the theory which he repudiated was popularly espoused by Methodist preachers and people. This fact notwithstanding, the strategy adopted by Cooke and his counsels failed again to carry the day on this last of the great debates.

Buckley reported that of the sixteen hours given to the entire trial, only ten were consumed by direct examination of the defendant.[96] And Elliott relates that for the last two charges there was time for "but little testimony" since most of the two-day sessions were given to the first, second, and third specifications.[97] It is to those latter indictments that we now briefly turn.

The Fourth Specification

Cooke's fourth charge against Bowne was that he taught views of the "divine government and of the future of souls" which were not consonant with Christ's teaching on "the future punishment of the wicked and the future reward of the righteous." [98] None of the Articles of Religion was cited as support for the allegation, but page references from two of Bowne's books were introduced as evidence against him: pages 66-67 and 83 from *The Atonement,* and pages 379-80 from *Metaphysics.*[99] These materials, together with a very brief excerpt in Elliott,[100] constitute the data presently available with respect to this specification. As in the case of the first charge, there is no mention made of this item in Cooke's pamphlet.

It is most likely that the elements of this indictment were chiefly two: (1) Bowne's alleged Universalism and (2) his rejection of an impersonally conceived divine sovereignty. None of Bowne's writings which are cited here make direct reference to the first of these. We have, then, only his testimony in response to a question put to him by Dr. Couch. Couch asked whether Bowne would "like to be" a Universalist and Bowne answered: "Only in this sense; I should like to believe that it was God's purpose finally to bring all souls into obedience unto himself. . . . I am not a Universalist." [101] Elliott's assessment of this response was that "Bowne was wholly in harmony with the desire of God to save all men, *if they would let him."* [102]

The second element offers even less demonstrable proof of what was being contended, though a relatively accurate hypothesis may be advanced. The earlier citation from *The Atonement* includes these revealing sentences:

Manifestly the only possibility of getting any conception of the case which will not revolt the moral reason lies in replacing the conception of the Divine Governor by that of the Heavenly Father, and the conception of the Divine government by that of the Divine family. . . . Whatever notions of government and justice we may form must be subordinate to the thought of this Divine Fatherhood of which every other fatherhood in heaven or in earth is named. Instead, then, of a Divine Ruler anxious mainly for his own claims and laws, we have a Divine Father in the midst of his human family, bearing with his children, and seeking by all the discipline of love and law to build them into likeness to and fellowship with himself.[103]

A contemporary treatment of "Wesleyan Theology" takes a counterview with which Cooke was apparently sympathetic. In this work "the grand purposes of the divine government" are said to be "to show God's hatred to sin" and "to show God's determination to punish the sinner." [104] Such purposes, moreover, are thought to become manifest according to a prescribed plan which the Scriptures sufficiently and unequivocally set forth. Toward such a view Bowne stood unalterably opposed.

In addition to Bowne's repudiation of an arbitrary divine action which asserts and intends only "his own claims and laws," the citation from *Metaphysics* leads one to suspect as another of Cooke's objections Bowne's dynamic conception of "soul." In *Metaphysics* Bowne adopts the principle that phenomena implies a conscious mind as the condition of its apprehension. He thus argues that "we cannot make mentality and materiality phenomenal without positing a conscious subject for whom the phenomena exist." [105] This epistemological position leads him, in the conclusion of the chapter on "The Soul," to contend for the theory known as traducianism, i.e., that the soul is neither introduced into the body after birth nor pre-existent but is somehow propagated with the body.

The development of the soul proceeds with that of the body. . . . This, of course, does not mean that the soul is ever half-made; this would be absurd. It means that the unfolding of the soul's powers is conditioned by the advance of the organism, and proceeds parallel with it.[106]

It is apparently the case that the basic conflict between Cooke and Bowne, in this specification, consisted in differing approaches to the questions of biblical interpretation and divine activity. Bowne argued for what we might today describe as an "existential" hermeneutic while Cooke defended a thoroughgoing biblical literalism. On the question of God's active governance of the world, Bowne rejected the notion of arbitrary divine action on the grounds that such was impersonal and hence immoral and Cooke, contrarily, maintained that God's sovereignty permitted him to act even in ways that were reprehensible to human moral sensibilities. Assuming the principles of analogy and correspondence, Bowne could not conceive the permissibility of any reputed divine activity which evoked outrage in the human breast.

Cooke did not cite any of the Articles of Religion as sanction for this charge, and one therefore suspects that "our established standards of doctrine" [107] constituted the basis for assessing Bowne's guilt or innocence. If this be so, Bowne's acquittal was plainly warranted. Wesley shows, in his notes on the New Testament, no reluctance to apply a critical eye to the text, amend it if need be, and even raise questions about authorship. So this much, at least, is defensible: neither Wesley nor Bowne was bound to a static and mechanical literalism. Furthermore, Wesley and Bowne were at one in their insistence that God's desire is to save all men if they will but allow him to do so. Wesley, in fact, states that "The God of love is willing to save all the souls that He has made. . . . But He will not force them to accept of it; He leaves them in the hands of their own counsel. . . ." [108] In addition, he argues explicitly in his sermon "On Living Without God" that it is better to leave the question of the fate of the "heathen" to the counsels of the Almighty than to sentence them to damnation for their lack of positive encounter with the Word.[109] Beyond reasonable doubt the documentary evidence certainly supports the verdict of the "Select Number."

The Fifth Specification

The final charge against Bowne alleged that his teaching on the Christian life did not represent "the views of the Methodist Episcopal Church as expressed in our standard works of theology." [110] Citations were introduced from his book on *Theism*,[111] page 208, and from the essay, *The Christian Life*,[112] pages 8, 34, 35, 38, 39, 50, and 119. Elliott states that Bowne was "called upon for but little testimony" on this and the previous specification, and none of that testimony is included in his excerpt of the trial transcript.[113]

The selections from both *Theism* and *The Christian Life* advance what is essentially an evolutionary view of Christian experience. Bowne did not insist that sudden and unambiguous experience of salvation is impossible; he merely argued that, when the experience is viewed as a totality, one will see a great variety of psychological and historical factors which have tended to shape, if not give final substance to, the event itself. His thoughts on the reality of "Christian nurture" are very similar to those of Horace Bushnell. What is at issue is that salvation does not occur *in vacuo* but is, in profound measure, interpersonally and socially oriented. Cooke probably held a more conservative position which would speak of redemption primarily in terms of atomic individualism. The "signs," then, by which Cooke and Bowne generally indentified God's activity in human life were poles apart; the former being more cataclysmic and catatonic and the latter being more evolutionary and progressive.

Conclusion

The "Select Number" concluded its deliberations and reported to the Conference on the morning of Friday, April 8. Frank Mason North, who served as chairman of the tribunal, presented the finding as follows:

The Select Number, to whom were referred the charges against Borden P. Bowne for "disseminating doctrines contrary to the Articles of Religion and our standards of doctrine," report: That all the evidence and testimony offered by the complainant and defendant in this case have been received and carefully considered, and that counsel for each has had ample opportunity for the presentation of argument; That the Select Number, by unanimous vote taken by ballot, find and decide that of the five specifications none are sustained, and that the charges are not sustained.[114]

Following this report and adverting to "Question 13," which called for the approval of each minister's character, the bishop recognized C. S. Wing, who two days earlier had presented Cooke's charges to the Conference. On motion of Dr. Wing the Conference passed the character of Bowne.

Two items of business intervened before Cooke, through Wing, offered a second set of charges against Bowne. J. M. Buckley, who had served as Bowne's counsel during the preceding trial, moved that since Cooke had communicated his new charges to the press before processing them through appropriate Conference channels he (Cooke) had "forfeited all rights to recognition of said charges." Bishop Foss, however, appointed a committee to investigate these latest allegations. Immediately prior to adjournment of the morning session G. E. Reed presented the following report from the committee, and it was adopted by the Conference:

The Committee to which the charges against Borden P. Bowne were referred begs leave to report that, after careful examination of the same, these members are of the unanimous opinion that there is nothing in the charges presented demanding the consideration of the Conference, and, therefore, respectfully move that the said charges be not entertained.[115]

Four years later, in what must appear a personal vendetta, Cooke again lodged charges against Bowne. In these charges he alleged defamation of character, intimidation, and hypocrisy. By this time Cooke's peripatetic pilgrimage had taken him to the Troy Conference. Following are the "crimes and offenses against the Discipline of the Methodist Episcopal Church" with which he charged Bowne:

CHARGE FIRST: *Defamation of Character.* Specification: Under cover of an editorial in *Zion's Herald,* of which Rev. Charles Parkhurst, D.D., is Editor, in the issue of Nov. 11, 1903, he published an article entitled, "Make the Criminal Industry [*sic*] Unprofitable," in which he falsely and maliciously assailed the character of some of his brethren in the Methodist ministry and branded them as criminals. CHARGE SECOND: *Intimidation*. Specification: In the article referred to in the first charge, which appeared in *Zion's Herald*, he virtually threatened to force out of our ministry ministers whom he had unjustly and falsely accused of being criminals. He closed the article with these threatening words, "Let them be headed off, and, if need be, off-headed." CHARGE THIRD: *Hypocrisy*. Specification: In writing the above mentioned article, viz.: "Make the Criminal Ministry [*sic*] Unprofitable," he assumed an air of lofty and superior morality, when in reality he was manifesting an unworthy and a wicked spirit. It is alleged, and we shall maintain, that he was engaging on a large scale in the very crimes he falsely accused others of being engaged in. In sustaining these charges we shall rely on evidence found in a book entitled *The Principles of Ethics,* of which Professor Borden P. Bowne is the author, and such other documentary and verbal testimony as may be necessary to prove the charges. George A. Cooke, Complainant.[116]

On the motion of J. M. Buckley, "the Conference refused to entertain them by a unanimous rising vote." [117] The anatomy of these proceedings is thus complete, at least insofar as available documentation allows, and Bowne continued the remainder of his life giving voice to these same tenets in his teaching at Boston University.

Given the paucity of reliable data, it would be hazardous to venture more than provisional and tentative assessments of this, American Methodism's last heresy trial. Perhaps the following judgments can, nevertheless, be advanced on the basis of the foregoing reconstruction. (1) Bowne was surely in advance of the popular theological constructions of his own time; but, even judged by contemporary views together with the accepted standards of Methodist orthodoxy, he was within traditional limits at four of the five points on which he stood accused. (2) Bowne should have been challenged more forcefully on the doctrine of the Atonement and the indictment either sustained or the defendant reprimanded for advocating a view which was at variance with then-accepted Methodist teaching. (3) The judgment that the trial was viewed with a degree of amusement is threatened by (a) the fact that extensive record of the trial proceedings was taken, (b) the fact that an Annual Conference invested sixteen hours in the trial, and (c) the obligation of the church always to take seriously allegations of heresy among its clergy. (4) That official record of the trial transcript was available eighteen years after the trial but is now a mystery gives rise to a host of scholarly speculations, none of which reflect credit upon the church's care for, and preservation of, official documents.

In the end, and taking a rather synoptic view of the proceedings, Bowne's innocence would have to be defended—in terms of his own times as well as ours. He was undoubtedly a liberal churchman and theologian; and while this in itself has often been taken as sufficient ground to suppose heresy, in the case of Bowne it is far from demonstrated fact.

NOTES

1. Francis John McConnell, *Borden Parker Bowne, His Life and His Philosophy* (New York: The Abingdon Press, 1929), p. 9. McConnell's biography is the definitive work on Bowne and this and subsequent historical data are largely dependent upon this source. McConnell has also appended a complete bibliography of Bowne's books and articles.
2. *Ibid.*
3. Indeed, Bowne's book *Metaphysics: A Study in First Principles* (New York: Harper & Brothers, 1882) is dedicated "in grateful recollection to the memory of my friend and former teacher Hermann Lotze." And he indicates in the Preface to the first edition (not, as McConnell mistakenly reports, in the Introduction [*Borden Parker Bowne*, p. 37]) that the "conclusions reached are essentially those of Lotze" and that "so far as their character is concerned, there would be no great misrepresentation in calling them Lotzian" (p. vii).
4. The most recent treatment of this subject is to be found in F. Thomas Trotter, "Methodism's Last Heresy Trial," *Christian Advocate*, IV (Mar. 31, 1960), 9-10. This brief essay is for a popular audience, although it does provide a general statement of Bowne's theological views.

5. "The Acquittal of Professor Bowne," *The Christian Advocate,*
   LXXIX (Apr. 14, 1904), 571.
6. George Elliott, "The Orthodoxy of Bowne," *The Methodist Review, CV* [Fifth Series, XXXVIII], (May-June, 1922), 399-413.
7. *Borden Parker Bowne,* pp. 189-201.
8. *Ibid.,* p. 181.
9. *Current Literature,* XL (Jan., 1906), 52-53.
10. *The Independent,* LIX (Nov. 16, 1905), 1178-80.
11. See George Albert Coe, "A Crisis in Methodism," *The Outlook,*
    LXXXI (Dec. 16, 1905), 933-35.
12. Cf. *General Conference Journal of The Methodist Episcopal
    Church,* 1908, pp. 482-83.
13. Cf. *Minutes* of The New York East Conference of The Methodist
    Episcopal Church, 1904, pp. 18 and 28; and *Minutes* of The New
    York East Conference of The Methodist Episcopal Church, 1908,
    p. 17.
14. *Ibid.,* 1904, p. 28.
15. Buckley, "The Acquittal of Professor Bowne," p. 571.
16. George A. Cooke, *The Present and the Future of Methodism: An
    Examination of the Teachings of Prof. Borden P. Bowne* (Bos-
    ton: The Cushman Press, n.d.), pp. 1-15. The dating of this
    pamphlet is critical for relating it to the charges which Cooke
    brought against Bowne in the fall of 1903. Buckley states in his
    Christian Advocate editorial that charges were initially filed
    "several months before the assembling of the Conference. They
    were defective and could not have been entertained. Feb. 26 new
    charges were sent" [p. 571]. Bowne himself was aware of this,
    or another, published pamphlet by Cooke as early as December
    of 1903. [Cf. Warren E. Steinkraus, "Five Letters of Bowne to
    James Mudge," *The Personalist,* 46 (Summer, 1965), 344-45.]
    Bowne's letter to Dr. Mudge credits publication of the pamphlet
    he had seen to the "Bible League," but there is no indication that
    the work by Cooke referred to above sustained any relationship
    to such an organization. What is of more moment to note is the
    fact that the title page of the pamphlet identifies Cooke as a
    "member of New England Conference, West Medford, Mass."
    Cooke was appointed to the Hillside and Trinity Methodist Epis-
    copal Churches, in West Medford, in April, 1902, and remained
    there until April, 1904, when he was appointed to the Millbury
    Church, Boston. [Cf. the *Minutes* of the New England Confer-
    ence of The Methodist Episcopal Church, 1902, p. 40; 1903, p.
    38; 1904, p. 37.] His pamphlet on *The Present and Future of
    Methodism* must, therefore, have appeared between April, 1902,
    and April, 1904; and it is not unlikely that it appeared prior to
    December, 1903, and was the one to which Bowne referred in
    his letter to Mudge. That his formal charges against Bowne were
    preferred "several months before the assembling of the Confer-

ence" (i.e., several months before April, 1904) also suggests that his formulation of the allegations was being worked out earlier, and probably in this pamphlet. Finally, the particular points at issue in the pamphlet are identical, even to specific references to Bowne's works, to those which later appear in Cooke's formal charges presented to the Conference of 1904.

17. It is perhaps worth noting that the author has contacted all the surviving members of the 1904 New York East Conference. Of those four men, two do not recall anything about Bowne's case. The Reverend E. Foster Piper wrote that he has "distinct recollection that the trial was considered in the light of a joke by most if not all of us. Dr. Bowne was held in highest esteem throughout the church and that a man of his unsullied character and scholarly attainments should be challenged by an obscure preacher from the wilds of New England was considered as simply ridiculous. . . . I well remember that we young fellows had only feelings of marked commiseration towards Professor Bowne's accuser, deciding that the poor fellow had in his heresy hunting merely disclosed his own incapacity to comprehend the writings and teachings of the man whom he would brand as heretic." (Personal correspondence, dated Feb. 8, 1965.)

The fourth surviving member of the Conference was also a member of the "Select Number" which tried the case. Bishop Herbert Welch does not recall any of the "details of the Bowne trial" but he does state that "My own recollection is that I think the N. Y. East brethren regarded the charges with a degree of amusement but of course had to go through the legal forms." (Personal correspondence, dated fall, 1965.)

Both these assessments are further substantiated by Dean Lynn Harold Hough, a student of Bowne's. "I can fairly see him [Bowne] in memory," wrote Dean Hough, "when after his vindication he said a number of things, which interested us all, ending with a chuckle by uttering these words, 'I have many more things to say unto you. But ye cannot bear them now.'" (Personal correspondence, dated Mar. 11, 1965.)

18. Buckley, "The Acquittal of Professor Bowne," pp. 571-72. Although there is no direct reference, in any extant documents relating to the trial of appeal, to what Cooke described in his specifications as "our established standards of doctrine," it should be noted that the "Select Number" acknowledged those standards to be the Articles of Religion, the fifty-three "standard sermons" of Wesley, and his *Explanatory Notes upon the New Testament*.

19. Cf. *The Doctrines and Discipline of the Methodist Episcopal Church*, 1900, para. 230, pp. 139-40.

20. Buckley, "The Acquittal of Professor Bowne," p. 571.

21. Steinkraus, "Five Letters of Bowne to James Mudge," pp. 342-43.

22. Cf. above, note 16.

23. Whatever irregularity may appear on the face of this fact, such a procedure was necessary under the requirements of the *Discipline*. Church law provided that charges should be presented to Annual Conferences by a Presiding Elder. Moreover, it stipulated that a member of an Annual Conference could be tried only by his respective Conference. It may appear strange, further, that Bowne, who resided and taught in Boston, should be amenable to the New York East Conference. But the *Discipline* provided then, as it does now, that a bishop might appoint teachers to schools which "are not under our care," i.e., which lie outside the boundaries within which a bishop is entitled to exercise appointive jurisdiction. Cf. *The Doctrines and Discipline of the Methodist Episcopal Church*, 1900, para. 173, p. 104.

24. Elliott, "The Orthodoxy of Bowne," pp. 399-400.

25. "Article I. *Of Faith in the Holy Trinity*. There is but one living and true God, everlasting, without body or parts, of infinite power, wisdom, and goodness; the maker and preserver of all things, visible and invisible. And in unity of this Godhead there are three persons, of one substance, power, and eternity—the Father, the Son, and the Holy Ghost.

"Article IV. *Of the Holy Ghost*. The Holy Ghost, proceeding from the Father and the Son, is of one substance, majesty, and glory with the Father and the Son, very and eternal God."

The Doctrines and Discipline of the Methodist Episcopal Church, 1900, pp. 19-20.

26. Buckley, "The Acquittal of Professor Bowne," p. 572.

27. Bowne, *Metaphysics: A Study in First Principles*.

28. Bowne (New York: Harper & Brothers, 1887).

29. Bowne, *Theism* (New York: The American Book Company, 1902). In 1902 Bowne revised and extended *Philosophy of Theism* and delivered the emended version as the Deems Lectures at New York University. These lectures were subsequently published under the title *Theism*. Buckley's pagination, when applied to *Philosophy of Theism*, discloses discussions on "God and the World" and "The World Ground as Ethical." The same pagination, when applied to *Theism*, refers to chapters on "The Metaphysical Attributes of the World-Ground" and "God and the World"; and specific reference in the former chapter is to a subsection titled "Unity." This later work, as regards the page references from Buckley, is undoubtedly more to the point of Bowne's alleged heresy in the first specification than the earlier one. This judgment is further supported by the page reference to *Theism* given for the fifth specification, viz. p. 208. In *Theism* this page falls in a discussion of "Pantheism" whereas in *Philosophy of Theism* it embraces the conclusion of a section on the divine government and the beginning of another on miracles. Finally, in Elliott's selections of the trial testimony, Bowne

addresses himself "In the next [second] place" to the question "as to the relation of the world to God." ("The Orthodoxy of Bowne," p. 401.) In *Theism* the discussion of "God and the World" is indeed in the second set of page references.

30. Cooke's pamphlet on *The Present and the Future of Methodism* makes reference only to Bowne's works on *The Christian Revelation, The Atonement,* and *The Christian Life.*
31. Bowne, *Theism,* p. 172.
32. *Ibid.,* p. 173.
33. *Ibid.,* p. 174.
34. *Ibid.,* p. 175.
35. *Ibid.*
36. Bowne, p. 451.
37. *Ibid.,* chap. II.
38. *Ibid.,* p. 487. Italics mine.
39. Elliott, "The Orthodoxy of Bowne," p. 401.
40. *Ibid.,* p. 402.
41. *Ibid.*
42. *Ibid.*
43. Cf. above p. 181, note 17.
44. Elliott, "The Orthodoxy of Bowne," p. 401.
45. *Ibid.,* p. 403.
46. "Article V. *The Sufficiency of the Holy Scriptures for Salvation.* The Holy Scriptures contain all things necessary to salvation; so that whatsoever is not read therein, nor may be proved thereby, is not to be required of any man that it should be believed as an article of faith, or be thought requisite or necessary to salvation. In the name of the Holy Scriptures we do understand those canonical books of the Old and New Testament of whose authority was never any doubt in the Church." [There follows a listing of the books of the Old Testament and acknowledgment of receipt and acceptance of the books of the New Testament.] Cf. *The Doctrines and Discipline of the Methodist Episcopal Church,* 1900, p. 4.
47. "The Acquittal of Professor Bowne," p. 572.
48. Bowne (Cincinnati: Curts and Jennings [New York: Eaton and Mains], 1898). Only a few copies of the first edition are still available. More accessible is the revised edition, published as the lead essay in Borden Parker Bowne, *Studies in Christianity* (Boston: Houghton Mifflin Company, 1909). I have therefore cited from the revised edition but noted parenthetically the corresponding pagination in the first edition.
49. *Ibid.,* p. 3. (Orig. ed., p. 6.)
50. *Ibid.,* p. 7. (Orig. ed., p. 10.)
51. *Ibid.*
52. Pp. 5-6.
53. In order, these occur on page 80, 7, 70, 69, and 70 (orig. ed., pages 106-7, 5-6, 10-11, 94-95, 93, and 94). Careful comparison of

the quotations in Cooke's pamphlet with both the 1898 and 1909 editions of *The Christian Revelation* reveals textual variation in all of these passages. Whatever the reason for this, Cooke's ability deliberately to misrepresent Bowne's teaching is attested to by Buckley during the trial. Cf. Elliott, "The Orthodoxy of Bowne," pp. 404-5, where Buckley states: "The complainant in this matter [Cooke] has mutilated the passage and withheld from the church and the committee a very remarkable passage which runs in the other direction." Buckley then gives the quotation in its entirety.

54. *The Present and Future of Methodism,* p. 6.
55. "The Orthodoxy of Bowne," p. 403.
56. *The Present and Future of Methodism,* p. 6. The citation is from p. 80 of *The Christian Revelation.* (Orig. ed., pp. 106-7.)
57. *Ibid.,* p. 7. The citation is from p. 70 in *The Christian Revelation.* (Orig. ed., p. 94.)
58. Elliott, "The Orthodoxy of Bowne," p. 408. The bracketed word in the quotation apparently expresses Elliott's misgiving about the stenographer's accuracy in ascribing the previous word to Bowne. Given the language employed in the concluding portions of the statement, a still more accurate transcription would probably be "conscience."
59. Pp. 39-40. (Orig. ed., pp. 58-59.) The concluding sentence is a revision of the original edition, but it is expressive of Bowne's consistent judgment.
60. *Ibid.,* p. 41. (Orig. ed., p. 61.)
61. Cf. *ibid.,* pp. 42-53. (Orig. ed., pp. 62-63.)
62. *Ibid.,* p. 68. (Orig. ed., p. 91.)
63. *Ibid.,* p. 69. (Orig. ed., p. 92.) Cf. Bultmann's essay, "Is Exegesis Without Presuppositions Possible?" in *Existence and Faith: Shorter Writings of Rudolf Bultmann,* Schubert M. Ogden, tr. (New York: Meridian Books, 1960), pp. 289-96. The original essay appeared as "Ist voraussetzungslose Exegese möglich?" *Theologische Zeitschrift,* XIII (1957), 409-17.
64. *Ibid.,* p. 77. (Orig. ed., p. 102.)
65. *Ibid.,* p. 78. (Orig. ed., p. 103.)
66. *Ibid.,* p. 61 (Orig. ed., p. 80.) Cf. Elliott, "The Orthodoxy of Bowne," p. 405.
67. Elliott, "The Orthodoxy of Bowne," p. 405.
68. *Ibid.*
69. *The Christian Revelation,* p. 81. While entirely consistent with Bowne's general view, this reference, together with the one which immediately follows, is to be found only in the revised edition.
70. *Ibid.,* p. 83.
71. *Ibid.,* pp. 24-25. (Orig. ed., pp. 36-38.)

72. Buckley, "The Acquittal of Professor Bowne," p. 573. Cf. Elliott, "The Orthodoxy of Bowne," p. 409.

73. Elliott, "The Orthodoxy of Bowne," pp. 409-10. See Bowne, *The Atonement* (Cincinnati: Jennings and Pye [New York: Eaton and Mains], 1900). See also Bowne, "The Incarnation and the Atonement," *Studies in Christianity* (Boston: Houghton Mifflin Company, 1909), pp. 85-193.

74. "Article II. *Of the Word, or Son of God, who was made very man.* The Son, who is the Word of the Father, the very and eternal God, of one substance with the Father, took man's nature in the womb of the blessed Virgin; so that two whole and perfect natures, that is to say, the Godhead and Manhood, were joined together in one person, never to be divided; whereof is one Christ, very God and very Man, who truly suffered, was crucified, dead, and buried, to reconcile his Father to us, and to be a sacrifice, not only for original guilt, but also for the actual sins of men."

"Article XX. *Of the One Oblation of Christ, finished upon the Cross.* The offering of Christ, once made, is that perfect redemption, propitiation, and satisfaction for all the sins of the whole world, both original and actual; and there is none other satisfaction for sin but that alone. Wherefore the sacrifice of masses, in the which it is commonly said that the priest doth offer Christ for the quick and the dead, to have remission of pain or guilt, is a blasphemous fable and dangerous deceit."

The Doctrines and Discipline of the Methodist Episcopal Church, 1900, pp. 19 and 25, respectively.

75. "The Orthodoxy of Bowne," pp. 409-12.

76. *The Present and Future of Methodism,* pp. 10-13.

77. Bowne, *The Atonement,* p. 21.

78. *The Present and Future of Methodism,* p. 11.

79. "The Orthodoxy of Bowne," p. 410.

80. Cf. Wesley's *Standard Sermons,* Edward H. Sugden, ed., Sermon I ("Salvation by Faith") and Sermon V ("Justification by Faith").

81. "The Orthodoxy of Bowne," p. 410. *The Atonement* may have been conceived as response to student inquiry, but it is a substantial theological monograph.

82. *Ibid.,* p. 411.

83. *The Atonement,* p. 22.

84. Elliott, "The Orthodoxy of Bowne," p. 411.

85. Bowne, *The Atonement,* p. 33.

86. Bowne, *The Christian Revelation,* pp. 39-40. (Orig. ed., pp. 58-59.)

87. Elliott, "The Orthodoxy of Bowne," p. 411.

88. Pp. 150-51.

89. *Ibid.,* p. 22-23.

90. *Ibid.,* pp. 125-26.

91. *Ibid.,* p. 139.
92. *Ibid.,* p. 152.
93. *The Present and Future of Methodism,* pp. 11-12.
94. "Ethical Legislation by the Church," LXXX (1898), 370-86.
95. *The Present and Future of Methodism,* pp. 13-14. Paragraph 248 states: "In cases of neglect of duties of any kind, imprudent conduct, indulging sinful tempers or words, the buying, selling, or using intoxicating liquors as a beverage, signing petitions in favor of granting license for the sale of intoxicating liquors, becoming bondsmen for persons engaged in such traffic, renting property as a place in or on which to manufacture or sell intoxicating liquors, dancing, playing at games of chance, attending theaters, horse races, circuses, dancing parties, or patronizing dancing schools, or taking such other amusements as are obviously of misleading or questionable moral tendency, or disobedience to the order and Discipline of the Church—first, let private reproof be given by the Pastor or Leader, and if there be an acknowledgment of the fault, and proper humiliation, the person may be borne with. On the second offense the Pastor or Leader may take one or two discreet Members of the Church. On a third offense let him be brought to trial, and if found guilty, and there be no sign of real humiliation, he shall be expelled."

The Doctrines and Discipline of the Methodist Episcopal Church, 1900, p. 145. The comparable paragraph is number 969 in the 1964 edition of *Doctrines and Discipline of The Methodist Church,* pp. 300-301. Parallel investigation of the texts would suggest that Cooke's fears were largely justified!
96. "The Acquittal of Professor Bowne," p. 571.
97. "The Orthodoxy of Bowne," p. 412.
98. *Ibid.,* pp. 399-400.
99. Buckley, "The Acquittal of Professor Bowne," p. 572.
100. "The Orthodoxy of Bowne," p. 412.
101. *Ibid.*
102. *Ibid.*
103. Bowne, pp. 66-67.
104. Thomas N. Ralston, *Elements of Divinity: Or, a Concise and Comprehensive View of Biblical Theology,* T. O. Summers, ed. (Nashville: Publishing House of the Methodist Episcopal Church, South, 1910), pp. 230-31. Ralston goes on to state, in language that Cooke would have happily embraced: "Now if it can be made to appear that the sufferings and death of Christ, as a substitute, will subserve these purposes, as fully as the exact penalty threatened in its precise kind and degree, then it will follow that, by this arrangement, the honor of the divine throne may be sustained, the demands of justice satisfied, and yet mercy be extended to a fallen world. All this, we conceive, is fully accomplished in the

to help support it in his youth. Consequently he had very little formal education. After serving as a drummer boy in the Civil War he engaged in business for a few years. When he was twenty he decided to enter the ministry and attended St. Stephen's College (later Bard) for two years. He entered the General Theological Seminary of the Episcopal Church in 1869.[2]

Crapsey said of the General Seminary, "I do not think there was ever an institution so inadequate to its purpose as this seminary when I was under its care." [3] The students were described as a "mediocre lot." These comments were made long after his trial. At the time of his lectures on "Religion and Politics" which caused his trial, he had said that seminaries "are the only institutions of learning which do not employ the scientific method in the investigation and establishment of truth," although in preparing the text for publication he observed that there were some exceptions.[4] Actually he had found the atmosphere of the General Seminary stimulating with its conflict between "ritualists and rationalists." Crapsey described himself as having been, at successive stages, under the influence of Newman, Darwin, and Marx. When he published his autobiography in 1924, a few years before his death in 1927, he said: "From first to last I have been a Humanist. God has never troubled me. I have taken Him for granted. I studied and in a measure mastered the theology of my church; but it was never vital to me. It was the humanity of Jesus and not His divinity that won and held my allegiance." [5] At the time of his trial, however, he had not yet progressed quite to this point. He might best be characterized as an enthusiastic and rather careless liberal of somewhat "Catholic" sympathies in his days as a clergyman.

After graduation from the seminary Crapsey served as an assistant in St. Paul's Chapel, New York, for a time. Here he came in contact with the then new "institutional Church" movement which greatly influenced his later work in Rochester. He was called to St. Andrew's Church in that city in 1879 and remained there until his conviction and consequent renunciation of the ministry in 1906. The mission had been organized on February 7, 1879, and had taken over the building of the recently defunct St. Clement's Church in Rochester. A new building was consecrated by the Rt. Rev. Arthur Cleveland Coxe in May, 1880, and four years later the bishop opened a new parish hall. The parish conducted a parochial school which had as many as 150 students and 20 teachers and also, around 1890, maintained an industrial school.[6] At the time of the trial in 1906 the parish was reported to have 342 families and 642 communicants.[7] Crapsey was greatly loved by the people of Rochester where he took a deep interest in civic affairs as well as in the immediate welfare of his parishioners. The trial was not held in Rochester, apparently because of the hostile attitude toward the prosecution there. The former mayor of the city commented in a letter to *The Churchman* at the time of Crapsey's trial that "no man has done more to invigorate the conscience of Rochester." [8]

As early as 1890 Crapsey had proposed the division of the Diocese of Western New York, a proposal which, in that year, was defeated by a narrow vote of the laity, the clergy being in favor of it.[9] Crapsey favored smaller dioceses and some years later published a plea for the division of the diocese. The book is of little permanent significance, but it is illustrative of Crapsey's viewpoint. He remarks that he was opposed to the election of the Rt. Rev. William David Walker until the division of the diocese had been effected, although Bishop Walker apparently did not favor the proposed division. It is unlikely that Bishop Walker was well disposed toward Crapsey as a result of his position on dividing the diocese. It is interesting to note that at this time Crapsey seems to have had a high regard for the creeds:

Little or no interest can now be excited in any question of doctrine or any point of ritual; not because the Church has become indifferent to these, but because she has settled them. She has asserted her unfaltering faith in the catholic creeds. She has made good her claim to all that is essential to catholic worship.

These things are to her mind no longer matters for discussion. The Church cannot be forever talking about the same thing. She always has an end of controversy.[10]

This strongly Anglo-Catholic position was slightly modified elsewhere in the book as Crapsey observed that the creed is not the same for every man. For, he urged, it is the Person of Jesus Christ, and not a definition, which is at the heart of faith.[11]

Crapsey's first book reflects the strong moralism always characteristic of him, but there is nothing in it to arouse even the most sensitive heresy hunter. His concern for morality is also shown in the report of a sermon preached in 1898 which said that "Dr. CRAPSEY expressed the belief that not only was there justification for perfect confidence in the high moral standards as well as the valor of our army and navy, but there was no excuse for hopelessness in regard to our capacity for civil administration." [12]

In 1899 Crapsey published the first of a series of tractates which attracted attention to him outside Rochester. Entitled *The Disappointment of Jesus Christ,*[13] it dealt with the causes and remedy for church disunity. He proposed seven points for the reunification of Christianity. These included the "subordination of the official organization of the Church" to the primitive practice of the church itself and emphasis upon the "pastoral rather than the priestly conception of the ministry." Christian doctrine must be brought into "accord with the facts of the visible universe" and must not "conflict with the great primal instincts of the human heart; the instinct for justice, mercy and truth." Crapsey further advocated "absolute intellectual freedom" in the church along with the "submission of the entire content of Christian tradition, both oral and written, to the trained intelligence." Finally, moral discipline in the church was to be restored "as the only true basis of her spiritual life."

The pamphlet had been written from a lecture Crapsey delivered in Toronto to the Canadian Society of Christian Unity. The seven points were reprinted in the New York *Ascension Parish Record,* presumably upon the suggestion of the rector, the Rev. Percy Stickney Grant.[14] The Rev. William Reed Huntington, rector of Grace Church, New York, was highly enthusiastic about much of the pamphlet, pronouncing it to be one of the best summaries of the principles of church unity he had ever seen.[15] He was greatly encouraged in the fact that it had been written by one known as a high churchman or Anglo-Catholic. Crapsey later said the letter of Huntington showed the "hopelessness of the clerical mind," presumably because of the following passage:

The only point on which I find myself disposed to criticize the contents of your Tractate is under the doctrinal head. It appears to me, I confess, that your waiver of creed-forms is a little too sweeping. I know you do not mean your words to apply to the baptismal symbol, but I am greatly afraid that by the casual reader they will be understood as doing so. Of "systems" we have had enough and too many, but surely there must be a minimum statement of the things commonly believed among us, if we are not to be all at sea. How can we, for instance, rally around the person of the Saviour, as you exhort us to do, unless we have the word-image of Him which the Apostles' Creed provides? Of course, you intended your strictures to apply to "confessions," the thirty-nine articles, and the like, but they will be misinterpreted as ruling out even the most elementary forms of faith.

"Who shall show thee words," said the angel, "whereby thou and all thy house shall be saved?" "Words" of that sort we certainly are bound to conserve in tolerably clear-cut shape.[16]

Huntington ordered one hundred copies of the tractate and offered his help in the cause.

Apparently Crapsey did not think the clerical mind was hopeless at that time, since in a later tractate he attempted to answer the criticism of Dr. Huntington in respect to the third and fourth points of the tractate. It is doubtful that the answer was satisfactory, in view of Crapsey's somewhat vague expression of his ideas. There are, he wrote, but two sources for statements about religion: individuals and religious bodies, and the latter (which are dependent wholly on external authority) are not as important as the former.[17] Herbert Spencer was quoted with great approbation. Science apparently was giving theology a new basis, and the days of creeds and creed-making were considered long since over, although Crapsey referred to the Apostles' Creed as a "form of sound words." In this he seemed not to have changed from his position of a few years earlier when, in the *Voice in the Wilderness,* he had said the creed was the "all-sufficient expression of our faith and love." [18] The fourth principle was dealt with in another tractate, *The Judgment of Abraham,* a strongly moralistic work which shows no real knowledge or understanding of Augustine or Calvin, both of whom it was supposedly to disprove.[19]

Crapsey's one novel, *The Greater Love,* was published in 1902. It was a novel of social protest described as a "realistic study" even though it was "crude, somewhat wanting in the elegance of polish, but then we defy any one reading it without emotion." The book dealt with the corruption of the rich and the oppression of the poor in New York City. Its heroine, Keturah Bain, had a drunkard father, an opium-eating mother, a crippled brother, and an only sister who was wild and heedless, involving the rector of a rich and fashionable parish in a good work of redemption which caused scandal among his parishioners. A reviewer concluded: "Books written for a purpose are not to be treated lightly, particularly when such familiarity is shown with those who people the slums and their vicissitudes so powerfully described." [20]

Until well after the turn of the century there was apparently no criticism directed against Crapsey's orthodoxy, although he was obviously not greatly interested in doctrine. Discussion as to his orthodoxy was aroused by the publication of a series of Sunday evening lectures on *Religion and Politics.* They were given in the evening after the regular evening prayer service, which was held in the afternoon. The lectures were printed much as they had been delivered. George Hodges, Dean of the Episcopal Theological School in Cambridge, Massachusetts, reviewed the book in the *Atlantic Monthly,* holding it to be in "substantial agreement" with Patrick J. Healy's *The Valerian Persecution* which also dealt with the early church. Dean Hodges noted that while Healy's book bore the imprimatur, the other book had led to an investigation of its author by a "diocesan committee appointed to examine his orthodoxy." Hodges felt that any heretical utterances were quite incidental.[21]

The series of thirteen "sermon lectures" dealt with such subjects as "The State," "The Attitude of Jesus to the State," "The Democratic Church in the Imperial State," "Jesus' Method of Government"; six were on church history, and others discussed "The Commercialized Church in the Commercialized State," "The Present State of the Churches," and "The American Church-State." The chapter on the present state of the churches aroused the most discussion, but the last chapter was also of interest. It was concerned largely with the corruption of the primary election, a matter apparently even worse to Crapsey than the prostitution of women. His patriotism expressed in the sermon of 1898 had suffered no diminution. The "perfect description of the Kingdom of God on earth" was to be found in the Preamble to the United States Constitution. The American established religion was already here:

When the people of the United States decreed by constitutional amendment that the government should never by law establish any religion, they did actually establish the only religion that could comprehend in its membership the whole American people. A religion having as its basis the principles of individual liberty and obedience to righteous law is really the religion of the golden rule. Nor has this religion been simply a theory powerless to work righteousness in the world. It has created a great and happy people. Never before in the history of the world have so large a number of human beings lived together under one government, so little restrained by governmental control; with so many opportunities, with so many advantages, intellectual, social, and physical, as are now living in the United States of America. . . . By a sublime instinct the American people have created the organ that has resolved race and religious differences into the larger life of a common citizenship. Gently, but firmly, the people withdrew the education of the children from under the hand of all lesser religions, and placed it in the power and keeping of the larger religion of the state. . . . But if religion be love, and joy, and peace in the holy air of God, then the public schools have done more to promote true religion than all the churches in the land.[22]

The chapter ends with an impassioned plea to his hearers to go to the primary, not only the Rochester primary, but to the primary of the heart. In the earlier chapter on the "Relation of Church and State in the United States," Crapsey had compared the coming of the Mayflower in its importance to the gathering of a little band of men and women "in an upper chamber in Jerusalem to wait for the promise of the Lord." He observed that "the present separation of the religious from the civil and political life of the nation is cause for grave apprehension for the future of the American people." These curiously chauvinistic passages with their deprecation of the "lesser religions" such as Christianity in favor of the "larger religion of the state" were not included in the later charges against Crapsey. They may serve, however, as a caution to those who have charged with no trustworthy evidence that Crapsey was tried for his social, economic, and political views.[23]

The chapters dealing with the history of church and state contain little that was not common to liberal scholars of the day. Crapsey was not a thorough or careful scholar, although he had done extensive reading on the subject. He had learned little history while a student in the seminary. Although they are hardly original, his views on historical criticism of "the facts" of Christianity are illustrative of his attitude at the time of his accusation. Christianity, like other great religions, was to be investigated using the methods of historical criticism. It was better, he said, for Christians to do this themselves than for "strangers" to do so, especially since "the true believer has nothing to fear from historic criticism." For faith is not dependent upon "any given interpretation of history," because "God is God, man is man, Jesus is Jesus, the Spirit of Holiness is the Spirit of Holiness in the eternal now, no matter what may have happened in the past." [24]

A lecture delivered in February, 1905, aroused the most discussion, particularly when it was reprinted in a Rochester newspaper. This lecture on "The Present State of the Churches" pointed out the need for the churches to become "scientific, democratic, and socialistic." It dwelt on the dangers of church disunity and the lessening influence of the clergy generally. Crapsey observed that Protestants rejected miracles when they were reported to occur in other religions or in the medieval church, yet their own religion is equally based on miracle. Seemingly Protestantism, like Roman Catholicism, is "the rearguard of the powers that make for religious progress," since it lacks both the democratic and scientific spirits. In a passage which caused much discussion upon its publication, he argued that the scientific spirit is particularly important for the Episcopal Church. Crapsey said that "there is not in all religious history a more saintly character than that of Charles Darwin" whose patience, self-restraint, and endurance of pain and calumny are the equal of St. Bernard or St. Teresa. Crapsey's critical faculties were not applied to science, which seemed to him to be supplying, finally, a truly firm and unshaken foundation for theology:

The scientific movement is not only constructing the thought world in which mankind must live for ages to come, but it is also profoundly influencing the political, social, and industrial life of the world. Science has unified the world to an extent and in a way that the old religions never dreamed of. The God of science is not the God of the Hebrew, nor of the Christian. He is the God of the whole earth, and not only of the earth, but of the infinite reach of the heaven. The man of science knows his God as God has never been known before. He is face to face with His God every moment of his life.[25]

The man of science "has a faith in his convictions which is beyond the faith of the medieval saint." From these and similar passages it appears that Crapsey was already more of a scientific humanist than he appeared to be in his more formally religious statements.

It was Crapsey's views on the Virgin Birth and the interpretation of the creeds that aroused bitter denunciation of him upon the publication of his lectures in the book *Religion and Politics* in 1905. The Episcopal Church press was filled with articles on the Virgin Birth and the interpretation of the creeds; editorials in the *Church Standard* and the *Living Church* denounced the "Rochester scandal," while *The Churchman,* disapproving of Crapsey's views, pleaded in more sober tones against the wisdom of a heresy trial.

The first important development in the case was the appointment of a committee of investigation by the bishop of western New York after Crapsey had refused Bishop Walker's request to repudiate or retract what he was reported to have said. The committee of five was requested to investigate the case to see if there were sufficient grounds for presentment for trial, somewhat in the manner of a grand jury. According to Dr. Crapsey's own report, the matter was at first settled amicably with the committee who were satisfied with his statement on the interpretation of the Scriptures and the Apostles' Creed. He implies that the bishop interfered with the submission of the statement agreed upon by the committee and Crapsey.[26] The final report of the committee, submitted to the bishop on November 11, 1905, is curiously vague and ambiguous. A majority of three found that there was "not sufficient evidence to secure conviction in case of a trial for heresy" in the book *Religion and Politics.* A minority of two found that the book did contain "sufficient grounds for the presentment of [the] author." All the committee agreed that

The Rev. Dr. Crapsey impresses us as being a man who easily surrenders himself to intellectual vagaries, and the thing which for the time being appears to him to be true he advocates with remarkable eloquence. . . . His writings indicate that while he recites and affirms his belief in the Creeds of the Church he virtually sets aside the historical sense in which their Articles have been and are received by this Church, and for it he substituted a "spiritual interpretation," claiming to retain the spiritual reality for which Christianity stands while dismissing as indifferent the historical facts asserted in the Creeds.

Your committee is unanimous in its condemnation of the Rev. Dr. Crapsey's position in this matter.[27]

This condemnation without presentment for trial stirred up much criticism in the Episcopal Church press and among the clergy. The *Church Standard* found that the report made the "scandal one degree more scandalous than it was" and criticized the committee's condemnation of Crapsey as "wholly gratuitous and impertinent" since the committee had no judicial function; at the same time the paper condemned the committee for not presenting Crapsey for trial.[28] The *Living Church,* a strongly Anglo-Catholic or high church publication, found the report a "ghastly and double-faced perversion of justice" in its editorial, "Is There No Evidence Against Dr. Crapsey?" [29] Some support for Crapsey's later charge that the bishop interfered with the committee may lie behind a sermon Bishop Walker preached at the laying of a cornerstone in Rochester: "I am here in this city to stand up for the faith of the Catholic Church as it is taught in the Gospel, as it is taught in the Creed. I cannot sympathize with the man who teaches anything contrary to that which he has promised to teach. God be thanked that there is a Church still, and that the faith still abides." [30] The sermon clearly expressed the bishop's attitude toward Dr. Crapsey's views. It is possible that the committee may have been influenced in its findings by the bishop's clearly derogatory attitude. It is interesting to note that while ten presbyters were willing to request the Standing Committee of the diocese to act in the case by having the committee of investigation appointed, the requisite number of three was not found willing to present Crapsey for trial.

Dr. Crapsey had not intended to write a theological treatise. His views on the creeds and the Virgin Birth were, as Dean Hodges had pointed out, incidental to the argument of the book. Crapsey referred to Jesus as "the son of Joseph, a carpenter of Galilee" and he had little patience with theological terms while emphasizing the humanity of Jesus. The emphasis of the book was on social reform, a fact which gives rise to the suspicion that Crapsey was tried for his social and economic views. There is, however, no evidence of this either in the trial documents or, more significantly, in the discussions in the secular press or in religious periodicals. In the strongly Anglo-Catholic context of the diocese at the time, Crapsey's vague and rather provocative comments on the creeds were unacceptable.

The committee report did not silence the controversy. The bishop, at the consecration of Christ Church in Rochester, delivered a vigorous attack upon "spiritual interpretation" of the creeds, which he said must be accepted literally. Bishop Walker took very seriously the statement of the Bishops' 1894 Pastoral Letter that "fixedness of interpretation is of the essence of the Creeds." [31] Along with the comment that the "Creeds are as technical and exact as any of the sciences," the bishop said: "The Creeds have not changed, nor have their forms, either. Those gathered Articles of Belief are a group of quartz crystals, clear and pure as the limpid spring water that wells forth from lofty mountain's heart." [32]

"Quartz crystals" recurred frequently in the discussion. Although none of the church papers was altogether calm in its discussion of the controversy, *The Churchman* took the most charitable position, one which seems in the light of the trial and its methods to have been the most reasonable and just. After observing that the attitudes of both the bishop and Dr. Crapsey were likely to arouse antagonism each in the other, *The Church-man* concluded:

The speculations of Dr. Crapsey, the committee reports, tend to undermine the Creeds, and surely the attitude of Bishop Walker, with his theory of "quartz crystals," would tend to destroy a belief in the Creeds as the truth of the "living Giver." But since both Bishop Walker and his priest, in spite of their peculiar opinions and speculations, declare that they are loyal to the Christ of the Gospels and the Creeds, we must believe, as we have no reason to doubt their sincerity, that each is entitled to a place in the Church's ministry.[33]

Early in 1906 the controversy was aggravated by the publication of a "Declaration of New Testament Criticism and Other Subjects" by a number of leading Episcopal clergymen and laymen including the dean and most of the faculty of the Episcopal Theological School, the Rev. Messrs. Percy S. Grant, J. Howard Melish, Edward L. Parsons, Endicott Peabody, and Elwood Worcester, and Messrs. Richard H. Dana, Seth Low, Brander Matthews, and George Foster Peabody.[34] The Declaration was similar to a letter circulated in England and signed by 1,700 clergymen of the Church of England. It pleads for an earnest effort to solve the problems posed by the critical study of the New Testament, asking for "authoritative encouragement to face the critical problems of the *New* Testament with entire candor, reverence for God and His truth, and loyalty to the Church of Christ." It warns that qualified men may be kept out of the ministry unless the door is open to historical scholarship which must face the question of the historical validity of the New Testament narratives. Old Testament criticism had been accepted in the Protestant Episcopal Church for some time, but New Testament criticism was more slowly accepted. The declaration concludes with "confidence that the faith of the Church in the years to come, whatever historical revisions may await us, will stand, without risk and without discontinuity" upon a firm foundation witnessed to by Christian experience and the creed.[35]

Crapsey was encouraged by the declaration and felt that it showed that his position was supported by a large number of churchmen. Many of the signers, including most of those mentioned above, were active in his defense, although few of them agreed with his position. Charles Lewis Slattery, later Bishop of Massachusetts, believed that the declaration had little effect one way or the other on the Crapsey case.[36] The high church *Living Church* denounced the broad church movement which the declaration represented as being "founded on an intellectual fallacy and on essential dishonor." [37]

Early in September, 1905, an article, "Honor Among Clergymen," [38] by Crapsey was published in the *Outlook,* a liberal New York publication. The article criticized the Bishops' Pastoral Letter of 1904 which had urged those who no longer held to the "fundamental verities" of the church to be silent or withdraw. Crapsey held that the letter would deprive clergymen of the sacred "right to form and express his own convictions." For Crapsey the "fundamental verities" were "given by Jesus himself in the two great commandments of the law, in the Lord's Prayer, and in the five laws of righteousness as we find them written in the Sermon on the Mount." The teaching of Jesus, the ultimate authority, was fundamental because it was true, not because it was the teaching of Jesus. The article is the clearest statement of Crapsey's beliefs in the period preceding his trial and may have played a part in that trial although the article was not cited in the charges against him. Neither the Virgin Birth nor the physical resurrection was discussed specifically. Crapsey does state that it is the duty of the clergyman to state his convictions to the church because he is a prophet who "must stand in his place and calmly abide the consequences of his position." Crapsey later did not reply specifically to any of twenty doctrinal questions raised in a letter to the *Outlook* by the Rev. Edward Abbott of Cambridge, Massachusetts.[39]

In all this discussion there was no mention of Crapsey's social, economic, or political views.

The article caused much public discussion of the Crapsey case. The *Outlook* reported that scores of clergymen in every denomination were perplexed by the questions raised in the case.[40] The *Church Standard* (Episcopal) advocated action by the diocesan authorities against Crapsey, or those authorities themselves would be guilty of encouraging heresy. The *Living Church* agreed, remarking that Crapsey's position was "one that divests the Church of all teaching authority." In New York the Roman Catholic *Freeman's Journal* said that the case was a good illustration of how the Protestant principle of private judgment leads to "rationalism, pure and simple." [41] Wide discussion was apparently ended with the committee report refusing to present Crapsey, although there was, as has been noted, criticism by some Episcopal publications of the committee's action.

The reasons for the presentment of Crapsey after the committee of investigation had found insufficient evidence for such presentment are not altogether clear. One recent scholar says that the trial "can be explained only by the fact that it occurred in the Diocese of Western New York, which represented a rigid theological conservatism." [42] G. Sherman Burrows, a member of the court, wrote in the official diocesan history that "further reports were abroad of heretical instruction" and that "with new evidence and new rumors at hand, the Standing Committee felt that something must be done to stop the discontent and the scandal." [43] The new evidence added little or nothing to what had been published in *Religion and Politics*. Crapsey's sermon on December 31, 1905, was the source of the new evidence. Notes on the content of the sermon were carefully taken by the Rev. Frederick James Kerr Alexander, ostensibly for the purpose of discussing the sermon with Dr. Crapsey, although his motives were clearly brought out in cross-examination at the trial. Alexander had been Crapsey's assistant.

The Standing Committee decided on February 23, 1906, to present Crapsey for trial. *The Churchman* pleaded against going "in the face of a principle so imbedded in the conscience of the Anglo-Saxon race as that a man shall not be put in jeopardy more than once for the same offence." [44] It found a grave threat to the liberty and integrity of the church and warned of the danger of persecution. The other major Episcopal Church papers all applauded the action of the Standing Committee.

The presentment charged that Crapsey "did openly, advisedly, publicly and privately utter, avow, declare and teach doctrines contrary to those held and received by the Protestant Episcopal Church in the United States of America." This was done chiefly by the sermons in *Religion and Politics*. Fifteen passages from the book were cited. Some of them seemed to deny the Virgin Birth, such as the first which said Jesus was "the son of Joseph, a carpenter of upper Galilee," or the eighth which implied that the Resurrection and Virgin Birth were legendary. The tenth and fifteenth appeared to cast doubt upon the Trinity and the latter also implied that the Incarnation was simply "the worn-out terminology of the Greek dialectic." The clearest denial of the Virgin Birth was the fourteenth passage cited:

In the light of scientific research, the Founder of Christianity no longer stands apart from the common destiny of man in life and death, but He is in all things physical like as we are, born as we are born, dying as we died, and both in life and death in the keeping of that same Divine Power, that heavenly Fatherhood, which delivers us from the womb and carries us down to the grave. When we come to know Jesus in His historical relations, we see that miracle is not a help, it is a hindrance, to an intelligent comprehension of His person, His character, and His mission. We are not alarmed, we are relieved when scientific history proves to us that the fact of His miraculous birth was unknown to Himself, unknown to his mother, and unknown to the whole Christian community of the first generation. (Pages 288-289.) [45]

The other sections cited simply assert the full humanity of Jesus and their inclusion is rather puzzling. Possibly their inclusion reflects the "impersonal humanity" of our Lord asserted by some Anglo-Catholics following Leontius of Byzantium, a concept hardly in accord with Chalcedon and biblical or modern thought.[46]

The doctrines which Crapsey was accused of denying or impugning were as follows:

1. The doctrine that our Lord Jesus Christ is God, the Saviour of the world, as contained and enunciated in the Apostles' Creed and the Nicene Creed, and as set forth, and declared in the Book of Common Prayer of the Protestant Episcopal Church in the United States of America.[47]

2. The doctrine that our Lord Jesus Christ was conceived by the Holy Ghost, as contained and enunciated in the Apostles' Creed and the Nicene Creed, and as set forth, indicated, and declared in the Book of Common Prayer of the Protestant Episcopal Church in the United States of America.

3. The doctrine of the virgin birth of our Lord Jesus Christ, as contained and enunciated in the Apostles' Creed and the Nicene Creed, and as set forth, indicated, and declared in the Book of Common Prayer of the Protestant Episcopal Church in the United States of America.

4. The doctrine of the resurrection of our Blessed Lord and Saviour as contained and enunciated in the Apostles' Creed and the Nicene Creed, and as set forth, indicated, and declared in the Book of Common Prayer of the Protestant Episcopal Church in the United States of America.

5. The doctrine of the Blessed Trinity, as contained and enunciated in the Apostles' Creed and the Nicene Creed, and as set forth, indicated, and declared in the Book of Common Prayer of the Protestant Episcopal Church in the United States of America.[48]

The first charge contained another specification:

Specification No. 2—That on or about the thirty-first day of December, 1905, the said presbyter did openly, publicly and privately utter, avow, declare and teach doctrines contrary to those held and received by the Protestant Episcopal Church in the United States of America, by the delivery of a sermon on said date, in the course of which, among others, he made in substance the following distinct statements:

(1) "Jesus was born of parents belonging to the middle class."

(2) "He was born of a simple father and mother."

(3) "He was the son of a carpenter."

(4) "The fact that the early Christians predicted a miraculous birth of Jesus was to be regarded as one of the greatest misfortunes that had ever befallen mankind." [49]

These statements were alleged to impugn and deny all of the previously mentioned doctrines except that of the Resurrection.[50]

The second charge against Crapsey was that he had violated the ordination declaration and vows. The vows which he was accused of breaking were the promises of faithfully ministering the doctrine and sacraments, of banishing all strange doctrines contrary to God's Word, of being diligent to frame and fashion himself and family to the doctrine of Christ, and of setting forward quietness, peace, and love among all Christian people.[51] The second charge noted that the whole of the first charge and specification were included in it, i.e., the lengthy series of excerpts from *Religion and Politics*. The presentment omitted Crapsey's footnotes giving biblical and other references. Part of one sentence dealing with the creeds was also omitted.[52]

The diocesan court consisted of two members elected by the Diocesan Council, one member appointed by the bishop, and two approved by the Standing Committee to take the place of two men challenged by the defense. The Standing Committee had made the presentment and the bishop had made his position in the case clear; nevertheless, the court was canonically constituted. The members of the court were all clergymen of whom Crapsey wrote: "They were country clergymen, far removed from the influences that were disturbing the intellectual life of the Church in the greater centers." [53] The court quickly denied a petition asking for an adjournment until after the next diocesan council when a new court would be elected, free from any possible charge of bias because of the selection of the court by the bishop and Standing Committee. The petition was signed by eight clergymen and seven prominent laymen, including the former mayor of Rochester and a justice of the State Supreme Court.[54]

The trial began in the parish house of St. James' Church, Batavia, on April 17, 1906. The church advocate or counsel for the prosecution was John Lord O'Brian, a Buffalo lawyer, assisted by the Hon. John H. Stiness, former Chief Justice of Rhode Island, and the Rev. Francis J. Hall, then professor of dogmatic theology in the Western Theological Seminary. Counsel for Crapsey was the Hon. James Breck Perkins, congressman from Rochester, assisted by Edward M. Shepard, a prominent New York lawyer.[55] Crapsey's counsel asked for an adjournment and the motion was denied. When the defense stated that the case would have to go by default without more time, it was allowed one week for further preparation.

The court reconvened on the twenty-fifth in the Court House at Batavia. Those present included the rector of the Church of the Advent, Boston, the Rev. Dr. Van Allen, and the rector of Emmanuel Church, Boston, Dr. Elwood Worcester who, says Crapsey, "sat opposite each other and glared their mutual hostility" during the course of the trial.[56] Some of the Cowley fathers, monks of the Society of St. John the Evangelist, were also present but took no part in the proceedings.[57] Whether Crapsey's friend and associate in Rochester civic reform, Walter Rauschenbusch was present at the trial is uncertain. Rauschenbusch supported Crapsey during the time of his trial, but took no part in it.[58] The defendant was present at his trial, but he did not testify.

The chief witness for the prosecution was Crapsey's former assistant, the Rev. James Alexander. Alexander was a reluctant witness under cross-examination when the defense proved that he had wanted to succeed Crapsey as rector of St. Andrew's and that long after the publication of *Religion and Politics* he had asked for a raise in salary. The request was denied shortly before Alexander took the notes on Crapsey's sermon of December 31 which formed part of the presentment against him.[59] One newspaper commented editorially that "the witness does not cut an attractive figure," although it felt that his testimony as to the content of the sermon was the thing which really mattered and that that had not been impeached.[60] Later Mr. Shepard remarked that it would be "a sad day for the influence of the church in this community, if a man with the standards of life of Dr. Crapsey must be thrown out, and a man with the standards of life of Mr. Alexander shall stay in." [61] The proposed testimony of a Rochester clergyman on conversations he had had with Dr. Crapsey was held to be inadmissible, and the prosecution rested its case, after having put in evidence the passages from *Religion and Politics* cited in the presentment, the constitution and canons of the church, and the greater part of the Book of Common Prayer.[62]

The defense commenced on April 27. The first witness called was the Rev. Joseph A. Leighton, professor of theology and chaplain at Hobart College. The defense then sought to introduce a number of books in evidence as had been done in the MacQueary trial of 1891. Those selected were: the *Encyclopedia Biblica* by T. K. Cheney; *A Word on the Virgin Birth* by W. S. Parker; Paul Lobestein's *The Virgin Birth of Christ;* a letter on the Virgin Birth from the Dean of Westminster to the Archbishop of Canterbury; an article, "The Person of Christ," by the Rev. W. R. Inge, then a lecturer at Oxford, in *Contentio Veritatis;* S. D. McConnell's *Christ;* Hensley Henson's *The Bible in Modern Life* and *Godly Union and Concord* (at the time Henson was rector of St. Margaret's, Westminster) ; and Frederic Palmer's *Studies on Theological Definition.*[63] The defense planned to have these works identified and characterized by Dr. Leighton and other expert witnesses, with the intention of showing that Dr. Crapsey's views were within the limits of interpretation generally held within the Anglican Communion.

The Church Advocate argued that Leighton had no more right to testify on doctrine than someone who had never heard of the Protestant Episcopal Church. The church, he said, was "not a Lutheran body; its doctrines are not determined by the consensus of opinion." O'Brian continued with the argument that no individual or group could decide what the doctrines are because those doctrines "are straightforwardly laid down in the most unequivocal language." He concluded that "the creeds as we have them were written in the most accurate and exact of all languages, and were expressly formed to exclude erroneous conceptions of doctrine." [64] Hence there was nothing for an expert witness, or any witness, to testify to regarding doctrine.

The defense attempted to meet this argument by saying that the

object of our evidence is this: that those learned in the law of the church, members of the church of recognized standing, whom no man has declared to be heretics or unfaithful members of it, should testify that what we have said does not deny those doctrines. We admit the publication, we deny the innuendo. We say we published these things, but we say in them we proclaim no disbelief in the creed. We assert that we say our creed as truthfully and conscientiously, and I hope as acceptably before God, as any other members of the Protestant Episcopal Church; and to sustain that the evidence is offered which is here produced.[65]

The court ruled, however, that such evidence was incompetent. The defense called a number of other prominent witnesses, but none were allowed to testify. These witnesses included the Rev. Messrs. Wilfred Lawrence Hoopes, then studying in Cambridge, Massachusetts; Alexis W. Stein, rector of Christ Church, Fitchburg, Massachusetts, and recently elected Chaplain of Columbia University; John Wallace Suter, rector of Epiphany Church, Winchester, Massachusetts; Edwin S. Hoffman, rector of Christ Church, Hornellsville, New York; George Clark Cox, rector of Calvary Church, Cincinnati; and Elwood

Worcester, rector of Emmanuel Church, Boston, and formerly professor of history of philosophy and experimental psychology in Lehigh University.[66] Clearly the defense had no chance to defend itself in the only way which seemed possible.

The trial concluded with lengthy arguments by each side. On Friday, April 27, the day began with a summary for the prosecution by Franklin D. Locke, a Buffalo lawyer, followed by a lengthy statement by Perkins for the defense. Perkins' statement included one by Crapsey which seems to have been unexpected.[67] This statement attempted to deal specifically with the doctrines he was alleged to have denied:

I have asserted the Incarnation. If the Word was made flesh and dwelt among us in Jesus Christ our Lord, then that flesh was human flesh and human blood, and the flesh in which the Word dwelt had its origin in the seed of man's flesh from which it is generated by a process so marvellous that it is an everlasting and constant miracle, and, therefore, instead of denying, I assert positively the incarnation of the Word of God in Jesus Christ my Lord.

. . . There are not three Gods, but there is one; and the Trinity is the unfolding of the one, not the addition of the three to make one. I see in Jesus the very substance of God the Father. He is of the same substance, not like substance. I see in Him a perfect union with the Father. I have in the Holy Ghost proceeding from the Father and coming to me the very substance of the Father Himself. I care not by what words these great spiritual facts are described, nor am I compelled by my ordination vows, or any other vows, to think in the terms of the Greek philosophy or in the terms of the Schoolmen. I have the right to think, and my generation has the right to think, in terms most apt to make these great truths real to our souls. To me God is not a definition; He is a living Being, and no definition can confine or fully describe His nature or my relation to Him.[68]

With respect to the Resurrection his statement said:

Jesus manifested his spiritual body to the spiritual apprehension of His disciples; and that apprehension was so keen and powerful that they saw the body of Jesus, they saw that Jesus whom they loved, they heard His voice, they knew He was dead, they knew He was alive again forevermore; He broke for them the bonds of death and hell; He made His presence a power, and in the strength of His resurrection they went forth to conquer the world.[69]

Crapsey's statement included an affirmation of the creed in its entirety with the claim that he interpreted it in accordance with his understanding of the Scriptures.

There were three more addresses that day; Elwood Worcester and Samuel McComb spoke for the defense and Francis J. Hall for the prosecution. Dr. Worcester distinguished between belief in the Incarnation and belief in the Virgin Birth. He appealed to the Holy Scriptures as the final court of appeal for the Episcopal Church. The resurrection of Christ was discussed at length with special emphasis upon I Corinthians 15 as the earliest and most trustworthy evidence of the Resurrection. Worcester concluded with an attack on the attitude of the prosecution in regarding the church "as if it were a political club or a voluntary society of persons who met together in Philadelphia in the year 1785, and who by the simple means of adopting a constitution and passing by-laws closed all the great questions of religious truth forever." He held that "the glory of the Protestant Episcopal Church is that it is, that it always has been a true catholic church." [70]

The Rev. Francis J. Hall spoke at length on the jurisdiction of the English Judicial Committee of the Privy Council in ecclesiastical matters. During his address Dr. Crapsey fell asleep and was awakened by his daughter. Hall's position was that the issue simply was that the "defendant intended to impugn in several statements of his certain of the fundamental doctrines of this church." As for Worcester's point about the ultimate authority of Scripture, Hall said that "that which the church teaches in controversies of faith is the doctrine which can and ought to be proved out of Scripture. In short, the Scriptures are to be interpreted, in controversy as to their doctrinal teaching, by the church." The individual priest has no right of private interpretation where the church has spoken. Hall defended the "quartz crystal" theory of the creeds saying that they "proclaim immutable truths" and that "they are legal documents." He added that such "documents do not grow." The sole issue before the court was that of enforcing the canon law of the Protestant Episcopal Church in the United States of America in the Diocese of Western New York. Hall dismissed the "formidable array of gentlemen of learning who have come here to testify to their private opinions" as being of no value.[71]

Dr. Samuel McComb of the Episcopal Theological School replied to Hall's speech. He said that Hall's view of the church was not catholic but was that of "a narrow, obscurantist, and intolerant sect." He took issue with the prosecution's view that the interpretation of the creeds was a simple matter, holding that it was a matter really of "the greatest questions of theology, the profoundest problems that tax the utmost wit of man to solve." With regard to the phrase of the 1894 Bishops' Pastoral Letter on "fixedness of interpretation," he said it would be a great blessing if it "could be possible to have a fixed and infallible interpretation" but God "has not willed to do so." We have been given reason and intelligence to seek the will of God "and to distinguish between what is of the essence and what is a mere accident of the faith." He reminded the court that Frederick Denison Maurice had been accused of heresy in the Church of England. He sought to establish a principle of judgment in the case:

I am certain that you will judge this man not from the fact of his using here or there a doubtful word, but you will ask yourselves: Is he loyal to the fundamental truths on which the church is built? Does he teach enough positive Christian truth, in spite of his negation, to warrant his retention in the church? You can then say to him: "We may not be able to agree with this or that point of your teaching, we cannot sympathize with your way of putting things;

still we believe you to be a true Christian and devoted son of the Church and as such you are innocent at this bar." [72]

The most eloquent plea on either side appears to have been that of Edward M. Shepard on Saturday, April 28. The basis of the defense was a brief prepared by the Rev. Alexander Viets Griswold Allen, professor of church history in the Episcopal Theological School and biographer of Phillips Brooks.[73] This brief was revised and expanded to form the basis of Allen's book, *Freedom in the Church,* which was a result of the Crapsey case.[74] Allen had no sympathy with Crapsey's views about the Virgin Birth, but he had agreed to give assistance after Crapsey had visited him in Cambridge.[75] Shepard's argument dealt primarily with what he conceived to be the larger issues of the trial, the liberty of thought and conscience which was to be permitted a clergyman. Shepard described two groups within the church:

It is the division between those who see the usefulness of organization, the necessity of rules, the necessity of discipline. That is one sentiment or intellectual habit, and a perfectly true one. Then on the other side are those who think of the church as a great living growth, something not technical or organized, but dynamic; something that, during God's ages here on earth and God's ages to follow, is to grow in beauty and usefulness never ceasing, and in the extent of its sacred ministry. They see the wisdom and necessity of permitting these diversities. They tell us that the mind of no man is like the mind of another, and therefore that the form and color of truth are to no man precisely what they are to another.[76]

The argument breathes a broad and catholic spirit as opposed to the narrow legalistic arguments of the prosecution which quite ignored any effects which the trial might have on the church at large, save as they were concerned with a rigorous enforcement of the letter of the laws. Shepard said that the diocesan court should not attempt to deal with questions of doctrine until there was an appeal court competent to handle such grave matters. He discussed the Colenso case and *Essays and Reviews* at considerable length in showing the limits of liberty in the Anglican communion. The larger question raised by the trial is nothing less than the liberty allowed in the holy catholic church while the specific question is whether the church will repudiate its comprehensive "practice and career" in rejecting Dr. Crapsey.[77]

Shepard held that the Reformation had settled the question of authority in the church, for it showed that both priest and layman are to search for the truth themselves "in their own conscience and, by the exercise of their own intelligence, in study of Holy Scripture." Shepard concluded his defense with a plea for comprehenseive liberty:

Gentlemen of the Court, I speak here in behalf of a true holy catholic church. If this Protestant Episcopal Church of ours be really the American branch of such a church, then today you can affect its growth and career as can no other men. From now on until the time a few days hence or a few weeks hence when you shall render your judgment, prayers unceasing will arise over our whole land—I might almost say over the earth—that the Almighty will guide you to the wisdom to see in this church of ours a vital reality, a living organization, with faculties fit to consummate the infinite mission of Christ upon earth. And with these prayers mingles a fear. If the contrary thing shall be done, will not Christ's garment be riven? Although there will rise other prayers no doubt just as sincere but to the contrary, they will come from those who would honor the creed in its letter and not its spirit, who would make of the church a thing no doubt precious but small, no doubt sacred but unfruitful, no doubt exalted but without infinite career or growth.[78]

Judge Stiness' reply saw no connection between the beautiful speeches of the defense and the point before the court. That point was perfectly clear to him, since Crapsey's book simply contradicted the plain words of the creed. The address of John Lord O'Brian was similar in content. He reminded the court of the

MacQueary precedent in 1891. O'Brian urged the court to do its duty: "Are we going to listen to this cry of heresy trial, heresy trial, and fail to do our duty; or are we going to look straight in the face, the fact that the Protestant Episcopal Church demands of a man obedience, that he shall say that he believes the articles of the faith as contained in the Apostles' Creed?" [79]

The Scriptures "were not written as a divine rule of faith" and, in any case, are to be interpreted by the church which wrote them. Presumably the Articles of Religion had little authority for the prosecution, since they were not referred to, even in passing. O'Brian concluded his address with an appeal to the truth since the "church must be in all things the Church of Truth." [80]

The court adjourned Saturday, April 28, 1906. It was announced that the verdict would be reached on or before May 15, 1906.[81]

Crapsey was not silenced by the event of the trial. The day after it closed he preached twice in Sage Chapel of Cornell University, taking occasion in the afternoon to question the physical Resurrection as told in the Gospels. In the morning sermon two paragraphs reported by the newspapers are of interest in showing Crapsey's views of Christ:

If we wait for some far-off Saviour, if we wait for a curtain of blue to open and for some mighty being to come and achieve our salvation, we shall wait forever. The day will never come. It is not necessary. It is a degrading idea that perfection exists the like of which we cannot attain, albeit be predicated on one hanging on a cross.

Jesus, mighty man of old, call Him what you please, divine, yet He was one of us and needs us almost as much as we need Him. We help saints and prophets of old to achieve perfection by our kind words, our noble deeds, and our tender thoughts. You cannot put on the righteousness of Christ like a garment over our own unrighteousness. The cross is a small price to pay to attain perfection, even as our Father is perfect.[82]

The morning's text was Hebrews 11:39-40 which Crapsey attributed to an "unknown writer, possibly a woman." Aside from Crapsey's desire to seem rather shocking, his theological views were clearly deficient in any real understanding of or appreciation for traditional Christian teaching. Whether a heresy trial was the proper means of dealing with such deficiencies is open to question.

The court's written verdict was delivered to Crapsey by the Chancellor of the Diocese of Western New York on Wednesday, May 15, 1906.[83] The lengthy decision convicted Crapsey of impugning and denying, in his book, the Virgin Birth and Resurrection; in his sermon the Virgin Birth; and in the book and the sermon of impugning the doctrines "That our Lord Jesus Christ is God" and the Trinity. He was acquitted only of the charge of violating the ordination vows dealing with framing and fashioning his life according to the doctrine of Christ and with maintaining and setting forward quietness, peace, and love.[84]

One member of the court, the Rev. Francis S. Dunham filed a brief minority report:

WHEREAS, The respondent constantly affirms his acceptance of all the articles of the Christian faith as contained in the Apostles' Creed; and,

WHEREAS, This creed declares the sacred mysteries of the incarnation of our Lord and Saviour Jesus Christ, and of the most Holy Trinity, and a belief in the resurrection of the body, concerning which eternal verities of the Christian religion the said respondent is called in question, I find from his own statements and the evidence submitted for his defense that his error consists rather in presuming to define what God has not been pleased to reveal, and to interpret those doctrines in a manner not generally received by the Church, rather than in a denial and rejection of their truth and authority.[85]

The deliberations of the court were overheard by newspaper reporters who stated that Dunham's argument was met by an-

other member of the court with the remark that "there is no
more divinity in Crapsey's Christ than there is in that tele-
graph pole." [86]

During the trial the defense had raised various technical
issues, presumably with an eye to a possible appeal. Shepard
condemned the trial court as simply representing the prosecuting
authority holding that the case was "practically foreclosed." He
charged that the majority had been predisposed to convict
Crapsey so that the trial was simply "a burdensome formality"
for them.[87] On the basis of alleged technical irregularities and
prejudice on the part of the court, an appeal was filed on June
6, 1906.[88] The Court of Review of the Second Department of
the Protestant Episcopal Church had jurisdiction over the
dioceses in New York and New Jersey, the present provincial
system not yet having been adopted. *The Churchman* felt that
the appeal was futile and harmful and would merely prolong
the legal controversy, a view representative of much Episcopa-
lian opinion.[89] The canons did not allow the review court to deal
with matters of faith or doctrine.

The first meeting of the court of review was held on Wednesday, September 5, in the Diocesan House on Lafayette Street,
New York City, with the Bishop of New Jersey presiding.
After brief discussion of whether the court could deal with
doctrine, it adjourned at the request of Mr. Shepard in order
to give him time to study the official trial record which he had
received only three days before the court of review met.[90]

The court reconvened on Friday, October 19, 1906, when
Shepard presented the argument of the defense for some three
hours. Despite its length and the sultry day, the argument interested the court which did not adjourn at its scheduled hour.
Shepard discussed the various technical faults of the trial court
and stressed the fact that many in the church believed as did
Dr. Crapsey. He asked that the final decision in the case be
held in abeyance until the constitution of an ultimate court of
appeal by the general convention.[91] The appeal of Shepard was
printed and helped to popularize the argument of the defense.[92]

The Rev. Dr. Henry Sylvester Nash, professor of New Testament interpretation in the Episcopal Theological School, wrote a letter urging that the New Testament supported Mr. Dunham's minority opinion and that the court of review should open the case more fully. Nash urged the church to heed the "voice of the New Testament pleading for emphasis where emphasis is needed and for kindly dealing with doubt where the Scriptures themselves have put no emphasis." He warned that the lower court had "magnified the letter of our Canon Law till it overshadowed the genius of the Church which the Court was serving." [93]

The decision of the court of review, announced Monday, November 20, 1906, upheld the diocesan court, finding that the court had been legally constituted, that it had jurisdiction in the case, and that there were no errors which would require a reversal of the decision of the lower court. It also denied the appeal to wait until the ultimate court of appeal was constituted.[94]

The sentence suggested for Crapsey by the original trial court had provided for his suspension from the ministry if he did not satisfy the bishop of his orthodoxy. Crapsey was hardly a man to recant. Consequently, he felt the only thing to do was to resign from the ministry. This he did in a lengthy letter to Bishop Walker on November 26, 1906. The letter was widely circulated and commented upon both within and outside his own denomination. Crapsey asked that the bishop depose him between the third and sixth of December. He noted that he was "not compelled to this action by anything that reflects upon my moral integrity or calls in question my faithfulness as a pastor." The court had found that he could not harmonize his own convictions with the creed. Although he recognized the right of the church authorities "to define the limits of interpretation," Crapsey held firmly to his conviction that he must interpret the creed in a "spiritual rather than a literally physical" manner. He had not ceased to believe in Jesus when he became convinced that "the infancy stories were not historical." [95]

Crapsey's letter urged that no one should feel that the decision in his case destroyed liberty in the church. He appealed to his "brethren of like belief to stay where they are." There appear to have been no resignations from the ministry nor were there any further heresy trials as a result of the Crapsey case.

Crapsey showed no bitterness toward the church which he left with deep regret and "gratitude for the opportunities of worship, of preaching, and of service which have been the privileges of my office." He had, he said, asked only for tolerance of his views, but that tolerance had been denied "and I must with a grief which only my own heart knows accept my dismissal from the service of the Church." God had further work for him, he believed, adding that perhaps "this is His way of calling me to that work." The letter concludes with an expression of good will toward his opponents and with deep gratitude to his friends, particularly to Seth Low, George Foster Peabody, James Breck Perkins, and Edward Morse Shepard who had all been helpful during the trial.[96]

Shepard deplored the situation which forbade the court of review dealing with questions of more than lesser matters of formal procedure. He stated that Dr. Crapsey refused to appeal to a civil court and felt that the controversy had opened to the church "the cause of intellectual honesty and free study." [97] The court of review may have felt that the decision of the lower court was unfortunate doctrinally, but it had no jurisdiction in the matter and could not comment on the doctrinal questions raised.[98]

Although Crapsey did not join the ministry of another denomination, he did not immediately give up his interest in religion. The year after his trial he published articles and a book on the passing of the old "dogmatic system" of religion, a system which had been "expressed and implied in the creeds and confessions of the various Churches." Crapsey urged the replacement of the old system with a new dogmatic of love and justice based upon morality and a God who is "simply a friend." For Crapsey "salvation comes not by way of definition, but by way of loving service; not he who rightly defines, but he who

truly loves, comes at last with Jesus into the Presence of God."
In an oblique reference to his trial Crapsey held that it was
ridiculous and that the ousted clergyman "finds that he can get
along very well without the Church." Undoubtedly Crapsey was
deeply hurt by his trial and deposition from the ministry even
though he argued that "the attempt to silence him has given
his voice clearer tone and farther reach." [99] Crapsey enjoyed a
certain reputation as a lecturer and writer after his conviction.
He formed an organization known simply as the "Brotherhood"
which disbanded after his economic views became too radical
for its wealthy members.[100] He was a delegate to the Interna-
tional Peace Conference at The Hague in 1907 and was appointed a parole officer for the state of New York in 1914.[101]
He had no direct influence upon the Episcopal Church after his
resignation since all connection with it was severed.

The Crapsey case aroused as never before discussion of the
great question of authority and freedom in the Protestant Episcopal Church. Crapsey represented an extreme position and
his understanding of the Christian faith was not shared by any
large group in the Episcopal Church. Yet it is in precisely such
a case as his that the actual limits of freedom are clearly raised.
The case did not provide a clear-cut legal answer since the decision of the court of review was binding only in the dioceses
within the states of New York and New Jersey. The church
was not moved, probably wisely, to attempt any final definition
of the matters involved either through action on the part of the
General Convention or by setting up an ultimate court of appeal
to deal with doctrinal issues. There were no other heresy trials
as a result of the Crapsey case nor were there any resignations
from the ministry. Whether any candidates for the ministry
were dissuaded from seeking ordination by the case is uncertain, but there were no repercussions of the case in the seminaries.

To some Episcopalians the Crapsey case was simply a matter
of a clear denial of certain clauses of the creeds which were absolutely binding in a literal sense upon the clergyman. To this

group there was no hesitation in claiming that a minister's liberty was restricted in interpreting the creeds or at the very least that that liberty did not extend to a literal denial of the clauses. This view is attractive not only because of its simplicity, but because it seems to be a plain avowal of honesty. Unfortunately perhaps, few theological questions are really simple. The Christian church cannot properly be compared to a business corporation, or indeed to any sort of secular organization or association, if the biblical view of the nature of the church is taken seriously. Surely even the most ardent of those advocating the conviction of Crapsey could not seriously have thought of the church as a purely human institution with a set of by-laws and constitution.

Biblical fundamentalism has never been a serious problem in the Protestant Episcopal Church, but a creedal traditionalism as illustrated by Bishop Walker's characterization of the creeds as "quartz crystals" has been a frequent source of controversy. If a large measure of freedom of interpretation has been generally accepted, the question of the limits of that freedom is a recurrent one. The Crapsey heresy trial did not solve the problem. Aside from the discussion it provoked, its chief result was the resignation of a kindly, zealous, and badly educated parish priest who had served the church faithfully and well. It is difficult to avoid the conclusion that the trial was hasty and ill-advised; certainly it settled none of the issues it raised. Theological questions are not amenable to courtroom solutions and the possible harm done by allowing the preaching of misguided views and opinions must be weighed against the more serious harm of stifling that sincere reverent search for truth which is involved in the theological enterprise.

NOTES

1. The other trial was that of the Rev. Howard MacQueary in the Diocese of Ohio in January, 1891. The threat of a trial occurred in 1923 at a time of heightened discussion over the significance of

the Bishops' Pastoral Letter of 1923 which urged the literal acceptance of the Virgin Birth narrative.

2. Biographical data is from A. S. Crapsey, *The Last of the Heretics* (New York: Alfred A. Knopf, 1924).

3. *Ibid.,* p. 85.

4. A. S. Crapsey, *Religion and Politics* (New York: Thomas Whittaker, 1905), p. 8. "The Union Theological Seminary in New York, Harvard Divinity School, Yale Divinity School, the Divinity School of Chicago University, the Episcopal Divinity School [*sic*] of Cambridge, Mass., are all schools of scientific as opposed to scholastic theology and are doing work of a very high order."

5. Crapsey, *Last of the Heretics,* p. vii.

6. *Inventory of the Church Archives of New York State—Protestant Episcopal Church Diocese of Rochester* (Albany: Historical Records Survey, 1941), p. 73.

7. Diocesan records quoted in Edward M. Shepard, *Argument of Edward M. Shepard as Counsel* (Oct. 19, 1906), p. 1.

8. Quoted in *The Churchman* CLXIX (July, 1955), p. 6.

9. *Inventory of the Church Archives of New York,* p. 18.

10. A. S. Crapsey, *A Voice in the Wilderness: Being a Plea for the Restoration of Primitive Christianity* (New York: James Potts, 1897), Part II, pp. 97, 138.

11. *Ibid.,* pp. 59-60.

12. *New York Times,* Aug. 6, 1898, p. 6.

13. (Rochester: Printed and published by the author, 1899).

14. Crapsey, *Last of the Heretics,* pp. 218-19.

15. *Ibid.,* pp. 222-23, letter to Crapsey, Nov. 6, 1899.

16. *Ibid.,* p. 223.

17. A. S. Crapsey, *The Answer to Pilate* (Rochester: Printed and published by the author, 1899), p. 28.

18. P. 12.

19. (Rochester: Printed and published by the author, 1899).

20. *New York Times,* Sept. 27, 1902, p. 642.

21. *Atlantic Monthly,* XCVII (1906), 413-20. Hodges had himself been accused of protecting heresy in the Cambridge school in the 1890's.

22. Crapsey, *Religion and Politics,* pp. 299, 305, 306-7.

23. Crapsey's statement that he was "condemned primarily not for theological, but for social, political, and economic heresy" is accepted at face value in *The Churchman,* CLXIX (July, 1955), p. 6.

24. Crapsey, *Religion and Politics,* p. 8.

25. *Ibid.,* p. 291.

26. Crapsey, *Last of the Heretics,* pp. 254-55.

27. "Report of the Committee," *Church Standard,* XC (Nov. 18, 1905), 77.

28. *Ibid.* (Nov. 25, 1905), 114-15.

29. *Living Church,* XXXIV (Nov. 18, 1905), 78-79.

30. *Ibid.*, XXXIV (Nov. 4, 1905), 20.
31. Protestant Episcopal Church in the U.S.A., *Journals of the General Convention, 1895*, pp. 416-17.
32. *Church Standard*, XC (Jan. 20, 1906), 389-90.
33. XCIII (Jan. 13, 1906), 46.
34. *Living Church*, XXXIV (Feb. 3, 1906), 486.
35. *Ibid.*
36. Charles Lewis Slattery, *Alexander Viets Griswold Allen, 1841-1908* (New York: Longmans, Green & Company, 1911), p. 234.
37. XXXIV (Feb. 3, 1906), 486.
38. LXXXI (Sept. 2, 1905), 25-29.
39. *Ibid.* (Sept. 30, 1905), 284-85. Crapsey's reply is concerned with a lengthy but vague discussion of the church as representing either "life" or an "organism" which, he said, was the view of his critics.
40. *Ibid.*, 253-54.
41. *Current Literature*, XXXIX (Nov., 1905), 523-24.
42. Walter Karl Malone, "The Impact of Naturalism and Higher Criticism Upon the Episcopal Church; 1860-1900" (Unpublished S.T.D. dissertation, Temple University, 1959), p. 201 n.
43. *The Diocese of Western New York, 1897-1931* (Buffalo: Diocese of Western New York, 1935), p. 129.
44. XCIII (Feb. 3, 1906), 157.
45. Algernon S. Crapsey, Defendant, *Proceedings on the Trial and Appeal of the Rev. Algernon S. Crapsey* (New York: Thomas Whittaker, 1906), pp. 4-8.
46. See "Appended Note on the Thesis of Impersonal Humanity," John Krumm, *Modern Heresies* (New York: Seabury Press, 1961), p. 138.
47. Without the words "and man" referring to Christ, this charge might itself be considered formally heretical according to the Chalcedonian definition.
48. Diocese of Western New York, *Journal of the Seventieth Annual Council of the Protestant Episcopal Church in the Diocese of Western New York, 1907*, pp. 96-97.
49. Crapsey, *Proceedings on the Trial*, p. 8.
50. *Ibid.*, p. 9.
51. *Ibid.*, pp. 10-12.
52. The omitted section is "but they are of immense value as attempts on the part of ordinary men to measure the greatest personality ever born into the world" (p. 83).
53. *Last of the Heretics*, p. 262.
54. Crapsey, *Proceedings on the Trial*, pp. 19, 24.
55. *New York Times*, Apr. 26, 1906, p. 7.
56. Crapsey, *Last of the Heretics*, p. 263.
57. George E. DeMille, *The Episcopal Church Since 1900* (New York: Morehouse-Gorham Co., 1955), p. 98.

58. Dores Robinson Sharpe, *Walter Rauschenbusch* (New York: The Macmillan Company, 1942), pp. 128, 378.
59. Crapsey, *Proceedings on the Trial*, pp. 56-67.
60. *New York Times*, Apr. 27, 1906, p. 10.
61. Crapsey, *Proceedings on the Trial*, p. 144.
62. *New York Times*, Apr. 26, 1906, p. 7.
63. Crapsey, *Proceedings on the Trial*, pp. 88-90.
64. *Ibid.*, pp. 91-2.
65. *Ibid.*, pp. 99-100.
66. *Ibid.*, pp. 106, 108-15.
67. *New York Times*, Apr. 28, 1906, p. 6.
68. Crapsey, *Proceedings on the Trial*, pp. 133-4.
69. *Ibid.*, p. 135.
70. *Ibid.*, pp. 161, 166.
71. *Ibid.*, pp. 185, 181, 171, 176, 177-78, 186.
72. *Ibid.*, pp. 188, 189, 193-94, 197.
73. Slattery, *A. V. G. Allen*, p. 235. Dr. Allen's views on the trial are discussed here.
74. (New York: The Macmillan Company, 1907).
75. Slattery, *A. V. G. Allen*, pp. 234-5.
76. Crapsey, *Proceedings on the Trial*, pp. 206-7.
77. *Ibid.*, pp. 208, 215-20, 210, 212.
78. *Ibid.*, pp. 213, 225.
79. *Ibid.*, pp. 226-37, 244, 254.
80. *Ibid.*, pp. 247, 257.
81. *New York Times*, Apr. 29, 1906, p. 11.
82. *Ibid.*, Apr. 30, 1906, p. 7.
83. *Ibid.*, May 16, 1906, p. 9.
84. Crapsey, *Proceedings on the Trial*, pp. 261-3.
85. *Journal of the Seventieth Annual Council of the Protestant Episcopal Church in the Diocese of Western New York, 1907,* p. 99.
86. Crapsey, *Last of the Heretics*, p. 268.
87. *New York Times*, May 16, 1906, p. 9.
88. *Ibid.*, June 7, 1906, p. 6.
89. *The Churchman*, XCIII, (1906), 957.
90. *New York Times*, Sept. 5, 1906, p. 16. In addition to the Rt. Rev. John Scarborough, the other members of the court were the Rev. Messrs. William Reed Huntington, A. B. Baker of New Jersey, J. G. Moses of Garden City, and Messrs. Frederick Adams, James Parker, and Charles Andrews, laymen of the Dioceses of Newark, New Jersey, and Central New York respectively.
91. *Ibid.*, Oct. 20, 1906, p. 7.
92. Edward M. Shepard, *Argument of Edward M. Shepard as Counsel* (Oct. 19, 1906).
93. *Ibid.*, Appendix II, p. 122.

94. "Judgment of the Court of Review," *Appeal by the Rev'd Algernon S. Crapsey to the Court of Review* (New York: Thomas Whittaker, 1906), pp. 187 ff.
95. *New York Times,* Nov. 26, 1906, pp. 1-2.
96. *Ibid.*
97. "Statement of Mr. Shepard," *Appeal by the Rev'd Algernon S. Crapsey to the Court of Review,* p. 220.
98. "Judgment of the Court of Review," pp. 189-90.
99. A. S. Crapsey, *The Re-Birth of Religion* (New York: John Lane Co., 1907), pp. 10, 216, 286, 297-98. Crapsey also wrote "The Historical Aspect of the Virgin Birth," *Arena,* XXXVII (1907), 337-46.
100. *New York Times,* May 23, 1924. It is not indicated whether this group was related to an organization of somewhat similar name founded by Rauschenbusch.
101. *Dictionary of American Biography,* IV, 513-14.

Conclusion
Heirs of the Faith

Open affirmation is at the heart of historical heresy. And in this respect the subjects of these chapters are genuinely Christian and legitimately Protestant. The finality of their commitment is to the God who has revealed himself in Jesus Christ. Their affirmation of this commitment has been couched in tentative forms, for they have imbibed the spirit of Protestantism which is basically "an openness to the judging and renewing activity of the living God made known in Jesus Christ." [1] The value judgment here suggested is not at all veiled. These men, and many others like them, are the more valid heirs of the faith. On the other hand, pride and that which approximates blasphemy reside at the heart of popular heresy hunting. The illustrations in these trials of this statement are too obvious to be noted. Let the records speak for themselves.

Though there remain glaring exceptions to the rule, the bulk of mainline American Protestantism no longer engages in the farcical *Inherit the Wind* type of trial. Interestingly enough, the formal and informal trials which *do* occur are very reminiscent of these presented in this volume. There are denominations, then, which have not read their history lessons in detail, indeed, if at all. To the contrary, however, the majority of the denominations have come to realize that academic freedom in the pulpit and at the lectern is an offensive weapon and not a defensive shield. The heretics of the late nineteenth and early twentieth centuries did not play hide-and-seek with this concept. Their maneuvers were affirmative and offensive.

In addition to a relatively proper understanding of academic freedom there has also emerged in our century a broader church-manship best expressed in the ecumenical movement. There is a confessionalism which rises above denominationalism. Neo-orthodoxy has at least taught us that we are finite creatures. And in our finiteness we have become humble and teachable (in our better moments) in the relationships we have with our fel-low finite men. This is the kind of relativism which leads to true humility and tolerance. That faith which is so shaky as to neces-sitate absolute dogma for its support senses anarchy in such relativism. But an heir of the faith is brought to finite sub-mission before God in the context of relativism. These chapters vividly portray the major role ecumenism played in the careers of these heirs.

In 1924 Rufus Jones expressed an insight descriptive of the contemporary attitude toward the heretics whose trials are presented here as he stated: "A heretic in one generation would have been a saint if he had lived in another, and a heretic in one country would often be a hero in another." [2] Three of these five trials resulted in "guilty as charged" verdicts with attendant penalties. Yet today the theological issues which were involved have become the normative standpoint of the schools and pulpits or at least a tolerated position. In a sense these heretics have come home, while others have left the churches, not because of the pressures of formal or informal trials but of their own ac-cord! They have become disenchanted with the institutional churches in their present structure. They have thus become the political, sociological, ecclesiological, theological heretics. The churches have not legislated against them; they have simply let them go, not bothering to answer their questions. Their questions are not those to which the churches are accustomed; they cannot be answered in traditional or "pat" forms.[3]

We have allowed our heretics to come home but others like

them have left. Though under different circumstances, they
have left for essentially the same reasons. For their interest has
been in the critical and correlating task of the churches. And
they have been better satisfied with the Sunday newspapers
than with the institutional churches in this regard.

Henry Preserved Smith was not included in this volume because his trial approximates so closely that of C. A. Briggs.
One of the engaging features of his story, however, is an autobiographical account which he composed more than twenty
years later. At the conclusion of his book he summarily states
the central issues of criticism and correlation:

And now the reader who has had the patience to follow me
thus far may ask the question that others have asked: "Was it
worth your while to unsettle the faith of the simple-minded Christian believer by your discussion of critical questions?" The answer
must be the answer to the general inquiry whether education has
any value. It would be possible to argue that the *sancta simplicitas*
of the peasant woman who brought her fagot to the fire that
burned John Huss should not be disturbed. In like manner the
good lady who complained to Doctor Roberts that the Lane Seminary professors were taking her Bible away from her might con-
ceivably be let alone in her belief in every statement of the sacred
Book; or the member of the Assembly of 1894 who protested that
he accepted the whole Bible "from Generations to Revelations"
might be spared by the scholars. But it is plain that in these cases
the remedy is in their own hands. No one can take the Bible from
them. All they have to do is to let the higher criticism alone. But the
teacher has others to consider. The minds of our young people are
keen to know all that has been discovered. Set them to read the
Bible, assuring them that it is the inerrant Word of God—that God
is "inverbate" in it as He was incarnate in Christ—and they will
at once raise questions that you will find difficulty in answering.
A minister asked me once whether he ought to give his people some
information concerning the higher criticism. My reply was:
"Better for them to get it from you than from the Sunday newspapers." [4]

A. S. Crapsey says the same thing in these words: "I have the right to think, and my generation has the right to think in terms most apt to make these great truths real to our souls. To me God is not a definition; He is a living Being, and no definition can confine or fully describe His nature or my relation to Him." [5]

There are hopeful signs in contemporary Christianity. Heretics who have already come home are putting out the welcome mat to those outside the church by means of the fresh experiments in renewal. House churches, lay institutes and academies, interracial efforts on the local level, and fresh methods of Christian education and curriculum are emerging in this country and abroad.[6] To be engaged in the business of criticism and correlation means different things to different people. And we are witnessing a variety of exciting developments.

The tradition of the heretics offers the finest opportunity of renewal which the churches have. Either the churches must make a place for these people within their fellowship or they run the risk of contemporary blasphemy and a rejection of the Protestant spirit. But when this place is made, the churches must not expect popular success or even absolute correctness from their "dissenters come home." They will occasion mistakes. The tradition of the heretics makes no firsthand claim to infallibility. In another context the same truth is uttered as follows:

But in the nature of things a really significant innovation is likely to be hard to appreciate, or even understand, in the old terms. Its advocates themselves may not understand it too well. Their easily stated tenets may seem self-exposing falsehoods to normal people (particularly if they deny something economically or emotionally precious), and may, indeed be wrong. The new generally resembles the old in one respect anyhow: not being perfect.[7]

But such dissenting heretics should be welcomed *and* heard— even though some of them (using hindsight) never make a distinct or unique contribution. In fact their contribution may simply be to prod others to devise more creative innovations than they were able to produce.

It is often alleged that the dissenter poses a terrible threat to free inquiry because of his cocksureness. But what of the cocksure orthodox? Indeed, "diehard adherence to a heresy is in general less menacing to free inquiry than matter-of-course adherence to orthodoxy; because the heretic, being constantly challenged, is deprived of the illusion that his rut is the whole road." [8]

The context for the homecoming is not one of suspicions, rigidity, or the threatened use of coercive power. It is rather one of trust—mutual trust. Effective creativity is never nurtured in an atmosphere that breeds suspicion. A breakdown of mutual trust is surely not conducive to Christian service; it only leads to a spirit of fear, frustration, and despair. Mutual trust involves a spirit of love and appreciation which leads to a creative witness.

And let the glaring exceptions among American Protestant denominations also put away their formal and informal trials in the relic trunk. Let them do their history homework. For the continued use of the trial tactic does real damage to the body politic and leaves other members in a state of loneliness and demoralization. The would-be-heretic who remains within the communion is completely stifled! And the tradition itself is thoroughly infeebled because it is deprived of confrontation by energetic heretics. May these denominations welcome their nineteenth-century heretics home so that, in turn, they may hang out the welcome sign for twentieth-century heresy.

The church must recover the heresy of Jesus if it is to speak effectively to the contemporary world. A part of this recovery is not only allowing but also nurturing its amateur or incidental as well as its professional heretics. In this way it will participate in the very obedience of the heretics. May there emerge a new kind of heresy hunt—the type that actively enlists and engages the heretic for service.

Protestant Christianity has never developed a doctrine of

sainthood. It has had a great deal to say about the priesthood of every believer, however. And does not this priesthood involve nonconformity to idolatry[9]—in whatever form, institutional or otherwise? In a vital sense, then, all of us poor priests of God are called to be obedient heretics at some time or another, "to the measure of the stature and fullness of Christ."

NOTES

1. R. M. Brown, *The Spirit of Protestantism* (New York: Oxford University Press, 1961), p. 40.
2. *The Church's Debt to Heretics* (New York: George H. Doran Co., 1924), p. 24.
3. Cf. Jaroslav Pelikan, *Obedient Rebels* (New York: Harper & Row, 1964), p. 206. Pelikan has included here an excellent section concerning the critical and the correlating task of the theology of the churches.
4. H. P. Smith, *The Heretic's Defense* (New York: Scribner's, 1926), pp. 123-24.
5. Cited above, p. 209.
6. For example, cf. Donald G. Bloesch, *Centers of Christian Renewal* (Philadelphia: United Church Press, 1964), *passim*.
7. Chandler Davis, "From an Exile," *The New Professors*, compiled by Robert O. Bowen (New York: Holt, Rinehart & Winston, 1960), p. 184.
8. *Ibid.*, p. 192.
9. Cf. Ernest Werner, "Remodeling the Protestant Ministry," *The American Scholar*, XXXIV (Winter, 1964-65), 47 ff.

Index